Critical Essays on
ZORA NEALE HURSTON

CRITICAL ESSAYS
ON
AMERICAN LITERATURE

James Nagel, General Editor
University of Georgia, Athens

Critical Essays on
ZORA NEALE HURSTON

edited by
GLORIA L. CRONIN

G. K. Hall & Co.

New York

G. K. Hall & Co.
1633 Broadway
New York, NY 10019

Library of Congress Cataloging-in-Publication Data

Critical essays on Zora Neale Hurston / edited by Gloria L. Cronin.
    p. cm. — (Critical essays on American literature)
    Includes bibliographical references and index.
    ISBN 0-7838-0021-5 (alk. paper)
    1. Hurston, Zora Neale—Criticism and interpretation. 2. Women and literature—United States—History—20th century. 3. Afro-Americans in literature. 4. Folklore in literature. I. Cronin, Gloria L., 1947–   . II. Series.
PS3515.U789Z67   1998
813'.52—dc21   98–19113
                                                        CIP

This paper meets the requirements of ANSI/NISO Z3948-1992 (Permanence of Paper).

10 9 8

Printed in the United States of America

Contents

◆

General Editor's Note

◆

This series seeks to anthologize the most important criticism on a wide variety of topics and writers in American literature. Our readers will find in various volumes not only a generous selection of reprinted articles and reviews but original essays, bibliographies, manuscript selections, and other materials brought to public attention for the first time. This volume, *Critical Essays on Zora Neale Hurston,* is the most comprehensive gathering of essays ever published on one of the most important modern writers in the United States. It contains both a sizable gathering of early reviews and a broad selection of more modern scholarship. Among the authors of reprinted articles and reviews are Henry Louis Gates Jr., Cheryl A. Wall, Richard Wright, Rachel Blau DuPlessis, Dolan Hubbard, Janet St. Clair, and Marion A. Thomas. In addition to a substantial introduction by Gloria Cronin, there are also two original essays commissioned specifically for publication in this volume, new studies by Phillip A. Snyder on *Dust Tracks* and Wilfred D. Samuels on heterosexual relationships in Hurston's short stories. Blaine L. Hall has compiled a comprehensive primary bibliography for inclusion in this volume. We are confident that this book will make a permanent and significant contribution to the study of American literature.

JAMES NAGEL
University of Georgia

Publisher's Note

◆

Producing a volume that contains both newly commissioned and reprinted material presents the publisher with the challenge of balancing the desire to achieve stylistic consistency with the need to preserve the integrity of works first published elsewhere. In the Critical Essays series, essays commissioned especially for a particular volume are edited to be consistent with G. K. Hall's house style; reprinted essays appear in the style in which they were first published, with only typographical errors corrected. Consequently, shifts in style from one essay to another are the result of our efforts to be faithful to each text as it was originally published.

Acknowledgments

◆

With grateful thanks to Lynne Facer, Diana Tanner, and Linda Hunter Adams for their contributions to the preparation of this manuscript.

Introduction: Going to the Far Horizon

GLORIA L. CRONIN

Zora Neale Hurston, the best-known woman writer to have emerged from the Harlem Renaissance, wrote nearly a dozen short stories before publishing her first novel, *Jonah's Gourd Vine*, in 1934. After this, she published two collections of folklore, three more novels, an autobiography, dozens of essays and articles, and many reviews. The critical response to her work is of particular interest not only for what it says about Hurston's work but for what it reveals about the changing values of the literary establishment and of the nation. Always at the mercy of her readers, editors, publishing houses, reviewers, critics, and the black intelligentsia of her generation, Hurston's reputation waxed briefly, waned quickly, and was all but obliterated after her arrest on morals charges in 1948, just as *Seraph on the Suwanee*, her final book, came off the press. By the late 1950s Hurston was little more than a footnote in literary history, and by the end of the decade she was dying of malnutrition and neglect in a black community that did not understand her importance to them, or to American letters.

Her posthumous literary resurrection in the early 1980s as a major twentieth-century American writer had much to do with the changing values of the literary establishment and of the nation. The emergence of feminism and multiculturalism as forces in the academy, the search by young black and white women writers for a literary matrilineage, the rise of black studies, and the subsequent willingness of publishers to reprint Hurston's works have brought her from near oblivion to literary center stage. The trajectory of Hurston's literary reputation provides an interesting window on American literary canon formation. Hurston criticism says as much about American ideologies and values as it does about Hurston and her work.

A bird of brilliant plumage and song, Hurston presented herself to both the black world and the white as a performance artist, a folk character, and a writer. In so doing she demonstrated her literary roots in a black oral and print culture. Early reviewers, failing to read both the black and white and the oral and written cultural aesthetics that informed her books, missed much of her intellectual complexity. Often confused by her hybridization of genres, many reviewers pegged her as a black local colorist whose use of black dialect, humor, and folk culture were alternately charming, annoying, or politically suspect, depending on the point of view. Even from within the mostly male black literary community her work was variously criticized as too pastoral, too black, too colonized, too sassy, or too outrageous.

From her first novel to her last, Hurston was engaged in a serious "womanist" ethnological critique of the social and political foundations of Western culture and, more specifically, of Christianity. In *Jonah's Gourd Vine* (1934), she described the plight of her mother, her preacher father, and herself in the patriarchal Christian South. In *Their Eyes Were Watching God*, she plots Janie's escape into feminocentric pantheism. In her retelling of the story of Moses and Exodus in *Moses, Man of the Mountain* (1939), she expanded her historical investigation of race, class, and gender into the origins of Judeo-Christianity. In her last book on the subject of poor white women in the South, *Seraph on the Suwanee* (1948), she remained faithful to these topics: women, race, and Christianity. Each book from its own microcosm provides an implied critique of a Judeo-Christianity that Hurston held responsible for the plight of blacks, women, nature, and all non-Christian forms of religious experience.[1] Many of her early reviewers entirely missed the "signifyin' " artistry and broad historical sweep of her mind, just as they failed to see the relationship between her personal history and her public persona. Critics have focused primarily on producing celebratory, triumphal feminist critiques of *Their Eyes Were Watching God* rather than fully exploring the thematic continuities. This coupled with uneven attention to Hurston's personal, intellectual, and artistic development has obscured a full understanding of both the very private Eatonville Hurston and the very public Hurston persona. Only recently has Hurston been celebrated as griot, actress, preacher, signfyin' ethnographer, trickster, and literary artist.

Hurston's adult professional study of anthropology and folklore led her to see theology as human discourse or narrative that arises out of an existential process informed by human desire.[2] She soon came to see narrative and its performance, not formal theology, as the guiding principle of African-American religious life. In addition to being a sustaining and organizing force within a community, narrative for Hurston was that remarkable spiritual force that emerged from the group ethos, a spiritual force from which stories of survival and triumph are transmitted through the charismatic power of the griot, African-American storyteller, and preacher. In writing her novels, folklore collections, and autobiography, Hurston repeatedly sought to appropriate the power of the tale teller as she attempted to narrate a new spiritual place for blackness and for femininity outside of formal Christianity.

Hurston's views on traditional Christianity are gathered mostly in *Dust Tracks on a Road*. Talking of her childhood, she writes, "You wouldn't think that a person who was born with God in the house would ever have questions to ask on the subject."[3] Yet she recounts that with her father, a preacher, and her mother, the Sunday school superintendent, she was thoroughly immersed in the theology, practices, and language of the Missionary Baptist Church of

Eatonville, Florida. She records with pride and enthusiasm, as well as with the hindsight of a trained anthropologist, the intimate rhythms of people's feet beating in the pews, her father's stories and sermons about the landscape of heaven and hell, and the high drama of the "love feast." Contained here, as well as in her folkloric collection *The Sanctified Church* (1981), are accounts of sermons, spirituals, and "shouting" as well as the visions of worshippers who "got close enough to peep into God's sitting room windows." Also recorded are her childhood observations that when the moment passed, these same visionaries "plowed, chopped wood, went possum-hunting, washed clothes, raked up back yards and cooked collard greens like anybody else." Mystified by this discrepancy, she wrote, "There were so many things they neglected to look after while they were right there in the presence of All-Power. I made up my mind to do better if ever I made the trip."[4] She thoroughly enjoyed the revival meetings, whose effects she ascribes to the bardic storytelling and poetry, moving musical expression, tense harmonic chants of call and response, and personal charisma of the black ministers. Yet no matter how much she reveled in the beautifully poetic and dramatic use of black folk vernacular in these religious forms, she was already skeptical. She puzzled over "passionate declarations of love for a being that nobody could see and who found fault constantly," and admitted to being afraid to reveal her doubts to her school chums for fear of rejection. She explained, "The questions went to sleep in me. I just said the words and made the motions and went on."[5]

Nature appears to have been a greater source of inspiration to her, even during these early years, and its influence remained. Even as a child, Hurston began to sense cosmic forces in nature, whose power went beyond the formulations of the communal Christian worship within her father's church. She described herself as a child making up tales after talking to a pine tree, the wind, and the lake.[6] Nature, even in these early accounts, became "Dame Nature,"[7] a goddess of awesome powers to this young religious initiate. She identified personally with this now-feminized force and declared, "I am the eternal feminine with its string of beads."[8] This feminocentric pantheism, which sustained her through most of her life, certainly hastened her disenchantment with such naively realistic religious forms of expression as those practiced in her Eatonville community by a father whose personal life steadily alienated her and slowly killed her mother.

Hurston quickly outgrew the Southern Baptist Christianity of her childhood and, ultimately, historical Christianity itself, but she did not abandon her quest for a fuller experience and understanding of the sacred. It was a quest centered in her search for a deeper understanding of the relationship between human necessity, myth, folklore, history, and religion. During her twenties, when Hurston studied under the famous Columbia University anthropologists Franz Boas, Ruth Benedict, and Gladys Reichard, she came to a more fully articulated belief in paganism and nature worship as the foundation of all world religions.[9] The force of God, she concluded, is conveyed through the power of nature. She had come to believe that most of the Bible and its heroes were folklore and that the spread of Christianity as a worldwide religion was due to the brilliant proselytizing efforts of Paul and the mighty converting power of Constantine's armies.

During this educational process, she acquired much academic knowledge about how the verbal and spiritual worlds relate to one another and hence about how to interpret them mythopoetically. In short, during these formative years of her university training, first at Barnard College and later at Howard University, Hurston became a serious and well-trained social scientist who understood how mythos, logos, and ethos coinhere and what Western Christian patriarchal culture means to black women in particular.

JONAH'S GOURD VINE (1934)

Jonah's Gourd Vine, Hurston's first novel, was published when she was 47 years old and had been in New York for seven years. She was well known on the black literary scene, and it was generally thought that she was trying to write a serious novel. Hurston did not, however, produce a book that pleased members of the New Negro movement. *Jonah's Gourd Vine* is a partly autobiographical account of Hurston's early personal pain over patriarchy, Christianity, the South, and religious authority. It tells a story that is absent from her autobiography, *Dust Tracks in the Road,* written eight years later. Though little read now, *Jonah's Gourd Vine* documents the psychological wounds she and her mother sustained from John Hurston's constant infidelities and abandonments of the family. The book concerns a gifted black man, John Pearson, who, through the devotion of a better-educated wife, Lucy, becomes a renowned preacher—only to lose all when his adultery and abandonments of family kill his wife, alienate his children, outrage his parishioners, and result in his own violent death. *Jonah's Gourd Vine* has excited relatively little interest either as a novel or as a book about the black community and its folk religious practices, yet it contains much of the linguistic richness of the black church as well as the pain of women and children held hostage by black preacher-poets who could never live up to the brilliance of their improvisational art. Into the work went more of Hurston's childhood trauma over her mother's plight and eventual death than she perhaps realized.

Jonah's Gourd Vine did not stir contemporaneous readers. Andrew Burris, writing in *The Crisis,* expressed his disappointment at its "failure" as a novel and thought Hurston had "used her characters and the various situations created for them as mere pegs upon which to hang their dialect and their folkways." Despite a few reviews to the contrary, thus began a long tradition of reading that persisted until Hurston's death in 1960, in which her works were trivialized as entertaining dialect contributions to black culture and folkways. Some reviewers celebrated the book for its juicy humor, telling depictions of black folkways, and "vivid pictures of Negro life"; others complained that "her style falls flat when she brings in events for which the reader is unprepared." Nick Aaron Ford, in his book *The Contemporary Negro Novel,* thought the story a failure because unlike Ben Hur, John Pearson does not rise from a rotten social order to win the applause of his enemies. Ford also raised an issue that has always plagued black writers: that less informed readers might find "a happy confirmation of what they already faintly believe: namely, that the Negro is incapable of profiting by experience or of understanding the deeper mysteries of life." Martha Gruening, writing in the *New Republic,* concurred that Hurston had written the story of John Pearson with "freedom from the conventional sentimentality so frequent in writing about Negroes." Margaret Wallace noted that "[i]ts essence lies . . . in the rhythm and balance of the sentences, in the warm artlessness of the phrasing." Only the *New York Herald's* Josephine Pinckney saw Hurston's "full grasp" of the "dramatic qualities" of the story, even though she found John Pearson's wife, Lucy, "too noble" and unconvincing. Hershel Brickell in the *North American Review* called John Pearson's sermon "simply magnificent," as did the *New York Age's* Mary Ovington White, who praised its magnificent phraseology. In short, the subtle ethnographic agendas, the womanist critique, and the biographical dimensions of the book were invisible to these early reviewers. Furthermore, a trivializing critical paradigm had been applied to Hurston that would remain in place for the next 14 years of her publishing career. Sadly, even after the resurgence of interest in Hurston from the 1970s on, critics have found little of interest in this novel.[10]

MULES AND MEN (1935)

Prior to publishing *Mules and Men,* Hurston had been involved in Negro theater and folklore concerts and had written essays on southern black Christian expressive forms. She spent the summer revising the manuscript while staying in a cabin situated in a sawmill camp in Loughman, Florida, where she had collected so much of her material. *Mules and Men* is a collection of 70 tales recorded by Hurston on several extended "expeditions" to the American South while under the patronage of Mrs. Mason Osgood and Columbia University. Written in New York between March 1930 and September 1932, after Hurston's return from the field, the work is divided into two parts, "Folk Tales" and "Voodoo." The tales, which are reported as actual performance, are unified by a narrator who shows the reader through her eyes the performance, social context, and social functions of the stories in the rural black community. Hurston's stories are a far cry from the dry and supposedly unsituated presentation of ethnographic material favored by the "scientific" anthropologists of the day. Franz Boas, realizing the value of her achievement with both the "folklore" and the "folk," noted in his preface to the novel that "the intimate setting in the social life of the Negro" was a feature largely absent from previous ethnographically presented folklore collections. He realized that Hurston had broken from the scientific method for good reasons but was puzzled to know how to treat the narrational structure and its presentation of the folkloric forms.

Few other reviewers and critics were aware of this departure from the formulas of "scientific" ethnographic reporting, though many praised the book for its entertainment value, charm, and authenticity. Henry Lee Moon in the *New Republic* called it "a valuable picture of the life of the unsophisticated Negro in the small towns and backwoods of Florida," though he was puzzled by its aesthetic rationale. H. I. Brock astutely recognized that the added value of this account was its ability to create the illusion that its outsider readers had somehow been admitted to the company of the insiders in a "listening in" sort of way, but he otherwise seemed to be at a loss. Such critics as Jonathan Daniels, who wrote in *The Saturday Review* that *Mules and Men* was a "remarkable" book, "rich enough to stand both skepticism and familiarity," were in the minority. Sterling Brown, who had problems with Hurston's depiction of the black storyteller as free of malice, complained that the characters lacked social consciousness and then raised the perennial question of a black writer's social and artistic responsibilities. He thought Hurston had provided a relatively uninflected, sentimentalized portrait of facile and superstitious blacks and was guilty of professional colonialism. Harold Preece of *The Crisis* dismissed her as a literary climber who had described her race as servile and who deserved the criticism of the black community. Only B. C. McNeill, writing in the *Journal of Negro History,* noted that whatever the book's intention, Hurston had successfully worked out how to form local atmosphere in modern novels dealing with "ethnic" or "local" characters. Others, such as Jonathan Daniels, simply erased both Hurston's presence and her racial identity in their reading of the book: "No advantage of skin or blood could have produced the book which Miss Hurston brought back from the gay 'woofing' of Florida's lumber camps and the tawdry rituals off the little sinister streets in New Orleans's Vieux Carré." Only Henry Lee Moon urged a larger meaning for the book.[11]

In the 1930s most black writers and critics were concerned about the Depression and the plight of urban black people. Hence Hurston's celebratory work was misread. Its implicit comments on racism and economic hardship were too subtle for an audience attuned to the blatant style of the proletarian novel or to the painful naturalism of such writers as Richard Wright. The book, which was published in the same year that the Scottsboro trial took place, seemed to many black intellectuals to be "disembodied." Many of Hurston's intellectual peers thought she had deliberately turned her back on the plight of the black community to reproduce pastoral images of a bygone era. They thought her too politically naive and too colonized to have a "black" viewpoint. That is a far cry from the current view, which now interprets Hurston as a writer very much involved with black consciousness, powerlessness, protest, and confrontation. Post-Depression critics, including James W. Byrd (1955), Robert Bone (1958 to 1966), Darwin T. Turner (1971), and Ann L. Rayson (1975), saw *Mules and Men* and *Tell My Horse* merely as standard collections of folklore. Darwin Turner, in his *In a Minor Chord: Three Afro-American Writers and Their Search for Identity*, lists almost apologetically *Mules and Men*'s numerous literary and scholarly sins as a supposedly ethnographic collection of folktales.[12]

Beginning mainly with Robert Hemenway's biography of Hurston (1977), however, *Mules and Men* came increasingly to be regarded as a new genre of African-American literature formed by "an ethnographic artist." Franz Boas, too, in his 1935 preface to *Mules and Men*, praises Hurston for providing what other (white) folklorists had not: "the intimate setting in the social life of the Negro." Hurston's sophisticated awareness of the processes of folklore in relation to context, as reflected in her break from the scientific and analytical to the journalistic and personal, would alter the way folklore was understood. It would also change the way critics would ultimately read her text. Hurston's intentions in the volume and its performance dimension were now addressed. Hemenway had gone back to Boas's preface and made his own comments on oral art functioning as narrative in community. He then commented on its natural setting, the craft with which Hurston mediated between self and materials, and her skillful creation of a narrator who would not intrude on the folklore event. Hemenway also talked about how she had chosen a narrative format for her "fieldwork account" and wrote always with a literary goal of incorporating scholarly conventions into her work as a crafted part of her story. Among this generation of commentators, however, only Marion Kilson saw *Mules and Men* as a unique literary work of art.[13]

In the 1990s it was Cheryl Wall who spearheaded a series of new scholarly conversations on this book, by calling *Mules and Men* an "under-discussed classic in Afro-American literature and American anthropology," a work in which Hurston, despite a title that singles out men, actually celebrates women. She demonstrates how Hurston carefully uses narrative strategies that "allow her to represent . . . the ways in which women are relegated to subordinate roles" and "the means by which women in that culture gain access to creative expression and power." Wall notes that the subtext of the book is the narrative of a successful female quest for "empowerment." She also points out that "Zora" first introduces herself as diffident and naive but that, as the journey South progresses, she is transformed from initiate to power player by her encounters with Big Sweet, her guardian and guide, and by the spirit of Marie Leveau, the great New Orleans voodoo priestess. Wall interprets the book as a paradigmatic immersion narrative that prefigures the movement of *Their Eyes Were Watching God,* a "mother text" in the tradition of black women's writing.[14]

Beulah Hemmingway (1991) sees in this slender volume Hurston's acceptance of Africanity and her protest against the sterility of white American culture. She recognizes Hurston's careful choice of rural black southerners as griots and tale tellers who were relatively uninfluenced by the larger white culture. For her, Hurston's characters are clever, proud, dignified people whose acute social awareness enables them "to parry harsh insults from other Blacks and glaring disrespect from whites" and who "collectively . . . shared an ethos by which their souls lived, readily defended their humanity, and shaped and controlled . . . their own world and destiny." She finds in *Mules and Men* "the legends, myths, proverbs, and games . . . [that] represent a satirical description of the world and the inter- and intragroup relations of its people." She concludes that future scholarship will "reveal a system of cultural values predicated on an African worldview." Howard J. Faulkner (1991) also praises Hurston's art, pointing out that *Mules and Men* is a complexly structured book that moves from simplicity to complexity and back to simplicity, employing techniques of exaggeration, figuration, dialect, punning, neologism, and the anticlimax customary in recorded tales. He sees that "Zora" the narrator has arranged the tales in an exceedingly complex set of frames within frames, all merging into the living expression of the narrator's natural discourse.[15]

Sandra Dolby-Stahl (1992) developed both Wall's and Faulkner's analyses by describing the first-person narrator in *Mules and Men* as a metafolklorist who has chosen the novelist's format rather than an ethnographer's. Dolby-Stahl notes how Hurston deliberately dispensed with classifications, index numbers, comparative notes, and informant data on 25 tales to offer contextual information of a different kind. She argues that the analytical commentary offered through the device of the narrator or through the informants is called "metafolklore," or folklore about folklores, and should be viewed as a literary technique.[16]

D. A. Boxwell (1992) adds much to the discussion of the construction and function of the narrator in *Mules and Men*. In his " 'Sis Cat' as Ethnographer," he claims that Hurston had an understanding far ahead of her time and cites anthropologist Clifford Geertz, who has argued for the essential fictionality of anthropological texts, for anthropology to recognize that its discipline requires the same kinds of imaginative acts that are necessary to create fictional literature. He notes that the characters in the stories are all subordinated to the ordering presence of Hurston as narrator. Hurston is "Sis Cat," a feline persona through whom she negotiates her own self-empowerment. "I'm sitting here like Sis Cat, washing my face and usin' my manners," says the narrator, thus re-creating herself as a magical creature who has broken free of her profession's constraints. Such recent commentary indicates a relatively new acceptance of Hurston's novelistic or narrative ethnography.[17]

THEIR EYES WERE WATCHING GOD (1937)

In 1935, the same year *Mules and Men* was published, Hurston proposed an ethnological study of African folklore in Haiti. By April 14, 1936, she was there on a Guggenheim Fellowship and preparing to study Obeah (magic) practices. She lived among the Maroons, descendants of people who fought their way out of slavery, and immersed herself in folk ritual, magic, medicine, and learning Creole. In just three months, she acquired a working knowledge of voodoo. However, the folklore project was aborted for the time being. In December Hurston took a trip to Ile de la Gonâve, near Port-au-Prince, and according to Hemenway fell in love with the languorous air, rich green foliage, and luminous sea. In just seven weeks she wrote *Their Eyes Were Watching God*. This love story took its impetus from her affair with a West Indian whom she had met in New York in 1931 and then again briefly while in graduate school. Trapped between his career and her own, Hurston, with a great sense of pain and loss, had severed the relationship. Subsequently, she made a failed attempt to enroll for graduate work in anthropology at Columbia, where she was unable to register for financial reasons. She began instead to revise the novel that she had submitted in draft form to Lippincott in the late spring of 1936. The book underwent very little revision prior to its publication in 1937.

Unfortunately for the reception of *Their Eyes*, the black urban protest novel was much in vogue, and Hurston's novel struck reviewers as unfashionable, if not downright anachronistic. One male reviewer described its central figure, Janie, as an "upstanding coffee-colored quadroon [who] outlasts all three of her men—the last only because she was quicker on the trigger than he was—goes back to her village to rest in peace and makes her friends' eyes bug out at the tales of what she and life have done together." He warned that southern readers would disregard the egalitarian groupings in the novel, whereas northerners would find much indigestible food for thought. Richard Wright, much influenced by the vogue of naturalistic and proletarian fiction, wrote in the *New Masses* that although "her dialogue manages to catch the psychological movements of the Negro folk-mind in their pure simplicity," Hurston was actually perpetuating minstrel images of the happy, laughing darkie. He dismissed the novel primarily because it did not address the race or class struggles of urban black people in America's northern cities. W. A. Hunton thought the book an argument for Negro isolationism, since it seemed to argue that this was the only condition under which the Negro could be himself, and Sterling Brown noted a "bitterness, sometimes oblique, in the enforced folk manner." Ralph Ellison commented on "the blight of calculated burlesque that has marred" most of Hurston's writing. But Alain Locke's review apparently disappointed her the most. He thought *Their Eyes* folklore fiction at its best and wondered when "Hurston was going to come to grips with motive fiction and social document fiction."[18]

These mixed responses indicate the typical confusion occasioned by Hurston's working outside of familiar literary genres. For instance, Lucy Tompkins noted Hurston's avoidance of the current vogue valorizing the primitive. She further noted that Hurston had created the perfect male-female relationship, that she had produced a novel "about every one, or at least every one who isn't so civilized that he has lost the capacity for glory." There were the usual comments on the book's technical flaws, its faulty style, its word-prettiness, and its aiming at "literary" effects. One reviewer even found the now-famous prologue confusing and unnecessary. Only Ethel Forrest found the book gripping, natural in style, and an accurate historical reflection of the times. Clearly, neither white nor black critics were prepared for this novel.[19]

In the last 15 years, many of these early mixed responses have been overturned by a radical reassessment of the novel. Virtually ignored from 1947 until Alice Walker's rediscovery of it in the 1970s, *Their Eyes* is now much celebrated and hailed as one of the great women's texts in American literature. The avalanche of books, essays, and doctoral dissertations on it that followed Walker's rediscovery of Hurston have virtually precluded attention to her other works. Robert Hemenway called *Their Eyes* the most truly coherent African-American narrative to date and a precursor to Ralph Ellison's great masterwork *Invisible Man* and to a host of other African-American narratives. The 1980s brought several new perspectives. *Their Eyes* was variously treated as a black woman's *Künstlerroman*, as the work of a black female blues singer, as by and about a black-identified woman, as a novel establishing a strong black female self-authorizing voice, or as an exposure of the struggle between black men and women.[20] Generally *Their Eyes* was raised to the status of icon of the Harlem Renaissance, a work featuring a black Colossa of heroic proportions who calls, recalls, fishes for life itself, and makes remarkable pictures.

Missy Dehn Kubitschek retrieved Hurston from her designation as socially uninformed romantic elitist by viewing Janie as a heroic figure who charts new territory and can now issue calls in the manner of the call-and-response patterns in black music and gospel. Houston Baker credits Hurston with being a blues singer of great lyrical power who has provided a critique of African-American women's psychic history from slavery to the present. He reads *Their Eyes* as a parody of a black middle class, thoroughly imbued with the worst values of capitalism and respectability. Deriving from slave narrative, Baker argues, *Their Eyes* enacts a "rupture" between traditional American literary history and an alternative Afro-American discourse by producing a fictive African-American history to stand alongside more popular or officially sanctioned fictions.[21]

The great majority of commentators provided womanist and feminist treatments of Janie's evolution from silence to namer to maker, one who reflects the self-division among black women. Others have seen the book as an intertext for later American feminist writing, a book employing free and indirect discourse that critiques male writing. There is much critical discussion of the book's revoicing of the typical African-American identity issue by providing a parable of race that crosses lines of color, class, and gender. Summing up this decade of critical commentary, Harold Bloom, in his introduction to *Zora Neale Hurston*, sees her as the inheritor of several traditions: American, vitalist, and feminist. He places the novel inside the heroic-vitalist tradition that extends from Richardson's *Pamela* to Dreiser and Lawrence.[22]

By 1990 over 200,000 copies of *Their Eyes Were Watching God* had been sold since the first printing, a phenomenon that began with the 1977 publication of Hemenway's biography, *Zora Neale Hurston*. But its immense popularity is also the result of academy-based critics seizing upon it as an agent of political change, to alter, subvert or explode the prevailing American literary canon. Sandra Pouchet Pacquet applauds *Their Eyes* because it shows the restorative and repository value of folklore in American literature and is a powerful spiritual and artistic resource that focuses on the typically modernist theme of alienation from one's ancestral roots. Sigrid King mines the book for its rituals and naming powers. Joseph Urgo and Michael Awkward see the novel as having become emblematic of the issues of canon exclusion, the female struggle for voice, the African-American search for literary heritage, and the validity of cultural criticism. Michael Awkward further credits *Their Eyes* with having given rise to the literary careers of Alice Walker, Gloria Naylor, Jamaica Kincaid, and Toni Morrison. Gabrielle Foreman explores the formal revisions, echoes, and parodies of earlier texts by Frances Harper, Jessie Fauset, and Nella Larsen. Nellie McKay calls this text a crosscultural, "crayon enlargement" of both an individual and a communal self that creates, through its female-journey motif, a new history.[23]

Hazel Carby sums up much of this critical interest by addressing the reasons for the immense popularity of this book in the 1980s and '90s. She suggests that its recent enthusiastic rediscovery derives from a combination of factors: support from the MLA, the book trade, special courses, women's studies programs, scholars, and teachers. She worries that its fate may be to evaporate at the end of the century, when women's and black texts are no longer in vogue or exotic. Otherwise Carby sees the novel as a nostalgic, romantic, and colonial work that chronicles the loss of a certain part of black culture that Hurston experienced during her childhood. The novel's tensions, she argues, arise from Hurston being simultaneously an intellectual and one of the folk, thus producing a form of the anthropological spyglass in which the anthropologist spies on herself. Carby also attributes the popularity of this novel with white readers in particular to the crisis in urban America of cities under siege. She believes it to be no coincidence that, during a period in American social history when one in four black males is in prison, awaiting trial or on parole, and when black children face the prospect of no adequate health care, *Their Eyes* has become the most widely taught black novel. *Their Eyes*, Carby argues, assures us that black folks are really happy and healthy.[24]

Early 1990s commentators began a serious discussion of the distinct African-American aesthetic *Their Eyes* demonstrates. Cathy Brigham sees the novel as a many-voiced text that divests the dominant discourse of its power and thus foregrounds the processes of cultural construction. In this reading Janie comes to represent pure possibility. Others see the book as distinctly modern, with its blending of realism, romance, myth, religion, psychology, and nostalgia. Vanessa Dickerson reads the novel as an illustration of how each community approaches God through metaphor, reminding us that "the gods we see and worship say more about [us] than about any supernatural being." Dolan Hubbard sees Hurston talking of religion as a model for making sense that externalizes through its language the values of black culture by providing a testimony or sermon that features the classical biblical image of the looker standing before the horizon watching ships and dreams on its far reaches. For Rachel Blau DuPlessis, the text is heterogeneous or heteroglossal, an incessant dialogue on color by a protagonist whose childhood name, Alphabet, suggests that she is literally made of conflicting signs regarding race, gender, roles, class, and age. Alphabet-Janie is multiplicity and plurality itself, she argues, a character through whom Hurston critiques the hegemonics of story making. As all the characters watch God before and after the storm approaches, she suggests, they watch warily, crossculturally, bifocally, and color-blindly.[25] Critical enthusiasm about this text seems far from exhausted.

TELL MY HORSE (1939)

Hurston's fourth book, *Tell My Horse*, is her three-part account of the voodoo cults of Jamaica and Haiti, for which did the field work in 1936, the year she instead wrote *Their Eyes Were Watching God. Tell My Horse* contains sections on Haitian culture, politics, personalities, and voodoo practices. In May of 1937, Hurston was back in Port-au-Prince on her second Guggenheim Fellowship. This time her focus of study had shifted from the rituals of the benign Rada gods to those of the more dangerous Petro gods. But she apparently failed to heed warnings about needing a spiritual guide for this research. By late June 1937, in a remote part of the bush, she became violently ill and had to be carried out to the home of the American consul. She was convinced that her illness and her voodoo studies were related. In Hemenway's words, "She had gone deeply enough into the Caribbean night. . . . In Haiti the material had engulfed her, and she needed the perspective of home."[26] But she would not complete the ambitious project to give a full account of voodoo or the voodoo gods. She went back to New York in September, left for Florida in February, and finished *Tell My Horse* in mid-March of 1938.

Contrary to Hurston's expectations, the book did not sell well. According to Hemenway, "It is Hurston's poorest book, chiefly because of its form. She was a novelist and folklorist, not a political analyst or traveloguist."[27] He points out that she did, however, see her topic as sophisticated and ancient, and thus subordinated the more lurid sexual and sensational aspects of voodoo that existed in the popular imagination to those aspects that were of interest to professional ethnographers.

Among the early reviews, the *New York Times* was the most flattering in its praise of the balance and level-headedness of Hurston's vivid, lyrical, and nonsensational style. The *New Yorker* reviewer, however, called the book a disorganized "witches' brew bubbling in the stewpot of a transplanted African culture." Harold Courlander in the *Saturday Review of Literature* believed the book warmer than comparable works by Constance Seabrook and Melville Herskovits because of its dialogue, humor, exaggeration, and honesty. He felt, however, that the material had not been fully digested. Only Carter G. Woodson, writing in the *Journal of Negro History,* found the book both important and entertaining.[28]

Tell My Horse has been given little critical treatment since its initial publication. Ishmael Reed, however, in his foreword to the 1990 Lippincott edition, praises Hurston's thorough account of the "Neo-African religion," of the main *loas* (gods). He finds her storytelling gifts immense and admires her intelligent and jargon-free comments on botany, anthropology, geology, and politics. Her greatest achievement, he claims, is her revelation about "the profound beauty and appeal of a faith older than Christianity, Buddhism, and Islam."[29]

MOSES, MAN OF THE MOUNTAIN (1939)

Published on the eve of World War II, *Moses, Man of the Mountain* is Hurston's assessment of 5,000 years of Judeo-Christian patriarchy, as manifested in Hitler's anti-Semitism and in American racism. Using a traditional reading of Exodus as a liberation story interpreted in the context of black America, Hurston set about disclosing the deleterious effects on women and men of a Judeo-Christianity founded on the ideologies of the hypermasculine nation-state building. In many ways, *Moses* is the culmination of Hurston's consistent fascination with racism, Christianity, Western culture, and women. Her choice of narrative methods was brilliant because, within the oral narrative and the sacred-music traditions of African-American Christianity, Moses is anointed by Yahweh to be the great emancipator of the dispossessed and enslaved. Hurston understood that for the black community this story is contemporary and tangible. Furthermore, writing *Their Eyes Were Watching God* as a feminocentric escape from southern Christianity and its social scripts for women opened the way for Hurston to perform a full-scale dismantling of the very foundations of Judeo-Christianity.

Hurston's purpose in this narrative was to rekidnap Moses for an older African religion. In her introduction, Hurston dismantles Moses as a Hebrew and as a charismatic culture hero and undercuts the exclusivity to Christians and Jews of the legend of Moses the lawgiver. As a trained folklorist, she is able to argue that Asia and all the Near East, not to mention Africa, are sown with legends of this character that are so numerous and varied that they cast doubt on Moses' exclusively Hebrew identity. In the Haitian pantheon, she explains, his full name is Damballa Ouedo Ouedo Tocan Freda Dahomey, and wherever Africans have been scattered by slavery Moses is the fount of mystic powers. "So all across Africa, America, the West Indies, there are tales of the powers of Moses and the great worship of him and his powers. But it does not flow from the Ten Commandments. It is his rod of power, the terror he showed before all Israel and to the Pharaoh, and THAT MIGHTY HAND."[30] Only Jews and Christians, she insists, revere Moses for delivering the Ten Commandments. Older African traditions revere him primarily for his powerful right hand, which commands the powers of nature and controls heaven and earth.

Hurston's deeper narrative strategies are even more subversive. She will be the female storyteller who will uncover the fundamental patriarchal error at the very foundations of historical Judeo-Christianity and provide a corrosive parallel commentary on both Nazi Germany and white America. Hurston will retell the story of Exodus, Egyptian bondage, and the escape to Israel under the leadership of a charismatic liberator not only to express her view that the American white settlers' promised land of milk and honey was, for black America, bondage to Egypt and slavery but also to critique the gendered and racially ordered foundations of Judeo-Christianity, Germany, and the U.S.

Though the tone of *Moses* is uneven and the book is ultimately a failure, it remains a fascinating minor work of American literature that opens a unique window onto a mid-twentieth-century black female perspective on the genealogy of modern racial and gender injustices. Yet Hurston creates Moses as the great voodoo man who is boastful, supernatural, impulsive, and even harsh with his followers, making it very clear that he has had an authentic religious experience with the burning bush, which profoundly altered him. For Hurston, the priest and conjure man coexist in the one man.

Moses has received relatively little critical attention. Early reviewers were skeptical of a book that seemed untouched by current literary trends. Ralph Ellison called it "chiefly lyrical" and accused Hurston of being unaware of the legacy of technical experimentation left by the great modernists: Joyce, Stein, Anderson, and Hemingway. He thought the book did nothing for "Negro fiction" with what he called its "affirmative" character. Other reviewers repeated the by-now standard mantra of praise for Hurston's mixture of colorful dialect, fact, folklore, and literature. Nearly all failed to recognize the book's intellectual seriousness and complexity and hence trivialized it by praising it as warm, humorous, and poetic. Percy Hutchinson commended it as "homespun" and a fascinating depiction of the "primitive," whereas others patronized its depiction of magic and primitive peoples. Worse, Carl Carmer, reviewing the book for the *New York Herald Tribune*, called it "a fine Negro novel" and concluded that Hurston was making a wonderful contribution to her race. He was patronizingly implying that there was one standard for white novels and a less exacting one for black ones. Alain Locke in *Opportunity* dismissed the book as full of "piquant thrills" and "anthropological gossip." Philip Slomovitz in *Christian Century* considered Hurston's rendering of Moses a magnificent story but chided her for not properly weighing the ethical accomplishments of the prophet and the laws handed down. He had entirely missed the point of her subversion of this typical Judeo-Christian depiction of Moses. Most reviewers failed to grasp even this much of her revisionist historical agenda in this novel.[31]

The year of Hurston's death, 1960, seemed to be a turning point for reassessment of the novel. Fannie Hurst in the *Yale University Library Gazette* paid tribute to Hurston for her contributions to the human race and called *Moses* a book written out of race memory. Darwin Turner called *Moses* Hurston's most accomplished book, saying that if she had written nothing else she should be recognized for this achievement. Richard Barksdale and Keneth Kinnamon, in their *Black Writers of America*, observed that *Moses* "combines fiction, folklore, and religion in an unusual amalgam." In 1974, Arthur Davis in *From the Dark Tower* complained that, despite its racy dialogue and unusual approach, the book does not quite work as a novel because characters, with the exception of Moses, are not fully developed. It was not until 1984, in his introduction to *Moses*, that critic Blyden Jackson recognized this as Hurston's most ambitious book, a work that transcends the genre of the protest novel. He argued that it constituted a significant achievement in Afro-American literature. Reviewing this new edition for the *New York Times*, Henry Louis Gates Jr. affirmed Jackson's reassessment by recognizing that "the myth and allegory in *Moses* protect Hurston from being guilty of mere propaganda." He pointed out that the work is an allegory, after all, of Moses' identity as an African conjurer.[32]

DUST TRACKS ON A ROAD: AN AUTOBIOGRAPHY (1942)

In 1941, Hurston's publisher, J. B. Lippincott, perhaps to dissuade her from writing another novel, approached her with the idea that she should write her autobiography. Hurston protested that she was in the middle of her career, having written two books of folklore, two novels, and a series of articles and short stories; she wanted to publish similar writing. But under financial pressure as always, she started the autobiography in the spring of 1941 while staying with a wealthy California friend, Katherine Mershon. Although she finished a draft of the manuscript by mid-July, she uncharacteristically took another six months to rewrite it. Hemenway suggests that this unusually long rewriting period had to do with her reactions to the bombing of Pearl Harbor. She hated the imperialist aspects of World War II and wrote unflatteringly about American marines. Lippincott, no doubt sensing the reactions of a patriotic American audience in wartime, edited these passages out. Finally published in November of 1942, the book subsequently has been received as the most problematic of all Hurston's works. Thwarted in producing another novel, Hurston wrote herself into this text as a folk character, narrator, and trickster in a quasi-historical, quasi-fictional account of her own life. This self-fictionalizing has baffled critics for years, though now that scholars assume that autobiography is also a fiction about oneself, the work has begun to be revalued. Hurston was always busy creating a public persona that was as much fiction as fact. In *Dust Tracks on a Road,* she simply wrote the most developed account of a lifetime spent developing and sustaining that persona. Writer Fannie Hurst expressed what nearly every reviewer and critic has commented on since, that what emerges from this autobiography is "a woman half in shadow."[33]

Hurston's problem was her racial anguish, her audience, and her time. She lived in an America in which only "primitive" blacks were considered authentic and in which rigid gender codes required obedience and submission of women and blacks to male and white superiority. This perhaps explains Hurston's depiction of a childhood unmarred by issues of race and poverty, or of a disrupted family that caused her to leave home at an early age. It also explains her creation of a woman writer and intellectual who would not be constrained by either white patrons or southern race and gender codes. Consequently, the figure who emerges did not feel entirely authentic to those who knew her. Hurston and J. B. Lippincott knew she would have thoroughly alienated both black and white worlds had she given full vent to the frustrations of a black woman within the male-dominated academic and publishing worlds of the early 1940s. Though she had been published almost at will up to the onset of World War II, Hurston was now considered passé. Failing to see the interplay of these factors, many black critics dismissed the book as "lyin'," make believe, or a propagandistic act of appeasement to the white readership.

Despite the fact that *Dust Tracks* won the Ainsfield Award in Racial Relations, Harold Preece in *Tomorrow* called Hurston's autobiography "the tragedy of a gifted, sensitive mind, eaten up by an egocentrism fed on the patronizing admiration of the dominant white world." Arna Bontemps gave the book a mixed report, calling it brilliant but accusing Hurston of ignoring the serious aspects of Negro life, even implying that this was the very reason she had done so well by herself in the kind of world she found. Darwin Turner took her to task for her conflicting attitudes, her impudence, and her general lack of credibility. In his *In a Minor Chord,* he notes scathingly that "in her artful candor and coy reticence, her contradictions and silences, her irrationalities and extravagant boasts which plead for the world to recognize and respect her—one perceives the matrix of her fiction, the seeds that sprouted and the cankers that destroyed." Further, he thought her conclusions on race were shallow. Other critics were less combative but also less incisive. Ernestine Rose thought the work crude as writing but a good basis for a documentary film on the state of the Negro intellectual. Rebecca Chalmers Barton described it as "the shooting off of bright sparks of personality." W. Edward Farrison, writing for the *Journal of Negro History,* complained of "a noticeable amount of hash-warming," that is, recycled material from *Jonah's Gourd Vine* and *Mules and Men.* The book also served to publicly roast many who had, in her estimation, done her wrong. Those thus depicted were not pleased. However, the *New Yorker* critic called the book "warm, witty, imaginative, rich." [34] Most reviewers were aware that *Dust Tracks* was a combination of fact and fancy, but only a much later generation of critics would appreciate and account for this sophisticated and provocative mixture.

Not until 1972 did this book begin to be taken seriously. Ann Rayson in *Negro American Literature Forum* reassessed it as a staging of myth, quest, anecdote, and narrative as well as a public performance done with charm, vision, and signification. Rayson also suggested that Hurston had inevitably been measured against the standards of black male autobiography and been found to have broken form for not revealing a typical life viewed at the end of a successful career. She saw the book rather as a picaresque story featuring a golden child, a Cinderella fantasy, a Ben Franklin myth, a visionary artistic questing isolato, and a folk heroine. In 1984, however, in his introduction to *Dust Tracks,* Hemenway argues that it fails as an autobiography because it describes neither the public career nor the private self and entirely ignores Hurston's career as a writer. He lists as significant omissions any mention of World War I, the Depression, her books, politics, presidents, the era, the missing 10 years in her life, and the mysterious Mister Neale. But he does describe the exhausting pressures Hurston faced at the hands of an American readership that warned black women writers not to offend. He demonstrates from her letters that Hurston knew she had to produce a book that would further racial harmony, a task that no doubt sent her into camouflage in an attempt to escape her own and society's paradoxes. Thus Hemenway concludes that the book was of necessity a study in subterfuge.[35]

Camouflage, subterfuge, and self-mythicization are all themes central to the next wave of criticism. In the 1970s, Shari Benstock and Elizabeth Fox-Genovese opened up the first discussions about the contingent self in autobiographical writing and about how an "ideal" self interacts with the everyday or "real" self. Autobiographies offer more screens than windows, they point out, and after all *Dust Tracks* is more a collective community history than an account of Hurston's life. In a parallel argument, Deborah G. Plant describes the Zora of the autobiographical production as a folk preacher who is entertaining and oratorically skilled as an actress and as a stand-up comic. She notes how the book is structured around a call, visions, conversions, resistance, suffering, conviction, and acceptance and thus places it as a sacred text in the folk sermonic literature of American culture. Plant was also the first to identify the antiphonal call-and-response patterns, the formulaic systems of thought, and the testimonial to individualism, all masking the book's revolutionary political agendas in religious rhetoric. Claudine Reynaud refuted Darwin's original criticism of Hurston, suggesting that Hurston was subverting the confessional goal of traditional autobiography to write for a white reader ignorant of black culture. She argues instead that Hurston's personal voice strove to become universal, a mask for representing a collective poetic truth in the form of the "signifyin' lying" tale. Thus Hurston avoided the confessional genre, concealed herself, and offered instead her black folklorist persona to the white reader.[36]

In the 1990s, Alice Walker opened a new critical conversation on *Dust Tracks* by commenting that "unctuousness" was out of character for Zora and therefore indicative of her dependency on her publisher. This provoked Kathleen Hassall to suggest that *Dust Tracks* is really a series of performances by an actress trained in Eatonville. For her, Hurston was a warrior in disguise who produced an encoded response to racism by reinventing facts, withholding information, blurring history and fiction, wearing masks, changing hats, lying as a celebration of the human voice, and contradicting herself to prevent closure. She is Gates's signifying monkey, a figure in disguise and a trope for the indeterminate. Through such performances she managed to slip through the ropes, concludes Hassall. Maya Angelou, however, in her introduction to the 1991 edition of *Dust Tracks*, does not let Hurston off so easily. She sees Hurston as the questionable character in the Langston Hughes poem "You've taken my blues and gone" and wonders at Hurston's significant historical omissions about race riots and the Ku Klux Klan, for instance. For Angelou, Hurston is a black liberationist one minute and a nationalist the next, hence too white for most black readers. Although she praises Hurston for her language and survival, Angelou questions such "imperious creativity."[37]

Reynaud, going back into the edited and revised manuscripts of *Dust Tracks*, provides one of the most insightful commentaries. She develops the narrative of the black writer and the white editor as the colonized and the colonizer. She paints a very sad story of the editorial excisions and reordering by Colonel J. B. Lippincott and his assistant, Mrs. Tay Honoff, that destroyed Hurston's original structures of meaning. Raynaud characterizes the book as a minefield of excisions and deletions that dilute the folk speech, alter the erotic voice, censor the profane voice, and eliminate the political voice that would address issues of sexism and race. More recently Paola Boi has suggested that the value of *Dust Tracks* is literary, not historical, since it bears multiple meanings, enacts subterfuge, destroys the dominance of time, and depicts a complex ego afflicted by self-division. For him it is a woman's song in which "I" is the mischievous "eye" that evades historical determinism and enacts conceptual repression.[38] Clearly this critical conversation is just beginning. *Dust Tracks* is now Hurston's most-read and commented-on text after *Their Eyes Were Watching God.*

SERAPH ON THE SUWANEE (1948)

In April 1947, Hurston left Lippincott Publishers for Charles Scribner and Sons, with whom she contracted for a book titled *The Sign of the Sun*. With the $500 advance in hand, she left almost immediately for Honduras. From May to November of 1947, she worked exclusively on this manuscript and changed the title many times. The latter was an indication that neither she nor the work was doing well. Scribner's was not entirely happy with the finished product either. Instead of looking for a lost city, her ostensible reason for going to Honduras, Hurston had had to abandon that project and return during a cold, wintry New York February to work on the revisions of the manuscript that was now titled *Seraph on the Suwanee*. It was her last publication during her lifetime and was not reprinted until 1991, long after all the other books had been reprinted.

With this last book, it appeared that Hurston had finally turned aside from race and religious issues. She had not, however, turned away from gender issues. She focused once again on marriage, only this time within the sphere of white womanhood. Early reviewers did not see the common ground, southern patriarchy, when they summarily dismissed the book because it seemed not to fit with the earlier ones. Their responses—puzzled, lukewarm at best, and few in number—were provoked by Hurston's departure from "Negro subjects." Many were surprised and even offended to learn that dialectal speech was also common to poor white southerners. For reasons of white racial pride, Hurston's expertise with white dialect did not please them, despite her principal reputation, up until this time, as an expert on southern dialect. Though Worth Tuttle Hedden in the *New York Herald Tribune* applauded her for knowing her southern whites as well as she knew her

Negroes, he could not find her in any fixed position. Hence he complained that "incompatible strains in the novel mirror the complexity of the author . . . [who] shuttles between the sexes, the professions, and the races as if she were man and woman, scientist and creative writer, white and Negro." The reviewer in the *Christian Science Monitor* thought the book "earthy" and "wholesome" as well as faithful in its depiction of Florida crackers and their dialect, whereas Frank Slaughter in the *New York Times Book Review* dismissed it as "a textbook picture of a hysterical neurotic, right to the end" and accused Hurston of reading too much Freud. Edward Hamilton, writing in *America,* liked the first two-thirds of the novel but thought it faded at the end. He complimented Hurston for producing a man's man successfully but then complained that the characters mostly reminded him of "half-human puppets." Carl Hughes, in *The Negro Novelist,* remarked on the very Freudian picture of a neurotic Arvay Henderson, but unlike other critics actually approved of Hurston's ending. Only Sterling Brown in *Phylon* noted that too many critics overpraised black dialect and actually seemed pleased at Hurston's ability to capture the speech and social ethos of this class of southern whites. Clearly, none of them looked very hard for the obvious thematic continuities between this latest novel and all the earlier works of fiction, folklore, and autobiography.[39]

When *Seraph on the Suwanee* was published in 1948, initial sales were satisfactory. About 3,000 copies sold after the first month or two, and 2,000 more were printed and ready for sale. But dreadful events were soon to overtake Hurston, causing her years of anguish and even making *Seraph on the Suwanee* a tool for negative publicity against her. According to Carby,

> On September 13, Hurston had been arrested on charges rising from allegations of sexual misconduct with a ten-year-old boy. She emphatically denied all charges, using her passport as evidence that she had been in Honduras at the time the immoral acts were supposed to have taken place. It must have absolutely astounded Hurston that *Seraph on the Suwanee* could become a tool in the publicity that was eventually generated from the allegations made about her. On October 23 the national edition of the Baltimore *Afro-American* published a distorted and inaccurate version of the original allegations, . . . [suggesting] that *Seraph on the Suwanee* advocated sexual aggressiveness in women[,] and then used selected sentences from the novel as if they provided evidence of the author's immorality. . . . [Hurston] was literally tried and found guilty in the widely syndicated story and in a subsequent editorial. . . . Charges against Hurston were not dismissed until March 14, 1949.

Hurston later indicated that betrayal by a black court clerk and a black reporter and libel by a black press had left her suicidal. After these events, she was in no position to promote the new novel, which Carby describes as one of Hurston's most experimental in the "very complexity and depth of Arvay's frustrated and unsatisfied desires. *Seraph on the Suwanee* is a very modern text that speaks as eloquently to the contradictions and conflict of trying to live our lives as gendered beings in the 1990s as it did in 1948," she concludes.[40]

Seraph received no other critical attention until 1989, when Janet St. Clair conceded that, although the "weaknesses of the novel are real, . . . the inconsistencies are the result of a subversive feminist substory that has so far gone unrecognized, a narrative of resistance and self-discovery that exists not between the lines but solidly on every page." She describes how carefully the story shows one woman's efforts "to reject both oppression and, more importantly, the mental submission to oppression." Withdrawal, resistance, and suspicion are motivated by her belief in her own intrinsic worth and in her rights to individual freedom and social respect. St. Clair then goes on to argue that because Arvay Henderson is "consistently denied access to the power of both word and deed, her progress is very slow [until] the end [when] she finds freedom, meaning, a sense of community, and the potential for continued growth in her discovery of an active, inclusive, unconditional love." St. Clair also points out how very anxious Hurston was to publish in the 1940s, an era when black culture and many of its authors lost much of their charm for a postwar America that was primed to resurrect "the [white] hearthside angel." Although St. Clair posits that Hurston may well have decided to signify on the phenomenon using her own observations on the plight of poor white southern women, she suggests that Hurston might also have wavered between courage and cowardice as she wrote this novel for a new era in American social history.[41]

A more complex picture of Hurston's motivations and intentions in *Seraph* emerges in Hazel Carby's historical contextualization of this postwar period in the mainstream and black literary establishments. In her foreword to the 1991 edition of Hurston's last novel, Carby suggests that *Seraph* might also have been her "attempt to realize two ambitions that the author had been working toward throughout the forties. Hurston wanted to sell a novel to Hollywood and to see her fiction transformed into film." But she also wanted to challenge "the apartheid American society" and "conventions [that] . . . she felt dictated that black writers and artists should be concerned only with representing black subjects." Carby points out how confusing the 1940s were for black writers who were torn between their identities as blacks and as Americans. She also notes that since the 1939 publication of *Moses*, Hurston had been writing nonfiction for white audiences. For this she was criticized by black intellectuals for "ignoring serious aspects of black life in order to pander to a white readership." At the same time, reviewers were busy panning the works of black writers for being too narrowly conceived, too much in the tradition of the proletarian protest novel of the pre-Depression era, and too contaminated with political and ideological issues. Furthermore, Carby points out, "Writing about white people was thought by many white critics, reviewers, and publishers to require more literary skill, and more talent, than writing about black characters." Carby also notes the ironies and ambiguities of a text that focuses on the "sometimes violent conflict between men and women that arises from the existence of incompatible and gender-specific desires." She concludes that it is yet to be shown how this last published work of Hurston's develops themes begun much earlier in her writings and treats them in even more complex ways.[42]

THE SANCTIFIED CHURCH (1981)

Written some 60 years before its publication, *The Sanctified Church* is a collection of innovative essays—some previously published, some not—on the folklore, legend, popular mythology, and spiritual configurations of the black Southern Baptist church. It preserves much of the speechways, musical performance, and signifyin' of rural black Florida. Hurston divided the book into three sections. Section 1, entitled "Herbs and Herb Doctors," contains pieces on cures and beliefs, Mother Catherine and Uncle Monday. Mother Catherine, founder of a voodoo sect, and Uncle Monday, a healer, conjurer, and herb doctor, suggest the intersection of Afrocentric voodoo culture and Christianity in this community. Section 2, entitled "Characteristics of Negro Expression," contains pieces on the tricksters, shamans, or conjurers, High John the Conqueror and Daddy Mention, legendary figures whose exploits are vividly reported by prisoners. Section 3, "The Sanctified Church," is rich in contextualized folk material about spirituals, neospirituals, conversions, visions, shouting, sermons, and the sanctified church itself.

As Toni Cade Bambara writes in "Some Forward Remarks," "Like recipes and remedies and vision pieces, [these essays] reflect a life-long interest in 'alternative,' as they say, channels of intelligence and being. . . . They represent too a life-long concern with spirituality." Marion A. Thomas, the work's principal commentator, calls it an important volume for anyone interested in Holiness-Pentecostal movements of the late-nineteenth and early-twentieth centuries. *The Sanctified Church* is an attempt to protest highbrow black Protestantism and to reclaim many of the elements of black religion brought from Africa and grafted onto Christianity soon thereafter.[43]

MULE BONE: A PLAY (1991)

In 1991, 60 years after Hurston and Langston Hughes wrote it, *Mule Bone* was finally published and performed. This folk comedy based on the Eatonville experience of the 1920s is written in the rural black vernacular, which caused consternation among black writers at the time. For 61 years, several black writers have feared that the play might reflect poorly on the black community with its emphasis on folk ways. Gates argues differently, suggesting that had Hurston and Hughes not had their famous falling out, this play, if staged on Broadway in the 1930s, might have significantly influenced the development of black vernacular theater. In 1991, the Lincoln Center Theater staged *Mule Bone* for the first time. It evoked a rather dubious response from such critics as Frank Rich, who wondered if the producer had "watered down" the original script or tried to "resuscitate" a lost, unfinished work. The result, he concluded, was "hokey" and "more folksy than folk."[44]

THE COMPLETE STORIES (1995)

This volume contains 19 previously published stories and 7 unpublished ones. Since its publication, a new short story entitled "Under the Bridge" has been discovered in a cardboard box with other Hurston memorabilia.

In their jointly written introduction, Gates and Lemke point out that as early as 1931, Hurston had secured the reputation of master storyteller. Her earliest critics, such as Lorenzo Dow Turner and Otelia Cromwell, commended her for her command of narrative voice and plotting, her concern with the themes of human justice, her delight in the southern black vernacular voice as a vehicle for narration, and the use of complex dynamics among a small group of Eatonville characters. This introduction is the first critical appraisal of the material. In it, Gates and Lemke point out that Hurston "is concerned to register a distinct sense of space—an African-American cultural space" and that she "is never in a hurry or a rush, pausing over—indeed, luxuriating in—the nuances of speech or the timbre of voice that gives a storyteller her or his distinctiveness." Both critics conclude that Hurston is a storyteller first and an anthropologist second.[45]

The chief value of this collection, argue Gates and Lemke, is the chance to examine Hurston's developing skill, from the Harlem Renaissance to the Korean War and up to the eve of the Civil Rights movement. In addition, they add, Hurston's great themes of love, betrayal, and death mark her as a significant modernist writer.[46]

UNPUBLISHED MANUSCRIPTS

In December 1996, Associated Press reporter Laura Meckler reported that several of Hurston's lost manuscripts had been found after being hidden in a cardboard box for many decades. Among the newly discovered memorabilia is the aforementioned short story titled "Under the Bridge." Also discovered was the text of another play, "Spear," which scholars know of but have never seen.[47]

Hurston's other unpublished writings include two novels, works that also show the persistence of her interest in issues of gender, race, and religion. "The Golden Bench of God" was rejected by Scribner's in 1951. Its subject is the life of Madame C. J. Walker (1867–1919), born Sarah Breedlove, who invents and manufactures products for straightening black women's hair and who is reputed to be the first black woman billionaire. Hurston told her literary agent, Jean Parker Waterbury, that the book was a "truly indigenous Negro novel" written from within the black American world.

During the last phase of her life, from 1953 to 1960, Hurston occupied herself with writing a major novel on the life of Herod the Great. She had read of him in Flavius Josephus, Livy, Eusebeus, Strabo, and Nicolas of Damascus. She thought Herod a great soldier, statesman, and lover and hoped to interest Cecil B. DeMille in making a major epic motion picture of Herod's story. She even asked Winston Churchill to write the introduction and came to refer to the project as her "great obsession." All that remains of the work, which was never published, is an incomplete, charred, and water-stained manuscript and a short story, "The Woman of Gaul," first printed in 1995.[48] Given Hurston's habit of moving frequently with manuscripts packed in her trunks, it seems likely that there will be more discoveries of her unpublished materials.

CONCLUSION

Despite her relative anonymity before her death, Zora Neale Hurston is now seen as the literary foremother of the twentieth-century African-American and women's literary traditions. Her reputation as a writer is no longer in doubt, nor is her place in the canon of major American authors. The enormous amount of attention currently devoted to *Their Eyes Were Watching God* and *Dust Tracks on a Road* suggests that once more she is being carried on a revivalist wave of interest by readers, the publishing industry, and the academy. This time, however, she is no longer lost and hidden in a field of weeds but finally monumentalized as "a genius of the South." Hurston's persistent feminocentric theological revisions of the Judeo-Christian narrative were her attempts to heal the divisions between blacks and whites, paganism and Judeo-Christianity, men and women, divisions that had deeply marked her life. But apart from this grand perspective and her attempts to explain her black community to her white readers, Hurston spoke powerfully from the position of an educated black woman for whom these divisions had become even more transparent, painful, and awe inspiring. Toward the end of *Dust Tracks,* she wrote:

I have walked in storms with a crown of clouds about my head and the zigzag lightning playing through my fingers. The gods of the upper air have uncovered their faces to my eyes. I have found out that my real home is in the water, that the earth is only my stepmother. My old man, the Sun, sired me out of the sea. . . . I know that destruction and construction are but two faces of Dame Nature, and that it is nothing to her if I choose to make personal tragedy out of her unbreakable laws.[49]

It was Hurston's particular genius to be able to connect the microcosm of her own black female experience growing up in Eatonville, Florida, with the larger Western Christian history of race and gender that informed it. In this respect, she took herself and her readers to the far horizons of time, place, and social ideology as narrator, poet, signifier, and ethnologist in parable and story.

Notes

1. Black women writers, such as Zora Neale Hurston, Toni Morrison, Paule Marshall, Alice Walker, Gloria Naylor, Toni Cade Bambara, Nzotake Shange, Audre Lorde, and others, have developed a substantial twentieth-century literary tradition of attempting to write themselves both into and out of the black Christian theological tradition. Some have done so through rejection of black and/or white Christianity by embracing various womanist and/or non-Christian Africanist religious practices. Others, also including Hurston, have engaged in a radical revisioning of those historical and theological structures that valorize masculine and white religious experience to the exclusion of the black and female religious experience. Although Hurston has finally been recognized for her contributions to black folklore and literature, the development of her religious views has captured only the passing interest of critics primarily interested in her feminist pantheism.

2. There are at least two major studies on black Christian attitudes of the post–World War I era that shed some light on the times. Not long after Hurston left Howard University, Benjamin Mays, then a professor of religion there, was preparing a book, *The Negro's God: As Reflected in His Literature, 1760–1937* (New York: Negro Universities Press, 1938), tracing black religion to the present. Strangely, Mays never sought Hurston's views, a matter of some significance since Hurston was well known at Howard as a woman with views on the subjects of race, gender, and religion. Published in 1938, this book concluded that the general trend in black thought about God was disillusionment in institutional Christianity and in the black church since the failure of black participation in The Great War to bring about social change. He concludes: "The Negro is not interested in any fine theological or philosophical discussions about God. *He* is interested in a God who is able to help him bridge this chasm that exists between the actual and the ideal" (255; italics mine). Had he interviewed Hurston he would have found a black female intellectual who was intensely interested in philosophical discussions about God and the failure of black Christianity to alleviate the social realities of the Jim Crow South, especially with regard to its female members.

The second major study, Henry Mitchell's *Belief of Blacks in American and West Africa* (1938; rpt., New York: Harper, 1975), captures a similar mood. Mitchell concludes that black Christians are more interested in "creative faith" than in formal theological development (95). He is referring to the practical application of Christian principles within the community rather than with the intellectual traditions of formal Christian theology. Hurston herself endorsed such a "creative faith" within community rather than any formal theology.

3. Zora Neale Hurston, *Dust Tracks on a Road* (1942; rpt., New York: Harper Collins, 1991), 193.

4. Hurston, *The Sanctified Church: The Folklore Writings of Zora Neale Hurston* (Berkeley, Calif.: Turtle Island Foundation, 1981), 194.

5. Hurston, *Sanctified Church*, 195.

6. Ibid., 69–71.

7. Ibid., 348.

8. Hurston, "How It Feels to Be Colored Me," *World Tomorrow* 11 (May 1928): 154–55.

9. See quotations from the 1927 and 1929 reports to her mentor, anthropologist Franz Boas, in Robert E. Hemenway, *Zora Neale Hurston: A Literary Biography* (Urbana: University of Illinois Press, 1977), 93, 125. See also a quotation from her 30 April 1929 letter to Langston Hughes in Hemenway, *Zora*, xx.

10. Andrew Burris, "The Browsing Reader," *Crisis* 41 (June 1934): 166–67; Martha Gruening, "Darktown Strutter," *New Republic* 79 (July 1934): 244–45; Margaret Wallace, *New York Times Book Review* 83 (6 May 1934): 6–7; Josephine Pinckney, "A Pungent, Poetic Novel about Negroes," *New York Herald Tribune Books* 10 (6 May 1934): 7; Hershel Brickell, review of *Jonah's Gourd Vine*, *North American Review* 238 (July 1934): 95–96; Mary Ovington White, review of *Jonah's Gourd Vine*, *New York Age* 48 (6 May 1934): 6; Nick Aaron Ford, *The Contemporary Negro Novel* (Boston: Meador, 1936).

11. Franz Boas, preface to Hurston, *Mules and Men* (1935; rpt., Philadelphia: J. B. Lippincott, 1990), xiii; Henry Lee Moon, "Big Old Lies," *New Republic* 85 (11 December 1935): 142; H. I. Brock, "The Full, True Flavor of Life in a Negro Community," *New York Times Book Review* 85 (10 November 1935): 4; Johnathan Daniels, "Black Magic and Dark Laughter," *Saturday Review* 22 (19 October 1935): 12; Sterling Brown, unidentified clipping, 25 February 1936, in Hemenway, *Zora*, 219; Harold Preece, "The Negro Folk Cult," *Crisis* 43 (December 1936): 364, 367; B. C. McNeill, *Journal of Negro History* 21 (April 1936): 223–25; Johnathan Daniels, "Black Magic and Dark Laughter," *Saturday Review* 22 (19 October 1935): 12; Henry Lee Moon, "Big Old Lies," *New Republic* 85 (11 December 1935): 142.

12. Hemenway, *Zora*, 220; James W. Byrd, "Zora Neale Hurston: A Negro Folklorist," *Tennessee Folklore Society Bulletin* 21 (June 1955): 37–41; Robert Bone, *The Negro Novel in America* (New Haven, Conn.: Yale University Press, 1966); Darwin Turner, *In a Minor Chord: Three Afro-American Writers and Their Search for Identity* (Carbondale: Southern Illinois University Press, 1971), 89–120.

13. Ann Rayson, "*Dust Tracks on a Road*: Zora Neale Hurston and the Form of Black Autobiography," *Negro American Literature Forum* (Summer 1975): 39–45; Boas, preface, xiii; Hemenway, *Zora*, 165–68; Marion Kilson, "The Transformation of Eatonville's Ethnographer," *Phylon* 33 (Summer 1972): 112–19; Hemenway, *Zora*, 163–67.

14. Cheryl A. Wall, "*Mules and Men* and Women: Zora Neale Hurston's Strategies of Narration and Visions of Female Empowerment," *Black American Literature Forum* 23 (Winter 1989): 661–80.

15. Beulah Hemmingway, "Through the Prism of Africanity: A Preliminary Investigation of Zora Neale Hurston's *Mules and Men*," in *Zora in Florida*, ed. Steve Glassman and Kathryn Lee Seidel (Orlando: University of Central Florida Press, 1991), 38–39, 44; Howard J. Faulkner, "*Mules and Men*: Fiction as Folklore," *CLA Journal* 34 (1991): 331–39.

16. Sandra Dolby-Stahl, "Literary Objectives: Hurston's Use of Personal Narrative in *Mules and Men*," *Western Folklore* 51 (January 1992): 51–63.

17. D. A. Boxwell, " 'Sis Cat' as Ethnographer: Self-Presentation and Self-Inscription in Zora Neale Hurston's *Mules and Men*," *African American Review* 26 (1992): 605–17.

18. Review of *Their Eyes Were Watching God*, *Time* 30 (20 September 1937): 71; Richard Wright, "Between Laughter and Tears," *New Masses* (5 October 1937): 25; W. A. Hunton,

"The Adventures of the Brown Girl in Her Search for Life," *Journal of Negro Education* 7 (January 1938): 71–72; Sterling Brown, " 'Luck Is a Fortune,' " *Nation* (16 October 1937): 410; Ralph Ellison, "Recent Negro Fiction," *New Masses* 40.6 (5 August 1941): 22–26; Alain Locke, review of *Their Eyes Were Watching God, Opportunity* (1 June 1938).

19.   Lucy Tompkins, "In the Florida Glades," *New York Times Book Review* (26 September 1937): 29; Otis Ferguson, "You Can't Hear Their Voices," *New Republic* (13 October 1937): 276; George Stevens, "Negroes by Themselves," *Saturday Review of Literature* (18 September 1937): 3; Sterling Brown, " 'Luck Is a Fortune,' " *Nation* (16 October 1937): 409; Ethel A. Forrest, review of *Their Eyes Were Watching God, Journal of Negro History* 23 (January 1938): 106–7.

20.   Robert Hemenway, "Are You a Flying Lark or a Setting Dove?" in *Afro-American Literature: The Reconstruction of Instruction*, ed. Dexter Fisher and Robert B. Stepto (New York: Modern Language Association of America, 1978), 122–52; Lorraine Bethel, " 'This Infinity of Conscious Pain': Zora Neale Hurston and the Black Female Literary Tradition," in *All of the Women Are White, All the Blacks Are Men, but Some of Us Are Brave: Black Women's Studies*, ed. Gloria T. Hull, Patricia Bell-Scott, and Barbara Smith (Old Westbury, N.Y.: Feminist Press, 1982), 176–88; Wendy J. McCredie, "Authority and Authorization in *Their Eyes Were Watching God*," *Black American Literature Forum* 16 (1982): 25–28; Roger Rosenblatt, "*Their Eyes Were Watching God*," in *Modern Critical Interpretations: Zora Neale Hurston's "Their Eyes Were Watching God*," ed. Harold Bloom (New York: Chelsea House, 1987), 229–33; Mary Jane Lupton, "Zora Neal Hurston and the Survival of the Female," *Southern Literary Journal* 15 (1982): 45–54.

21.   Missy Dehn Kubitschek, " 'Tuh De Horizon and Back': The Female Quest in *Their Eyes Were Watching God*," *Black American Literature Forum* 17 (1983): 109–15; Houston A. Baker Jr. "Ideology and Narrative Form," in *Blues, Ideology, and Afro-American Literature: A Vernacular Theory* (Chicago: University of Chicago Press, 1984), 35–39; Barbara Johnson, "Metaphor, Metonymy, and Voice in *Their Eyes Were Watching God*," in *Black Literature and Literary Theory*, ed. Henry Louis Gates Jr. (New York: Methuen, 1984), 205–19; Elizabeth Meese, "Orality and Textuality in *Their Eyes Were Watching God*," in *Crossing the Double Cross: The Practice of Feminist Criticism* (Chapel Hill: University of North Carolina Press, 1986), 39–53; Barbara Johnson and Henry Louis Gates Jr., "A Black and Idiomatic Free Indirect Discourse," in *Modern Critical Interpretations: Zora Neale Hurston's "Their Eyes Were Watching God*," ed.

22.   Bloom, 73–85; Barbara Johnson, "Thresholds of Difference: Structures of Address in Zora Neale Hurston," *Critical Inquiry* 12 (Autumn 1985): 278–89; Harold Bloom, introduction to *Modern Critical Interpretations: Zora Neale Hurston's "Their Eyes Were Watching God*," ed. Bloom, 1–4.

23.   Sandra Pouchet Paquet, "The Ancestor as Foundation in *Their Eyes Were Watching God* and *Tar Baby*," *Callaloo* (Summer 1990): 499–515; Sigrid King, "Naming and Power in Zora Neale Hurston's *Their Eyes Were Watching God*," *Black American Literature Forum* (Winter 1990): 683–97; Joseph R. Urgo, "The Tune Is the Unity of the Thing: Power and Vulnerability in Zora Neale Hurston's *Their Eyes Were Watching God*," *Southern Literary Journal* (Spring 1991): 40–54; Michael Awkward, " 'The inaudible voice of it all': Silence, Voice, and Action in *Their Eyes Were Watching God*," in *Black Feminist Criticism and Critical Theory*, ed. Joe Weixlmann and Houston A. Baker Jr. (Greenwoods, Fla.: Penkevill, 1988), 57–109; Gabrielle Foreman, "Looking Back from Zora, or Talking out Both Sides My Mouth for Those Who Have Two Ears," *Black American Literature Forum* (Winter 1990): 649–67; Michael Awkward, *Inspiring Influences: Tradition, Revision, and Afro-American Women's Novels* (New York: Columbia University Press, 1991); Nellie McKay, " 'Crayon Enlargements of Life': Zora Neale Hurston's *Their Eyes Were Watching God* as Autobiography," in *New Essays of "Their Eyes Were Watching God*," ed. Michael Awkward (Cambridge, England: Cambridge University Press, 1990), 51–70.

24.   Hazel V. Carby, "The Politics of Fiction, Anthropology, and the Folk: Zora Neale Hurston," in *New Essays of "Their Eyes Were Watching God*," ed. Awkward, 71–93.

25.   Cathy Brigham, "The Talking Frame of Zora Neale Hurston's Talking Book: Storytelling as Dialectic in *Their Eyes Were Watching God*," *CLA Journal* 37 (June 1994): 402–19; Vanessa D. Dickerson, " 'It Takes Its Shape from de Shore It Meets': The Metamorphic God in

Hurston's *Their Eyes Were Watching God,*" *Literature, Interpretation, Theory* 2 (1991): 221–30; Dolan Hubbard, " '. . . Ah said Ah'd save de text for you': Recontextualizing the Sermon to Tell (Her)story in Zora Neale Hurston's *Their Eyes Were Watching God,*" *African American Review* 27 (1993): 167–79; Rachel Blau DuPlessis, "Power, Judgment, and Narrative in a Work of Zora Neale Hurston: Feminist Cultural Studies," in *New Essays of "Their Eyes Were Watching God,"* ed. Awkward, 95–123.

26. Hemenway, *Zora,* 248.

27. Ibid., 248–49.

28. "Lore of Haiti," *New York Times Book Review* (23 October 1938): 12; review of *Tell My Horse, New Yorker* (15 October 1938): 71; Harold Courlander, "Witchcraft in the Caribbean Islands," *Saturday Review of Literature* 18 (15 October 1938): 6–7; Carter G. Woodson, review of *Tell My Horse, Journal of Negro History* 24 (January 1939): 116–18.

29. Ishmael Reed, foreword to Hurston, *Tell My Horse* (1938; rpt., New York: Harper-Collins, 1990), xi–xv.

30. Hurston, author's introduction to *Moses, Man of the Mountain* (1939: rpt., New York: HarperCollins, 1991), xxiii–xxiv.

31. Ralph Ellison, "Recent Negro Fiction," *New Masses* (5 August 1941): 22–26; review of *Moses, Man of the Mountain, New Yorker* (15 November 1939): 75; Percy Hutchinson, "Led His People Free," *New York Times Book Review* (19 November 1939): 21; Carl Carmer, "Biblical Story in Negro Rhythm," *New York Herald Tribune Books* (26 November 1939): 5; Alain Locke, "The Negro: New or Newer," *Opportunity* (February 1939): 38; Philip Slomovitz, "The Negro Moses," *Christian Century* 6 (December 1939): 1504; Hemenway, *Zora,* 275–76.

32. Fannie Hurst, "Zora Neale Hurston: A Personality Sketch," *Yale University Library Gazette* 35 (1960): 17–22; Turner, *In a Minor Chord,* 109; Richard Barksdale and Keneth Kinnamon, *Black Writers of America: A Comprehensive Anthology* (New York: Macmillan and Co., 1972), 611–13; Arthur Davis, *From the Dark Tower: Afro-American Writers, 1900–1960* (Washington, D.C.: Howard University Press, 1974), 113–21; Blyden Jackson, introduction to Hurston, *Moses, Man of the Mountain,* vii–xix; Henry Louis Gates Jr., "A Negro Way of Saying," *New York Times Book Review* (21 April 1985): 1, 43.

33. Hurst, "Zora Neale Hurston: A Personality Sketch," 17–22.

34. Harold Preece, review of *Dust Tracks on a Road, Tomorrow* (February 1943), qtd. in Hemenway, *Zora,* 289; Arna Bontemps, "From Eatonville, Fla., to Harlem," *New York Herald Tribune Books* (22 November 1942): 3; Turner, *In a Minor Chord,* 90–91; Ernestine Rose, review of *Dust Tracks on a Road, Library Journal* 67 (1 November 1942): 950; Rebecca Chalmers Barton, *Witnesses for Freedom: Negro Americans in Autobiography* (New York: Harper, 1948), 101–14; W. Edward Farrison, *Journal of Negro History* 28 (July 1943): 352–55; review of *Dust Tracks on a Road, New Yorker* 18 (14 November 1942): 79.

35. Rayson, *"Dust Tracks on a Road,"* 39–45; Robert E. Hemenway, introduction to Hurston, *Dust Tracks on a Road,* (1942; rpt., Urbana: University of Illinois Press, 1984), ix–xxxix.

36. Elizabeth Fox-Genovese, "My Statue, My Self: Autobiographical Writing of Afro-American Women," in *The Private Self: Theory and Practice of Women's Autobiographical Writings,* ed. Shari Benstock (Chapel Hill: University of North Carolina Press, 1988), 63–89; Deborah G. Plant, "The Folk Preacher and Folk Sermon Form in Zora Neale Hurston's *Dust Tracks on a Road,*" *Folklore Forum* 21.1 (1988): 3–19; Claudine Raynaud, "Autobiography as a 'Lying' Session: Zora Neale Hurston's *Dust Tracks on a Road,*" in *Black Feminist Criticism and Critical Theory,* ed. Joe Weixlmann and Houston A. Baker Jr. (Greenwood, Fla.: Penkevill Press, 1988), 111–38.

37. Kathleen Hassall, "Text and Personality in Disguise and in the Open: Zora Neale Hurston's *Dust Tracks on a Road,*" in *Zora in Florida,* ed. Glassman and Seidel, 159–73; Maya Angelou, foreword to Hurston, *Dust Tracks on a Road* (1942; rpt., New York: HarperCollins, 1991), vii–xii.

38.   Raynaud, " 'Rubbing a Paragraph with a Soft Cloth'? Muted Voices and Editorial Constraints in *Dust Tracks on a Road*," in *De/Colonizing the Subject: The Politics of Gender in Women's Autobiography*, ed. Sidonie Smith and Julia Watson (Minneapolis: University of Minnesota Press, 1992), 34–64; Paola Boi, "Zora Neale Hurston's *Autobiographie Fictive:* Dark Tracks on the Canon of a Female Writer," in *The Black Columbiad: Defining Moments in African American Literature and Culture*, ed. Werner Sollors and Maria Diedrich (Cambridge, Mass.: Harvard University Press, 1994), 191–200.

39.   Worth Tuttle Hedden, "Turpentine and Moonshine," *New York Herald Tribune Books* (10 October 1948): 2; review of *Seraph on the Suwanee, Christian Science Monitor* (23 December 1948): 11; Frank Slaughter, "Freud in Turpentine," *New York Times Book Review* (31 October 1948): 24. Edward Hamilton, review of *Seraph on the Suwanee, America* (1 January 1949): 354–55; Carl Milton Hughes, *The Negro Novelist* (New York: Citadel Press, 1950), 172–78; Sterling Brown, "Negro Folk Expression," *Phylon* 21 (Fourth Quarter 1949): 318–27.

40.   Hazel Carby, foreword to Hurston, *Seraph on the Suwanee* (1948; rpt., New York: HarperCollins, 1991), xiii–xvi.

41.   Janet St. Clair, "The Courageous Undertow of Zora Neale Hurston's *Seraph on the Suwanee*," *Modern Language Quarterly* 50 (March 1989): 38–57.

42.   Carby, foreword, x–xii.

43.   Toni Cade Bambara, foreword, to Hurston, *The Sanctified Church* (Berkeley, Calif.: Turtle Island, 1981), 7–11; Marion A. Thomas, "Reflections on the Sanctified Church as Portrayed by Zora Neale Hurston," *Black American Literature Forum* 25.1 (Spring 1991): 35–41.

44.   Henry Louis Gates Jr., "Why the *Mule Bone* Debate Goes On," *New York Times* (10 February 1991): 5; Frank Rich, "A Difficult Birth for *Mule Bone*," *New York Times* (15 February 1991): 1.

45.   Henry Louis Gates Jr. and Sieglinde Lemke, eds., introduction to Hurston, *The Complete Stories* (New York: HarperCollins, 1995), ix–xxiii.

46.   Ibid., xxiii.

47.   Laura Meckler, "Writings of Noted Harlem Author Found in Boxes," *The Provo, Utah, Daily Herald* (19 December 1996): D9.

48.   Hemenway, *Zora*, 338–39, 343–44; Hurston, "The Woman in Gaul," in *The Complete Stories*, ed. Gates Jr. and Lemke, 261–83.

49.   Hurston, *Dust Tracks*, 254.

JONAH'S GOURD VINE (1934)

♦

A Pungent, Poetic Novel about Negroes
[Review of *Jonah's Gourd Vine*]

JOSEPHINE PINCKNEY

This novel of Negro life is the product of a fortunate combination of circumstances. The author writes as a Negro understanding her people and having opportunities that could come to no white person, however sympathetic, of seeing them when they are utterly themselves. But she writes as a Negro whose intelligence is firmly in the saddle, who recognizes the value of an objective style in writing, and who is able to use the wealth of material available to her with detachment and with a full grasp of its dramatic qualities. Considering her especial temptations, her sustaining of the objective viewpoint is remarkable. She writes of her people with honesty, with sympathy, without extenuation. The white man is portrayed but little and then without bitterness. This is a novel about Negroes and she is not to be deflected by controversy from her preoccupation with her characters as the stuff of art.

The story unfolds in pages and pages of talk, and delighting talk it is—the pungent, expressive idiom of the country Negro, full of humor and folknotions; poetic, whether on the secular side or transposed into the biblical phraseology required by the many church scenes. Miss Hurston makes effective use of biblical rhythms in the passages that describe mass emotions quickening and becoming richer as they mount to a climax. John Buddy, the central figure of "Jonah's Gourd Vine," becomes later the Rev. Pearson, and his sermons are poems in Old Testament style, exemplifying that affinity of the Negro for the strong rhythms of Hebrew poetry.

The Rev. Pearson made the most of the instrument his church provided and of his talent for playing on it, which talent was an emotionalism that often strayed off into dissonance. In spite of having a virtuous and adoring wife, he couldn't let women alone. People tried to discipline him, but nothing stopped him except a railroad train quite unexpectedly on the last page, as he crossed the track in his new Cadillac. A woman was responsible for that.

There is some uncertainty in the handling of the narrative. Quarrels, trial proceedings, conflicts occur which are never resolved but merely slip out of the story as though the author had conceived them as links in a progression

Reprinted from *New York Herald Tribune Books* (6 May 1934): 7. Reprinted by permission.

but had forgotten her intention. Yet the character of John Buddy on which the story hangs is clearly realized. Lucy, his wife, is not equally convincing. Her unremitting nobility appears sentimental against a background of figures set off by the chiaroscuro of their humanity. When all is told this background is what lingers most vividly in the mind—a group composed of many deftly-drawn personalities, childlike, shrewd, violent, gay; and all the colors drawn together by the strong ingredient of Negro humor.

The Browsing Reader
[Review of *Jonah's Gourd Vine*]

ANDREW BURRIS

As the author of "Spunk," one of the best short stories in "The New Negro" (edited by Alain Locke, New York, 1925), Zora Neale Hurston was in the vanguard of the movement which took its name from that book. Some of us have had the pleasure of hearing Miss Hurston tell, in her inimitable way, stories about the people in her native village, Eatonville in Florida, or have read and enjoyed the lusty humor, the rich folkways and authentic speech of the characters in her (as yet unproduced) play "Mulebone," done in collaboration with Langston Hughes, or have seen the interesting folk sketches resulting from her anthropological studies that were produced for a brief run at the John Golden Theatre in New York City two years ago; and we have felt that a great delight lay in store for us when finally Miss Hurston committed herself to a book.

We have believed that Zora Hurston was not interested in writing a book merely to jump on the bandwagon of the New Negro movement, as some quite evidently were; but we felt that she was taking her time mastering her craft, and would as a result, produce a really significant book.

Now Miss Hurston has written a book, and despite the enthusiastic praise on the jacket by such eminent literary connoisseurs as Carl Van Vechten, Fannie Hurst and Blanche Colton Williams, all sponsors of the "New Negro," this reviewer is compelled to report that *Jonah's Gourd Vine* is quite disappointing and a failure as a novel.

One must judge Miss Hurston's success by the tasks she has set herself—to write a novel about a backward Negro people, using their peculiar speech and manners to express their lives. What she has done is just the opposite. She has used her characters and the various situations created for them as mere pegs upon which to hang their dialect and their folkways. She has become so absorbed with these phases of her craft that she has almost completely lost sight of the equally essential elements of plot and construction, characterization and motivation. John Buddy emerges from the story through his mere presence on every page, and not from an integrated life

Reprinted from *The Crisis* 41 (June 1934): 166–67.

with the numerous others who wander in and out and do things often without rhyme or reason.

It is disappointing when one considers what Miss Hurston might have done with John Buddy, illegitimate offspring of a white man and a Negro woman, who at an early age leaves the thankless toil and hovel of a home provided by a shiftless, jealous stepfather and a protecting mother, and loves, prays, preaches and sings his way up to the eminent position of moderator in the Baptist church. In John Buddy she had the possibility of developing a character that might have stamped himself upon American life more indelibly than either John Henry or Black Ulysses. But like the chroniclers of these two adventures she has been unequal to the demands of her conception.

The defects of Miss Hurston's novel become the more glaring when her work is placed beside that of contemporary white authors of similar books about their own people such as the first half of Fielding Burke's novel of North Carolina hillbillies, "Call Home the Heart," or two novels of Arkansas mountaineers, "Mountain Born" by Emmett Gowen and "Woods Colt" by T. R. Williamson. The first two named are, like Miss Hurston's, first novels and we feel that it is not asking too much of her to expect that in writing novels about her own people she give us work of equal merit to these.

Lest this criticism of *Jonah's Gourd Vine* seem too severe, let us add that there is much about the book that is fine and distinctive, and enjoyable. Zora Hurston has assembled between the pages of this book a rich store of folklore. She has captured the lusciousness and beauty of the Negro dialect as have few others. John Buddy's sermon on the creation is the most poetic rendition of this familiar theme that we have yet encountered in print. These factors give the book an earthiness, a distinctly racial flavor, a somewhat primitive beauty which makes its defects the more regrettable. We can but hope that with time and further experience in the craft of writing, Zora Hurston will develop the ability to fuse her abundant material into a fine literary work.

MULES AND MEN (1935)

◆

The Full, True Flavor
of Life in a Negro Community
[Review of *Mules and Men*]

H. I. BROCK

Here, to put it so, is the high color of Color as a racial element in the American scene. And it comes neither from Catfish Row nor from Harlem with a Jazz tempo affected by the rhythm of Broadway to which contribute so many exotic strains newer to that scene than the African. In this book a young Negro woman with a college education has invited the outside world to listen in while her own people are being as natural as they can never be when white folks are literally present. This is an environment in the deep South to which the Negro is as native as he can be anywhere on this Western Continent.

The writer has gone back to her native Florida village—a Negro settlement—with her native racial quality entirely unspoiled by her Northern college education. She has plunged into the social pleasures of the black community and made a record of what is said and done when Negroes are having a good gregarious time, dancing, singing, fishing, and above all, and incessantly, talking.

The talk (as those fragmentary memories of long ago come back to remind us) runs on such occasions generally to competition in telling what are unashamedly labeled "lies." These "lies" are woven out of the folklore of the black race in the South—with its deeper African background dimmed by years and distance. It is the same folklore, of course, out of which have been rescued for our nurseries the mildest elements—the tales of Br'er Rabbit, Br'er Fox and the rest of the talking animals that children reared in the South had listened to long before Uncle Remus made them classic for the whole country.

But as the feast is spread here it is not always nursery fare. Not by any means. Some of it is strong meat for those who take life lustily—with accompaniment of flashes of razor blades and great gusts of Negro laughter.

Reprinted from *New York Times Book Review* (10 November 1935): 4. © 1935 New York Times Company. Reprinted by permission of the publisher.

The book is packed with tall tales rich in flavor and alive with characteristic turns of speech. Those of us who have known the Southern Negro from our youth find him here speaking the language of his tribe as familiarly as if it came straight out of his own mouth and had not been translated into type and transmitted through the eye to the ear. Which is to say that a very tricky dialect has been rendered with rare simplicity and fidelity into symbols so little adequate to convey its true values that the achievement is remarkable.

At the end you have a very fair idea of how the other color enjoys life as well as an amazing round-up of that color's very best stories in its very best manner—which is a match for any story-telling there is in the two qualities of luxuriant imagination and vivid expressive language.

At the back of the book you find a glossary, the words and music of some of the songs these people sing to the banjo or guitar, and sundry recipes of the hoodoo doctors for success in love or compassing the sudden death of an enemy. Several chapters of the narrative are devoted to the writer's personal investigation of the mysteries of hoodoo or voodoo. Included is the record of her initiation by several eminent witch-doctors into the deepest mysteries of their black art and of the part which she took as their assistant in the "conjur" business. No mock modesty is invoked to veil the details of the initiations or the elements and procedure involved in producing for paying clients the death of persons whose living presence is obnoxious—as no-longer-wanted husbands or wives or the like. It is flatly stated that after the conjur work was done, with the writer assisting in the mummery, some of these persons did actually die approximately on schedule. You can think what you please about that.

Descriptions of the preparation of charms and of midnight incantations in the swamp seem to take us all the way back to Africa—and darkest Africa at that. We are told that hoodoo is, in fact, ancient religion of the Negro race, still carrying on. If that is so and if it does carry on as here reported, we have a revealing account of a very curious personal adventure in a region far on the African side of the color line. That adventure, however, carries to this reviewer no such conviction of solid interest and value as the collection of competitive "lies" from the treasury of Afro-American folklore.

[Review of *Mules and Men*]

B. C. McNeill

In Part I from the vantage ground of "the inner circle," the writer has written of her adventures in Eatonville, and Polk County, Florida. She has deftly woven in not only a picturesque account of the social customs, games and work of every day life, but has also re-created creation and other myths, "massa," animal and devil tales, poetical sermons and prayers, folksongs, and even children's games. The collected folklore ranges from the consciously extemporized lie of the "swapping-contest" to the traditional myth. Here with their ancient animosities, rove Brer Rabbit, Brer Dog, Brer 'Gator. Trouble and "monkies" with their uncertain interpretation mingle with the goat, the mule, the snake, and the lizard; the cat retains its sinister effect on man. Along with the old idea of outwitting supernatural forces, generally—the devil in particular—goes the God and man myth, the former easily accessible and indulgent, though firm. All are here, as in varied form they have hitherto appeared in *Uncle Remus* of Joel Chandler Harris, or *Black Genesis* of Samuel Stoney and Gertrude Shelty.

Miss Hurston presents here something unique for a collection of folkways, the sort of running dialogue that would, in moderate use, form the local atmosphere of modern novels dealing with characters drawn from this milieu. Recorded here are storms of laughter over the repartee that is so spontaneous, and sensitiveness resulting from the barbed personalities based on blackness of complexion, obesity, ugliness, and the like. The schooled or college-trained is ridiculed.

Even as many of the tales concern the old massa and slave theme with first one and then the other winning, so others with modern ideology suggest present day attitudes. The swampers dislike the swamp boss, so ugly that "if a spell of sickness ever tried to slip up on him, he'd skeer it into a three-weeks' spasm"; "the foreman, too mean to let them knock off but, when there's no work in the swamps sends them to the mill." "God made the world and the white folks made work" is the theme of one tale.

Miss Hurston's contribution is significant because of her close contacts, first with the men and women of Eatonville, her native city "of five lakes,

Reprinted from *Journal of Negro History* 21.2 (April 1936): 223–25. © 1936 Morehouse College. Reprinted by permission of the publisher.

three croquet courts, three hundred brown skins, three hundred good swimmers, two schools and no jail house." The men during their leisure sat on the store porch, doing nothing or playing Florida-flip. Her other contributors were employees of the Everglades Cypress Lumber Company—several hundred Negroes from all over the South—"a rich field for folklore." Her laughing acceptance of "woofing," together with her assumed role of "bootlegging," determined her success in gathering voluminous material, through both a public lying contest and private conversations.

The novelist, more than the student of cultural history, seems to have won out toward the end of Part I, for her account becomes worthwhile largely as a record of jookhouse epithets and gambling terms. The action illustrates the defense mechanism of an in-group of a lower strata of society against the inroads of an outside group, culminating in a razor fight with the writer herself as one of the intended victims.

In Part II the scene shifts to New Orleans, and Miss Hurston records her personal training in the arts and practices of Voodoo or Hoodoo, as she calls it. The origin of the beliefs, the initiation ceremonies and rituals of several practitioners are given without restraint. In great contrast with the broad humor of Part I do we find the serious portrayal of the dependence of Negroes of the Deep South upon "conjure" when the police, physicians, and banks fail.

Most effective is the account of her preparation for the initiation ceremony under one Luke Turner, associated with the famous Marie Leveau. That she became proficient is evidenced by his request for her to remain with him, by agreement of others that "Mother Kitty had done well to take me." Certainly the writer, if she has not convinced all readers of the powers of Voodooism, has offered new evidence of widespread ignorance and superstition.

Literary Objective:
Hurston's Use of Personal Narrative in *Mules and Men*

SANDRA DOLBY-STAHL

What do Charlotte Brontë's *Jane Eyre* and Zora Neale Hurston's *Mules and Men* have in common? You could say that they are both works written by women, but you might be hard pressed to find any other commonality. Still, you might remember that they are both written in the first person singular; they both appear to be written personal narratives. In *Jane Eyre* the primary *dramatis persona* and the person telling the story are one and the same, Jane Eyre. Furthermore, research since the publication of *Jane Eyre* and Brontë's three other novels has contended that Jane's story is at least in part autobiographical for the author. In *Mules and Men* the primary *dramatis persona* is Zora Neale Hurston, and the story is told by Hurston supposedly as a segment of her life story. Does this mean that *Jane Eyre* and *Mules and Men* are examples of a single genre? And just what would that genre be? *Jane Eyre* is generally recognized as a novel, most people would say quite a good one, but there is no such consensus on the genre (or quality) of *Mules and Men*.

Brontë chose to cast her novel in the first person singular for "literary" reasons, we must assume. The book is autobiographical in many ways; that is, it does reflect certain real events from the author's life. Still, the decision to have the character Jane Eyre tell her own story was motivated by literary objectives. We must assume that Brontë chose the personal narrative format because she felt that in this work it would most effectively call forth the kind of response good literature is supposed to evoke. It would allow her to move her audience; it would give her the power of a well-executed literary performance.

Contrast this understanding of Brontë's objectives with the usual view of Hurston's objectives in writing *Mules and Men.* Typically, scholars assume that Hurston's objective is to present a collection of folklore, to be the ethnographer, the scholar, rather than the "creative writer," at least in *Mules and Men.* Unfortunately, the academy has been slow to acknowledge and celebrate the

Reprinted from *Western Folklore* 51 (1992): 51–63. © 1992 The California Folklore Society. Used by permission of the publisher.

literary talents of good ethnographic writers. In fact, we must assume that over the years many scholars have had to stifle expressive urges continually while adhering to prescribed formats and styles of academic discourse. Recently, much of this has changed. Students of anthropology, literature, folklore, sociology, history, and philosophy are increasingly self-conscious, aware of their own role in gathering and presenting whatever they have chosen to study. The collection of essays titled *Writing Culture* edited by James Clifford and George E. Marcus (1986) is a prime example of the growing acceptance accorded those who would attend to their own writing as a necessary "literary" dimension of the ethnographic or critical enterprise.

Long before Clifford and Marcus and other contemporary scholars brought such concerns out into the light of day, Zora Neale Hurston showed us how a good writer does it best—with a writer's skill *and literary objectives* taking precedence over the conventions of scholarship. Clifford in his "Introduction," identifies the self-reflexive, autobiographical "fieldwork account" as a new subgenre of research emerging in the late 1960's and 1970's and finding academic respectability only in the 1980's. And yet, when Hurston's *Mules and Men* was published in 1935, the world was offered one of the finest examples of such reflexive, literary ethnography ever written. It is time to go back and take our cue from Hurston—not on the necessity for self-reflexive scholarship but rather on how to do it well.

For most critics, *Mules and Men* is a collection of folklore. Robert A. Bone (1958), one of the first critics to offer serious commentary on Hurston's work, discusses *Jonah's Gourd Vine, Their Eyes Were Watching God,* and *Seraph on the Suwanee* as three novels that focus upon "aspects of the racial past." He regards both *Mules and Men* and *Tell My Horse* as well as *Moses, Man of the Mountain* as books of folklore. Ann L. Rayson (1974) considers both *Mules and Men* and *Tell My Horse* "collections of folklore" though she does discuss *Moses* as a novel rather than folklore. James W. Byrd, in an article in the *Tennessee Folklore Society Bulletin* (1955) describes *Mules and Men* as a "treasury of Negro folklore," an entertaining and impressive collection. Even one of Hurston's contemporary champions, Darwin T. Turner (1971), deals with *Mules and Men* only briefly, and then apart from the novels, as a folklore collection.

A sociologist, Marion Kilson, writing in 1972, grouped all of Hurston's narrative works together as the products of an "ethnographic artist." To Kilson, *Mules and Men* was comparable to *Their Eyes Were Watching God* as a narrative fiction. But it wasn't until Hurston's biographer, Robert Hemenway (1977), addressed the underlying issue of genre that attention was given to Hurston's objectives and performance as an author in *Mules and Men.* Hemenway writes of the "intimacy" that Boas noted in the manuscript of *Mules and Men:*

> The intimacy of *Mules and Men* is an obtained effect, an example of Hurston's narrative skill. She represented oral art functioning to affect behavior in the

black community; to display this art in its natural setting she created a narrator who would not intrude on the folklore event. A semifictional Zora Neale Hurston is our guide to southern black folklore, a curiously retiring figure who is more art than life. . . . It is easy to overlook Hurston's craft as she mediates between self and material in this presentation; yet she shaped *Mules and Men* in somewhat the same manner in which Henry David Thoreau created a unified experience in *Walden*. (1977:164–65)

Hemenway's suggestion that "it is easy to overlook Hurston's craft" brings us to the heart of "folklore and literature" historiography. It is "easy" to overlook her craft precisely because critics have not been looking at the work as literature but rather as a rich but vaguely unsatisfying folklore collection. The sub-field of "folklore and literature" supports scholarly consideration of a novel such as *Their Eyes Were Watching God* more readily than it does a mere collection such as *Mules and Men*. Still, as Hemenway suggests, there is much literary artistry at work in *Mules and Men*. More importantly, there is as well a shining example of how a new generation of folklorists might consider presenting the folklore they study to a literate and eager public.

Hurston chose a narrative format, the "fieldwork account," a kind of personal narrative potentially a product of any ethnographer's or folklorist's research career. However, she also chose to take her literary obligations seriously. She wrote always toward a literary goal, incorporating scholarly conventions into her work as a "crafted" part of her story. She developed this kind of literary performance not out of disdain for or ignorance of proper descriptive models in ethnographic research but rather through a positive regard for the effectiveness of literature.

Mules and Men is literature rather than ethnography through the clear intention of its author. Zora Neale Hurston was a trained anthropologist; she was familiar with the terminology, methodology, and proper publishing format for ethnographic research. Among her instructors in graduate studies at Columbia University were the well-known American anthropologists Franz Boas and Ruth Benedict. Her field projects won her support through competitive grants and fellowships, and much of her research was published initially in reputable ethnographic journals, including the *Journal of American Folklore* (see Turner 1971). That Zora Neale Hurston could have presented the stories, sayings, practices, and beliefs she collected in Florida and Louisiana as "pure ethnography" is undeniable; that she chose not to is both significant and fortunate.

Having decided upon a novelist's format rather than an ethnographer's, Hurston did not in consequence throw out the ethnographer's viewpoint as well, but rather she integrated it subtly into the literary format she had chosen and blended it with the creative writer's skill and literary focus. This is the point Darwin Turner overlooks in his evaluation of the book as a "disappointingly superficial" ethnography. Turner maintains that in *Mules and Men*

Hurston offers no evidence of scholarly procedure, fails to classify her material meaningfully, and fails to ask essential, analytical questions (1971:117). These, he anticipates correctly, are the complaints folklorists and anthropologists would offer in response to the book. However, a closer look at the book can acquit Hurston of these charges but only if substance itself rather than its sometime lack of conventional, academic dressing is accepted as evidence.

It is true, for example, that Hurston does not classify her material into generic categories. Nor does she include comparative notes for the stories or index numbers for the traditional tale types. As Turner no doubt recognizes, we would expect a professional folklore editor to identify and group the material by conventional genres, provide brief data on the informant and context for each item, and annotate each item, citing relevant index numbers and analogues. It is initially disappointing to note that Indiana University Press, in reissuing *Mules and Men* in 1978, did not require that notes be added by Robert Hemenway, who did write a new "Introduction" to the book. On second thought, the lack of added annotation seems a telling tribute to Hurston's success in writing a book that "stands" as a piece of literature.

Within the frame of a "fieldwork account"—a written personal narrative—Hurston offers contextual information in sufficient quantity to allow any readers so inclined a chance to speculate on the functions of the folklore or to devise descriptive generalizations on typical context. And the selection of material in the book is purposefully representative of a wide variety of genres rather than a limited number of "preferred" categories. Where a standard ethnography might narrow its focus to only narrative categories or only customs or beliefs, or perhaps only mythological narratives, *Mules and Men* records examples of well over twenty-five different categories of folklore material.

There are tall tales, including the Texas mosquito and the Great Hunt; etiological tales explaining how there came to be black and white races or why cats have nine lives or why the 'possum has no hair on its tail; animal tales about the rabbit, 'gator, and dog; "ordinary" folktales about Jack and the Devil; and some prime examples of the category of stories called "John and Old Massa" tales which have since received considerable attention (see Oster, for example). There are stories "explaining" the Bible and stories explaining where Hoodoo beliefs and practices came from, legends about Marie Leveau and formulaic recitations of her hoodoo routines. There are memorates or personal narratives about experiences with the supernatural, such as Jim Allen's account of seeing the wind after squirting sow's milk in his eyes. There are descriptions of customs and traditional skills, children's games, folk cookery, and hoodoo conjurations.

The text for one folk sermon is provided in full, as fine and full of formulas as any in more recent studies of folk sermonizing (see Rosenberg 1970 or Davis 1985). There are examples of entertaining cumulative rhymes, traditional rhymes that begin or end longer prose narratives, traditional insults or "dozens," blues lyrics and their music, a text of the well-known ballad "John Henry," citations of religious songs, street cries, and proverbial expressions. There are esoteric usages and items of folk speech explained in notes or in the glossary and several examples of the patterned repartee known as signifying or "woofing."

All of these kinds of folklore are scattered throughout the book in what appear to be natural contexts or at least realistic settings. They seem to be recorded in the sequence and verbal context in which they were heard by the collector. They would seem to be "grouped" then simply by their real occurrence in time as the collector entered the contexts of their performance. It is of course Hurston's skill as a writer of mimetic fiction that creates the illusion of natural, context-bound ordering. She has in fact manipulated the grouping of material not toward the scholarly goal of generic classification but rather toward the literary goal of mimesis. She wants her readers to experience the "reality" of folkloristic contexts and authentic folklore material, and she acts upon the assumption that the more effective way to elicit a profound appreciation for the material and people who perform it is to manipulate the material toward a literary goal. That literary goal is to move her readers, and to do that she must not leave the response of her readers to chance. She must influence it by making art appear as reality, by turning ethnographic rawness into a personal narrative, a literary performance. She does this by "hiding" the ethnographer's observations within the very fabric of the narrative. Like Brontë, she lets dialogue between characters convey the message about belief in ghosts.

There are other instances in which evidence of ethnographic methodology is visible yet subtly integrated into the dominant literary framework. Fieldwork methodology frequently involves an "induced natural context." Hurston records the use of this technique in her discussion of the "get-together" at Mett's, held for the express purpose of collecting stories but made "natural" through the adherence to routine grouping and even the usual refreshments—gingerbread and buttermilk. Or, again, the role of the fieldworker is often the subject of objective comment in ethnographic reports, especially in current anthropological studies. Hurston presents—dramatically rather than in an essay—a number of common role-related problems a fieldworker faces. In one instance she demonstrates the necessity for temporary role-playing in an effort to gain the trust of potential informants: She (or rather Zora in the story) pretends to be a bootlegger's woman. In another she points to the trying task of remaining objective in the role of participant-observer during an emotional event: She tells us when she went through the Black Cat Bone ritual that she experienced "indescribable noises, sights, feelings. Death was at hand! Seemed unavoidable! I don't know. Many times I have thought and felt, but I always have to say the same thing. I don't know. I don't know" (Hurston 1978:229). All of these are aspects of field methodology that would and should be discussed operationally in conventional ethnographic works. Hurston incorporates them into the ongoing narrative, demonstrating but not generalizing their use.

Another technique she uses is the presentation of analytical commentary through the words of the characters themselves rather than through her own formalized observations. Comments on folkloric or ethnographic concepts, generalizations on the variety of performance situations and abilities, and other analytic statements are put into the mouths of the "informants" the fictionalized Zora encounters, and the statements appear natural or realistic because Hurston so skillfully mimics the actual phenomenon of metafolklore. "Metafolklore" is a concept identified well over two decades ago by Alan Dundes and discussed along with a related concept, "orally literary criticism," in an article published in *The Monist* (Dundes 1966). Metafolklore is essentially folklore about folklore or folklore in which an allusion is made to some frame of reference known to be a part of the popular notion of folklore. For example, someone might refer casually to the familiar characteristics of a specific genre of folklore (the "once upon a time" opening to fairy tales), or to a well-known ballad, legend, or story as a model for another, or perhaps to a shared belief or proverbial expression, as in the punch lines to "shaggy dog stories." Dundes expanded the concept into the realm of "oral literary criticism," which may be identified as comments about the folklore offered by the performers themselves or their audiences (see Bauman and Briggs 1990 for a historiographic expansion on the effects of reflexive attention to contextualization in folklore research). Hurston, drawing upon an intuitive recognition of metafolklore, presents analytic comment and culture-specific observations through realistic dialogues spoken by her "untrained" characters.

For example, the concept of etic and emic categories, the distinction between passive and active bearers, the recognition of the "esoteric-exoteric" factor, or the identification of traditionality are all concepts that an anthropologist or folklorist might use in discussing analytically the body of folklore Hurston collected. Hurston's admirable achievement is in having the other characters in her personal narrative use these same concepts themselves in dialogues with her. We assume that these characters do not know the social scientist's jargon for the concepts, but Hurston suggests convincingly that they do "know" the concepts, nevertheless. It is unlikely that her "real" informants were as consistently well-informed as her characters appear to be. Still, she presents their layman's articulation of conceptual concerns so skillfully that we are convinced that she has reported her actual experiences in collecting rather than scenes manipulated for literary effect.

Consider the case of Officer Richardson, for example, who says when asked to recite "the white man's prayer": "Ah don't know it well enough to say it. Ah jus' know it well enough to know it" (Hurston 1978:95). Without jargon but with an obvious understanding of the concept, he is saying that he is a passive bearer rather than an active bearer of the item. Similarly, Luke Turner, discussing Marie Leveau, says:

Now, some white people say she hold hoodoo dance on Congo Square every week. But Marie Leveau never hold no hoodoo dance. That was a pleasure dance. They beat the drum with the shin bone of a donkey and everybody dance like they do in Hayti. Hoodoo is private. She give the dance the first Friday night in each month and they have crab gumbo and rice to eat and the people dance. The white people come look on, and think they see all, when they only see a dance. (Hurston 1978: 201–2)

Here Luke Turner has clearly documented the "esoteric-exoteric" factor, the folklore of "what we think about them, what they think about us, what we think they think about us, etc." identified by William Hugh Jansen (1965).

Generalized statements on context, audience, and tellers are often a part of folkloristic analysis. Hurston offers very few formal observations on such topics; rather, she again uses the technique of casting her generalizations into the form of metafolklore and allowing her "informants" to present this information to the reader. For example, when young Julius Henry begins a long John and Ole Massa story, two older men interrupt with a discussion of the approved or conventional age for a teller of such stories—a social factor often investigated in depth in standard ethnographies. The metafolkloric discussion of the two men is as follows:

"Let de dollars hush whilst de nickel speak," Charles Jones derided Julius' youth. "Julius, what make you wanta jump in a hogshead when a keg will hold yuh? You here dese hard ole coons lyin' up a nation and you stick in yo' bill."

"If his mouf is cut cross ways and he's two years ole, he kin lie good as anybody else," John French defended. "Blow it, Julius" (Hurston 1978:45).

The beauty of this passage is that it is rich with folklore, much richer, I am persuaded, than any "real" dialogue would be. Hurston has not only provided an example of a metafolkloric commentary on the appropriate age for a story teller but she has allowed the reader to see proverbial expressions used in an appropriate ("realistic" if not actual) context, she has used colorful examples of folk vocabulary in a "realistic" context, and she has offered a rare direct articulation of a folk idea ("If his mouf is cut . . .").

It is important that Hurston's use of metafolkloric dialogue be viewed as a literary technique. We might more easily suppose that the metafolkloric material is simply the transcribed content of her collection, written down and presented to the reader exactly as the informants, the characters in her book, had related it to her, the collector. Hurston of course wants her readers to accept the reality created within the framework of the book; she wants us to suspend any disbelief that the events, stories, and dialogues occurred in reality exactly as they are presented in the book. She is telling us the story of her experiences while collecting folklore, and she wants to create the illusion that her role as author is simply that of recorder and transcriber. And the illusion is most convincing. But an appeal to either field experience or literary theory, especially as these have informed the study of personal narrative, will yield a verdict of literary craft, of manipulation, fictionalizing, and "improving" on the part of the author.

Field experience supports a number of objections that could be made to Hurston's supposed verbatim transcriptions. In the field one rarely finds stories without some false starts, some backtracking for significant details, and occasionally some incongruities. In fact, William Hansen used this bit of field wisdom in arguing once and for all in support of the oral source of Homer's *Odyssey* (Hanson 1972, see also Stahl 1979). One finds even more rarely the smooth contextual "scenes" recorded in *Mules and Men*, where every exchange, whether involving more structured storytelling or simply casual conversation, is meaningful, aesthetically balanced, and representative (see again Bauman and Briggs 1990 on implications of the "ethnography of speaking" and the effects of "entextualization" in ethnographic research). Hurston's dialogues in *Mules and Men* are not verbatim transcripts of real speech events but rather artistic fictions created by the author.

Nevertheless, it is clear that Hurston did indeed do fieldwork. It is precisely because she was a skilled observer that she was able to draw upon the unspoken "rules" of performance (the "ethnography of speaking") when constructing her realistic dialogues. She taught herself the rules and the "stuff" of performance and incorporated them into her book. And lest anyone doubt her ability to do this, consider this comment from her autobiography *Dust Track on a Road:*

> On my return to New York in 1932, after trying vainly to interest others, I introduced Bahaman songs and dances to a New York audience at the John Golden Theater, and both the songs and the dances took on. The concert achieved its purpose. I aimed to show what beauty and appeal there was in genuine Negro material, as against the Broadway concept, and it went over. . . . I had no intention of making concert my field. I wanted to show the wealth and beauty of the material to those who were in the field and therefore I felt that my job was done when it took on (Walker 1979:61).

Hurston knew how to "perform" the material she collected—in the fullest sense of the word. A song can be sung, a dance danced, and the rules and materials of verbal expression can be used in the writing of plays and novels. Hurston learned the "rules" that direct real speech events, condensed them into manageable scenes, and incorporated the raw field "texts" into these realistic contexts. The stories, sayings, rhymes, and even some patterned verbal exchanges were likely told to Hurston in much the same form in which they are found in *Mules and Men*. But the ordering of the stories in their verbal contexts, the augmenting of telling events with metafolkloric comment, and especially the balancing and enrichment of the scenes of dialogue were tasks Hurston took upon herself as author.

An appeal to literary theory, too, would convince the reader that Hurston's book is fashioned through literary technique rather than conventional field observation and ethnographic methodology. Consider, for example, the tight structuring toward thematic statement in the following passage:

"John sho was a smart nigger now. He useter git de best of Ole Massa all de time," gloated Sack Daddy.

"Yeah. but some white folks is smarter than you think," put in Eugene Oliver.

For instance now, take a man I know up in West Florida. He hired a colored man to clear off some new ground, but dat skillet blond was too lazy to work. De white man would show him what to do then he's g'wan back to de house and keep his books. Soon as he turned his back de nigger would flop down and go to sleep. When he hear somebody comin' he'd hit de log a few licks with de flat of de ax and say, "Klunk, klunk, you think Ah'm workin' but Ah ain't."

De white man heard him but he didn't say a word. Sat'day night come and Ole Cuffee went up to de white man to git his pay. De white man stacked up his great big ole silver dollars and shook 'em in his hand and says, "Clink, clink, you think I'm gointer pay you, but I ain't."

By that time somebody saw the straw boss coming so everybody made it onto the mill (Hurston 1978: 99–100).

The juxtaposition of a story about a black man not working when he is expected to and the arrival of the white "straw boss" on the scene where the tellers are "goofing off" is an example of careful and effective structuring by the author. The story is traditional, and the text probably represents a near-verbatim transcription. But the verbal context preceding the telling of the story and especially the thematically significant arrival of the boss are perhaps more than simply realistic; they are supportive, effective, persuasive; in short, they are fictional and therefore charged with literary meaning.

Rhetorical theory would suggest that because Hurston's scenes of dialogue are imbued with meaning, because her storytelling events are thematically solid rather than simply topically sequential, reality in *Mules and Men* has been manipulated toward an artistic goal. Like any writer of realistic fiction, Hurston has drawn upon the "epic laws" of good fiction (see Olrik in Dundes 1965). Just as the Grimms or other great collectors of fairy tales in the nineteenth century used their sense of what a good tale is like to "help" transcribe the tales into versions that would appeal to readers, so Hurston has used her keenly developed sense of rules for appropriate and effective speech in publishing her ethnographic material for her readers.

She has given us a work of realistic fiction based on a real life experience event (her time in the field in Florida and Louisiana). She has written a personal narrative that, like most oral personal narratives, is based on a true experience but enhanced by the demands of a literary genre. Her use of the personal narrative format is effective. It invites our trust and acceptance of the material she presents. And as Boas noted, it creates a sense of intimacy between the author and the reader that would be hard to achieve in any other form. Perhaps we have not seen Hurston's real character in the fictionalized Zora of the book, but we have learned something of her values and her appreciation for the folk she has studied. As with any personal narrative (see Stahl 1989) we have discovered what she most wanted us to know about her, that she values the folklore and ideas of the people she met.

Works Cited

Bauman, Richard and Charles L. Briggs. 1990. Poetics and Performance as Critical Perspectives on Language and Social Life. *Annual Review of Anthropology* 19:59- 88.

Bone, Robert A. 1958. *The Negro Novel in America.* New Haven: Yale University Press.

Byrd, James W. 1955. Zora Neale Hurston: A Novel Folklorist. *Tennessee Folklore Society Bulletin* 21:37–41.

Clifford, James and George E. Marcus, Eds. 1986. *Writing Culture: The Poetics and Politics of Ethnography.* Berkeley: University of California Press.

David, Gerald L. 1985. *I Got a Word in Me and I Can Sing It. You Know: A Study of the Performed African-American Sermon.* Philadelphia: University of Pennsylvania Press.

Dundes, Alan. 1966. Metafolklore and Oral Literary Criticism. *The Monist* 50:505–16.

Hansen, William F. 1972. *The Conference Sequence: Patterned Narration and Narrative Inconsistency in the Odyssey.* Berkeley: University of California Press.

Hemenway, Robert E. 1977. *Zora Neale Hurston: A Literary Biography.* Urbana: University of Illinois Press.

Hurston, Zora Neale. 1978 [1935]. *Mules and Men.* Bloomington: Indiana University Press.

Hurston, Zora Neale. 1984 [1942]. *Dust Tracks on a Road: An Autobiography,* ed. Robert E. Hemenway. Urbana: University of Illinois Press.

Jansen, William Hugh. 1965. The Esoteric-Exoteric Factor in Folklore. In *The Study of Folklore,* ed. Alan Dundes, pp. 42–51. Englewood Cliffs, N.J.: Prentice-Hall.

Kilson, Marion. 1972. The Transformation of Eatonville's Ethnographer. *Phylon* 33:112–19.

Olrik, Axel. 1965. Epic Laws of Folk Narrative. In *The Study of Folklore,* ed. Alan Dundes, pp. 129–41. Englewood Cliffs, N.J.: Prentice-Hall.

Oster, Harry. 1968. Negro Humor: John and Old Marster. *Journal of the Folklore Institute* 5:42–57.

Rayson, Ann L. 1974. The Novels of Zora Neale Hurston. *Studies in Black Literature* 5(3):1–10.

Rosenberg, Bruce A. 1970. *The Art of the American Folk Preacher.* New York: Oxford University Press.

Stahl, Sandra K. Dolby. 1979. Style in Oral and Written Narratives. *Southern Folklore Quarterly* 43:39–62.

Stahl, Sandra K. Dolby. 1989. *Literary Folkloristics and the Personal Narrative.* Bloomington: Indiana University Press.

Turner, Darwin T. 1971. *In a Minor Chord: Three Afro-American Writers and Their Search for Identity.* Carbondale: Southern Illinois University Press.

Walker, Alice, ed. 1979. *I Love Myself When I Am Laughing: A Zora Neale Hurston Reader.* New York: The Feminist Press.

Mules and Men and Women:
Zora Neale Hurston's Strategies
of Narration and Visions of
Female Empowerment

CHERYL A. WALL

Mules and Men, Zora Neale Hurston's first book of folklore, is a widely recognized if under discussed classic in Afro-American literature and American anthropology. Unlike many of its predecessors in the field, it presents lore not to patronize or demean Afro-American culture, but to celebrate it. The shift of purpose is encoded in the book's title, with its dual reference to the status accorded blacks from without and the status they assume within their own community. Of course, the title also privileges the male. Analyzing its narrative strategy rather than its ethnographic data, one sees that, despite its title, *Mules and Men* shares the female focus typical of Zora Hurston's writing. Hurston's narrative strategies allow her to represent, first, the ways in which women are relegated to subordinate roles in the culture she otherwise celebrates and, second, the means by which women in that culture gain access to creative expression and power.

In effect the subtext of *Mules and Men* is the narrative of a successful quest for female empowerment. In the opening scenes, the narrator, "Zora," introduces both herself, diffident and naïve, and her hometown, where, despite its unusual customs and memorable patterns of language, all too familiar gender roles are strictly imposed. On the journey south, the narrator is changed by her encounter with Big Sweet, the powerful figure who becomes Zora's guardian and guide. Finally, under the providential guidance of the spirit of Marie Leveau, the great New Orleans hoodoo priestess, "Zora" is completely transformed. In this outline, *Mules and Men* is a paradigmatic immersion narrative that prefigures the movement of Hurston's classic novel *Their Eyes Were Watching God.* As much as that novel, *Mules and Men* deserves to be considered a "mother text" in the tradition of black women's writing.

Reprinted from *Black American Literature Forum* (currently *African American Review*) 23.4 (Winter 1989): 661–80. © 1989 Indiana State University. Reprinted by permission of the journal.

I

The first line of *Mules and Men* reads, "I was glad when somebody told me, 'You may go and collect Negro folk-lore' " (3). The Biblical allusion establishes both Hurston's sense of mission and the high value she places on the material she is out to preserve. Hurston's joy in her ability to document Afro-American cultural practices from shouting to signifying has been widely documented.[1] Divided into two parts, headed "Folk Tales" and "Hoodoo," *Mules and Men* is a compendium of expressive forms, featuring tales and aphorisms, prayers and sermons, children's rhymes and games, blues and work songs, curses and cures. It is, in sum, the brief Hurston offers the world in support of her contention that the "unlettered Negro has given the Negro's best contribution to America's culture" (Hayes).

After its initial joyous proclamation, however, the introduction is ambivalent at every turn. First, the narrator declares collecting would not be a new experience for her since she had known the lore "from the earliest rocking of my cradle." On the other hand, she had not been able to appreciate this old experience until college had given her the "spy-glass of Anthropology" (3), through which to view it. "New" to the field, she was relieved and happy to make the familiar ground of Eatonville her first stop. Seasoned in their ways, she knew how jealously black folk guarded "that which the soul lives by" (4). Even "Lucy Hurston's daughter, Zora," (3) might have problems probing the minds of strangers, but her Eatonville homefolk would be eager in every way to help. She would, it seemed, need all the help she could get.[2]

At its close, then, the introduction leaves us with a persona who is idealistic but timid, inspired but insecure, and one who is far more sure of her mission than of herself. The shy self-consciousness is at odds with everything we know about the real-life Hurston in the late 1920's—a woman for whom the adjective *bodacious* could have been coined—, but it is totally consistent with what the book's Eatonville expects of Lucy Hurston's daughter.

Driving across the Maitland-Eatonville township line, a line that separates the white world from the black, the narrator is delighted that her first sight is the store porch. In all of Hurston's writing, of course, the porch is a transformative space. The preeminent description is found in *Their Eyes Were Watching God:*

It was the time for sitting on porches beside the road. It was the time to hear things and talk. These sitters had been tongueless, earless, eyeless conveniences all day long. Mules and other brutes had occupied their skins. But now, the sun and the bossman were gone, so the skins felt powerful and human. They became lords of sounds and lesser things. They passed nations through their mouths. They sat in judgment. (9–10)

No such lyrical interpretation is offered in *Mules and Men,* where the transformation explained above is presented as a given. But Hurston dramatizes the importance of the lore in an exchange between Zora and one of the porch sitters.

When B. Moseley wonders who would be interested in " 'them big old lies we tell when we're jus' sittin' around here on the store porch doin' nothin',' " Zora responds, " 'they are a lot more valuable than you might think. We want to set them down before it's too late' " (9–10). How much more than nothing goes on on the store porch is evidenced by a narrative that seems often filled to overflowing with word play and incident (an effect Hurston reinforces by representing informants interrupting each other in their eagerness to share the lore). At bottom, of course, the opposing views of folklore as "valuable" and "nothing" represent a conflict less between Zora and her informant than between Hurston and the audience for her book. Ultimately, leaving the "we" unspecified invites the reader to identify with Hurston's project.

On the store porch a card game is in progress, and, significantly, all of the participants and onlookers are male. The narrator's comment is typically slant. " 'Hello, boys,' I hailed them as I went into neutral" (9). Read figuratively, this comment connotes Zora's desire to praise her homeboys as well as her need to assume the objectivity fieldwork requires. Neutrality is also the mask the narrator dons when confronted by the issues of sexual politics that soon prove to be the subject of the first section of *Mules and Men.*

Throughout the early scenes of the text, Hurston represents the ways in which gender roles are imposed, resisted, and more often than not accepted. The scenes range from the overtly benign to the protoviolent. An example of the former is the first event Zora attends, a toe-party, at which women stand behind a curtain, revealing only their feet, as men bid for their company. Not surprisingly, the totally passive Zora, who defers to someone else for every decision made in the first chapter, is selected five times. After the toe-party, this Zora recedes from the narrative, and a presumably more assertive figure begins to choreograph the action. The group that gathers on the store porch at Zora's invitation the following morning is made up of women and men. Interspersed among the tales are highly charged exchanges between couples; these constitute another narrative, the subject of which is male-female relationships.

This narrative is constructed of what Hurston once referred to apologetically as the "between-story conversation and business" she added to make her book appealing to commercial publishers. She feared, rightly, that it would damage the reputation of the book among professional folklorists. For a long time it did. More recent commentary from folklorists emphasizes the value of the context Hurston provides because of what it conveys about folklore process.[3] Literary critics are apt to praise it for the narrative skill it demonstrates. One aspect of that narrative skill, the manipulation of the "between-story conversation and business," is the means through which Hurston is able to give voice to women in her text.

Drawing on the same field notes from which she produced *Mules and Men*, Hurston penned a groundbreaking essay on Afro-American aesthetics, "Characteristics of Negro Expression," in which she argued:

> Every phase of Negro life is highly dramatized. No matter how joyful or how sad the case there is sufficient poise for drama. Everything is acted out. Unconsciously for the most part of course. There is an impromptu ceremony always ready for every hour of life. No little moment passes unadorned. (49)

Here Hurston states one of the principles that informs the structure of *Mules and Men*. In accord with this principle, the text presents a series of brilliant performances that reflect what Hurston termed the Afro-American's "will to adorn."[4]

Anticipating the work of current-day anthropologists by several decades, Hurston in the 1930's both theorized about and put into practice the concept of performance. For Hurston, performance is, as Bauman defines it, "the enactment of the poetic function, the essence of spoken artistry" (3). What becomes clear in *Mules and Men* is the extent to which the most highly regarded types of performance in Afro-American culture, storytelling and sermonizing, for example, are in the main the province of men.

Only three of the tales told in the Eatonville section and cited in the Table of Contents are told by women; only one is about women. The relative scarcity of woman-centered tales in the oral tradition must have been one of the revelations of Hurston's fieldwork. Although tales about women created by men, many of them virulently misogynistic, exist in some quantity, tales about women told from a female point of view are rare. In "Characteristics" Hurston had noted the "scornful attitude towards black women" expressed in Afro-American folk songs and tales (64). Yet, she noted they were respected in "real life." How women "assert their image and values as women" is not found in the folklore literature because, according to Roger Abrahams, women negotiate for respect in the "apparently spontaneous interpersonal exchanges of everyday interactions" (58). Only apparently spontaneous, black women's presentations in these exchanges are in fact often as formulaic as the more formal performances in which men engage. "Ideally [a woman] has the ability to *talk sweet* with her infants and peers but *talk smart* or *cold* with anyone who might threaten her self-image" (62).[5] Respect is never a permanent given, as the "between-story conversation" in *Mules* amply demonstrates.

Some of the fiercest exchanges on the store porch take place between a man and woman named Gene and Gold. After one tale (25–26) which uses " 'rounders and brick-bats' " as terms of address for women, Gold negotiates for respect by commenting that the teller knows he has told a " 'lie.' " He laughingly denies and thus confirms her charge, which encourages Gold to continue: " 'Dat's all you men is good for—settin' 'round and lyin'. Some of you done quit lyin' and gone to flyin'.' " Though he is not the storyteller, Gene responds, and his retort shifts the focus from the tale to the tensions between men and women. Initially, the tensions stem from economics; Gene allows that " 'you women ain't good for nothin' exceptin' readin' Sears and Roebuck's bible and hollerin' 'bout, "gimme dis and gimme dat" as soon as we draw our pay.' "

Continuing the formulaic exchange, a woman named Shug interjects that the only way women get anything is to work for it: " 'You mens don't draw no pay. You don't do nothin' but stand around and draw lightnin'.' " The tension escalates when Gold moves from the general to the specific and addresses Gene directly: " 'Aw, shut up, Gene. . . . You tryin' to talk like big wood when you ain't nothin' but brush.' " At this point another woman, Armetta, sensing "a hard anger creepin' into the teasing," defuses it with a joke. With a similarly humorous gesture, Hurston defuses the anger with a prayer that the group conveniently overhears in the pause it takes to restore good humor to the porch. In this instance Hurston is, to borrow Barbara Johnson's formulation, both describing and employing a strategy. (325)

The strategy described proves ineffective, and the porch sitters soon break down into two camps. The comments of the men grow more crudely sexist; George Thomas proposes, for example, that a woman " 'could have had mo' sense, but she told God no, she'd ruther take it out in hips . . . [so] she got plenty hips, plenty mouf and no brains' " (33). These lines, which resonate in the dialogue on Joe Clarke's porch in *Their Eyes Were Watching God*, evidence the way in which Hurston reworked the "between-story conversation and business" into her novels. In *Their Eyes*, of course, the power relations at issue here are encapsulated in the metaphor that the black woman is the mule of the world.

The metaphor is drawn from a folk tale, "Why the Sister in Black Works Hardest." That tale is recounted in *Mules*, but interestingly, it is told by a male informant as part of a discussion on the relation of blacks to work. Race, not gender, is the topic. Similarly, "mules" in the book's title refers to the exploitation of black people's labor, not to black women. In *Their Eyes*, as Sherley Anne Williams points out, the metaphor of the mule becomes a metaphor for the female condition; the burdens borne are not only those imposed by physical labor, but by sexist attitudes. Reading backwards from the novel to this narrative, the title *Mules and Men* situates black men both in relation to work, and therefore implicitly to white men, and in relation to black women. In the former, black men, though oppressed and treated as mules by whites, create alternative spaces where they succeed more often than not in asserting their selfhood. In the latter, black men frequently suppress and treat black women as mules, while women respond by constantly negotiating spaces in which to assert their selfhood. The doubled thematic pattern anticipates one frequently noted in current writing by black women.[6] Hurston's tone is, however, decidedly more celebratory; it reflects her emphasis on the cultural riches these diverse negotiations both reflect and produce.

Among the formal devices Hurston employs throughout *Mules and Men* is the incorporation of the structural patterns of the folktales into the unifying narrative. In this section both the folk stories and the between-story conversation follow the thematic parallel of people asking God for the wrong thing. George Thomas's remark anticipates the structure of the tale Mathilda Moseley jumps in to tell in women's defense. While her ability to respond to Thomas's challenge proves she can *talk smart*, "Why Women Always Take Advantage of Men" finally reinscribes the inferior position of women.

The story begins with an invocation of a faraway past in which "de woman was just as strong as de man and both of 'em did de same things" (33–34). This, to summarize briefly, is more than the man can stand, and he entreats God to give him more strength than woman. God grants his request. When the woman finds out what has happened, she angrily asks God to restore the balance. He refuses to comply. Turning then to the Devil, she gains the keys to the kitchen, the bedroom, and the cradle; with these she can counter man's greater power.

As is true of most of the women on the porch, Mathilda Moseley's smart talking or "sass" is ultimately resistance of a passive kind. It produces important transformations: Women become subjects in their own discourse rather than the objects they generally are in the discourse of black men and white men and women.[7] But the discursive transformations do not make them the subjects of their own lives. Before the scene is concluded, more stories are told, but, between men and women, nothing is changed. When Zora explains that her townspeople have " 'lied good but not enough,' " one of them suggests that she go down to Polk County " 'where they really lies up a mess' " and " 'where dey makes up all de songs and things lak dat' " (60). On this journey, Zora crosses a boundary as significant as that which divides white Maitland from black Eatonville: "Twelve miles below Kissimmee I passed under an arch that marked the Polk County line" (64). She has reached Polk County where, according to the blues, the water tastes " 'lak cherry wine' " (60). Following the directional markers the narrative provides, she has traveled south, *down* to an almost mythic space which, like the muck in *Their Eyes,* represents the matrix of Afro-American expressive culture.

II

In Polk County both the narrator and the women of the book grow more assertive. When Zora arrives at the Everglades Cypress Lumber Company camp, she avers, "I saw at once this group of several hundred Negroes from all over the South was a rich field for folk-lore" (65), but they resist her inquiries. Her shiny gray Chevrolet and $12.74 Macy's dress arouse their suspicions that she is a revenue officer or a detective of some kind. Unlike the diffident daughter of Eatonville, this Zora is able to spin a few "lies" of her own, and she quickly claims to be a bootlegger on the lam. She later shows that she appreciates good "woofing" (stylized talk) and passes the final test by singing a few verses of "John Henry." Through this rite she wins acceptance in the community. "By the time that the song was over, before Joe Willard lifted me down from the table I knew that I was in the inner circle. . . . After that my car was everybody's car. James Presley, Slim and I teamed up and we had to do 'John Henry' wherever we appeared" (70).

One of the singers in this scene is Big Sweet, who proves in short order to be the most assertive character in the book. Although the text provides few details about her appearance, the woman's name—with its suggestions of physical power and sexual attractiveness, of strength and tenderness—aptly defines her persona. At the same time, the lack of a conventional proper name makes her seem larger than life.[8] The space associated with Big Sweet is not the porch but the jook—in Hurston's definition, a combination dance hall, gaming parlor, and pleasure house. It is the incubator of the blues. As Alice Walker would demonstrate anew in *The Color Purple,* the ethics of the jook, and of the blues, give women far more personal freedom and power than the women on the store porch enjoy. Free of the constraints of ladyhood, the bonds of traditional marriage, and the authority of the church, women improvise new identities for themselves.[9]

In her autobiography, *Dust Tracks on a Road,* Hurston describes her first encounter with Big Sweet. Significantly, Hurston hears Big Sweet before she sees her; and it is her talk that attracts Hurston's attention. Big Sweet is "specifying," "playing the dozens" with an outmatched male opponent. Before a large and appreciative audience, she breaks the news to him "in one of her mildest bulletins that his pa was a double-humpted camel and his ma was a grass-gut cow." This performance gives Hurston a "measure of this Big Sweet," and her judgment is soon verified by the opinions of others on the job (*Dust Tracks* 187). Though fearsome, Big Sweet is not feared as much as she is respected, because the community draws a distinction between meanness and the defense of one's integrity. Hurston sees the wisdom of acquiring her friendship and hence protection. Big Sweet becomes the author's guardian and guide. She identifies informants, awards prizes in "lying" contests, and eventually saves Hurston's life.

Whereas the folktales are told by informants, the narrator recounts the story of Big Sweet. In keeping with the strategies employed in the earlier section, it is told through the between-story conversation. Formidable though she is, Big Sweet contributes only two folktales to *Mules and Men:* Neither focuses on female identity. In the general narrative of her experiences in Polk County and in her descriptions of the specific situations in which stories are told, however, Hurston shows how Big Sweet asserts and maintains her identity. From these descriptions, readers can take their own measure of this woman.[10]

The dramatic performance of Big Sweet's "specifying" is not recounted in *Mules and Men;* her first words here are low-keyed. Indeed, they offer a weak contrast to the series of memorable tales of John the slave outwitting his master which dominate the scene. Big Sweet's two tales, "Why the Mocking Bird Is Away on Friday" and "How the 'Gator Got Black," are told matter of factly, but the second is preceded by an exchange that reveals a bit of her mettle. Someone else has recited "How Brer 'Gator Got His Tongue Worn Out," which has reminded Big Sweet of the tale she knows. Before she gets a chance to begin her story, however, Big Sweet is interrupted and must reclaim her place in the discussion. " 'When Ah'm shellin' my corn, you keep out yo' nubbins' " (115) wins her readmission, and the tale is told.

Later, as the others joke and lie good-naturedly, Big Sweet interjects a personal and pointed warning to her lover. The scene that follows prefigures the oft-cited one in *Their Eyes,* when Janie takes the floor against Joe. " 'And speakin' 'bout hams,' " Big Sweet begins apropos of nothing, but "meaningly, 'if Joe Willard don't stay out of dat bunk he was in last night, Ah'm gointer sprinkle some salt down his back and sugar-cure *his hams*' " (133). A leader of the group and very much a man of words, Willard tries initially to shrug off Big Sweet's challenge. " 'Aw, woman, quit tryin' to signify' " (133). But she is undeterred and announces she will signify as much as she pleases. Making an appeal to male solidarity, Willard tries to draw the other men to his side. But they know they can't beat Big Sweet signifying. Her declaration of independence cuts right to the heart of the matter: " 'Lemme tell *you* something, *any* time Ah shack up wid any man Ah gives myself de privilege to go wherever he might be, night or day. Ah got de law in my mouth' " (134). These words are emblematic of her power, for they signal her ownership of self.

Big Sweet's behavior conforms to the pattern Roger Abrahams outlines; she can *talk sweet* and *talk smart* as circumstances require. She uses "Little-Bit" as a term of endearment for Zora in *Mules and Men,* warns her that collecting songs from one of the men has provoked his lover's jealousy, and promises to defend her. A conversation between her and Hurston quoted in *Dust Tracks* further evidences her ability to *talk sweet.* Not understanding why Hurston wants to collect "lies," she pledges to aid her in doing so. Such conversations are held privately; the public smart talking she does earns Big Sweet respect.

A crucial incident recounted in *Mules and Men* pits Big Sweet against her arch rival Ella Wall, a woman whose feats are also chronicled by Leadbelly and other country blues singers. With characteristic sexual assertiveness, Ella Wall enters the camp "jook" and sends a message to Big Sweet's man. The two women exchange verbal insults, then physical threats, until the conflict is halted by the arrival of the white quarters boss. While Ella Wall is disarmed and thrown off the job, Big Sweet stands up to the white man and refuses to yield her weapon. In a telling compliment, Joe Willard expresses the admiration of the group; he also offers a self-serving response to the incident: " 'You wuz noble! . . . You wuz uh whole woman and half uh man. You made dat cracker stand offa *you*' " (162). To be sure, Willard confirms and honors the androgynous ideal Big Sweet embodies. But for understandable reasons, given his own culpability, he reads the incident in racial rather than personal terms. The courage he praises is the courage Big Sweet has shown in her struggle with the white man. Her fierce conduct in that struggle enhances her value as a woman. In its wake, her lover proudly escorts her home.

Zora Hurston knew that approval of Big Sweet was not shared by the world outside the lumber camp. The life of this hard-living, knife-toting woman was the stuff of myriad stereotypes. Hurston's narrator seems all too aware of this judgment when she reflects, "I thought of all I had to live for and turned cold at the thought of dying in a violent manner in a sordid sawmill camp." A dramatic realization follows: "But for my very life I knew I couldn't leave Big Sweet even if the fight came. She had been too faithful to me" (160). She vows to stand by her friend. Passages such as this have caused some critics to accuse Hurston of being condescending and self-serving in her presentation of the rural black community. She does seem to be playing to her audience here: "Sordid" voices the audience's opinion of the camp and its people; it also reimposes the good/bad woman dichotomy this section of the narrative otherwise suspends. Hurston's problem was to legitimize Big Sweet's conduct without apologizing or positing sociological explanations for it. Her solution was to identify the sources of its legitimacy within the culture itself.

Just before the fight scene, Hurston interpolates "a little drama of religion." A traveling preacher arrives in the camp. His sermon, "Behold de Rib," is a variant of the Biblical creation myth; its text is Genesis 2:21; its message is female equality:

> So God put Adam into a deep sleep
> And took out a bone, ah hah!
> And it is said that it was a rib.
> Behold de rib!
> A bone out of a man's side.
> He put de man to sleep and made wo-man,
> And men and women been sleeping together ever since.
> Behold de rib!
> Brothers, if God
> Had taken dat bone out of man's head
> He would have meant for woman to rule, hah
> If he had taken a bone out of his foot,
> He would have meant for us to dominize and rule.
> He could have made her out of back-bone

And then she would have been behind us.
But, no, God Amighty, he took de bone out of his side
So dat places de woman beside us
Hah! God knowed his own mind.
Behold de rib!

(150–51)

Its rhythm and imagery place "Behold de Rib" squarely in the tradition of black American preaching, but its message is anomalous. Hurston had transcribed other sermons in her field notes, including the one that became the centerpiece of her novel *Jonah's Gourd Vine*. The purposeful selection of "Behold de Rib" allows her both to celebrate a verbal art she greatly admired and to register a protest against the tradition that shaped it, a tradition which for the most part neither welcomed women's participation nor fostered their equality.

Hurston draws no connection between the sermon and the agon between Big Sweet and Ella Wall. Here and throughout the book her method is presentational, not analytical. Nevertheless, the reader's approbation of Big Sweet seems won in part by the juxtaposition of the two scenes. The care Hurston took to legitimize Big Sweet's behavior intimated the expected reaction to an assertive woman. Tellingly, the spiritual sanction for Big Sweet is located in only the most heterodox form of Christianity existent in the black community; it comes from the words of a much maligned figure in the oral tradition, the jack-leg preacher, who is here relegated to ministering to pick-up congregations in lumber camps. The spiritual sanction is functional nonetheless. Unlike, for example, the conventional Christianity followed by Delia Jones in Hurston's early story "Sweat," this revisionist tenet allows a woman to assert her self without risking her soul's salvation. Big Sweet has no qualms about her behavior; as she puts it, " 'Ah got jus' as good uh chance at Heben as anybody else' " (187).

Throughout the text, Big Sweet is empowered to speak and to act. But in the interim between her conflict with Ella Wall—when she fights to defend her honor and keep a faithless man—and her final appearance in the narrative—when she fights to defend her honor and her faithful friend Zora—, Hurston interpolates a series of tales that allude to an alternative or complementary spiritual tradition, hoodoo. Clearly, Big Sweet, who keeps a piece of gambler's lucky hoodoo in her hair to help her win at cards, is conversant with this tradition too.

To explore it more fully, the narrator Zora must journey farther south, this time to the Crescent City, New Orleans. Well-tutored and emboldened by her encounter with Big Sweet, she is now prepared to navigate spiritual mysteries. These in turn unlock the key to her personal power, the power of the word.

III

The final section of *Mules and Men* locates the sources of female empowerment firmly within the pre-Christian, Afro-centric belief system of hoodoo.[11] For Hurston, hoodoo was an intrinsic part of that "which the soul lives by"; it was a means by which Afro-Americans could exert control over their interior lives. Metaphysically decentered and clerically nonhierarchal, hoodoo offered some women a more expansive vision of themselves than did Christianity. Within hoodoo, women were the spiritual equals of men. They had like authority to speak and to act.[12] Both the first and last hoodoo practitioners introduced in *Mules and Men* are women, while the greatest teacher of all is the dead New Orleans priestess Marie Leveau. Under the providential guidance of her spirit, Zora is completely transformed.

Hoodoo—with its curses and cures, its prescriptions to rent a house, make a man come home, and ease illnesses of the body and spirit—offered its adherents instruments of control. To represent that point, all the formulae prescribed and all the ceremonies conducted in *Mules and Men* yield the desired results. If *Mules* does not stint on representing the mundane, however, it seems more concerned finally with the sacred.

As Levine abstracts the metaphysical underpinnings of nineteenth-century Afro-American sacred beliefs from which hoodoo is derived, the fundamental premise was that life was not random or accidental. Events were meaningful, and human beings could divine and understand their causes. Human beings could "read" the phenomena surrounding and affecting them because people were "part of, not alien to, the Natural Order of things, attached to the Oneness that bound together all matter, animate and inanimate, all spirits, visible or not." Personal misfortunes were not accidental or due to bad luck; once people understood the root cause of their trouble they could end or reverse it (58–59).

Psychologically, hoodoo empowered all of its adherents; it allowed them to perceive themselves as actors in the world, not the passive reactors the dominant society held them to be.[13] Conversely, hoodoo put the masters' power in a new perspective. As a result of their belief, Blassingame observes, "many of the slaves constructed a psychological defense against total dependence on and submission to their masters. Whatever his power, the master was a puny man compared to the supernatural" (45). Indeed, hoodoo could be used to exact justice from the master as well as revenge against fellow slaves (see *Mules* 240–2). Finally and most pertinently, power in hoodoo was decentered; the absence of clerical authority militated against male dominance within the slave community. Consequently, hoodoo was particularly empowering for women. Unlike the slave preacher, the plantation conjurer could as easily be a woman as a man. As Hurston documents, these features remained operative in the early decades of the twentieth century.

The first scholar to undertake a formal investigation of hoodoo, Hurston originally published her research in an extended article, "Hoodoo in America," in the *Journal of American Folklore*. Writing in the dispassionate tones of the social scientist, she compared and contrasted the beliefs of blacks in the United States and the Caribbean, outlined the ways in which hoodoo took on the prevailing religious practices of its location, listed the means by which a man or woman could become a hoodoo doctor, and catalogued the "routines" associated with each practitioner. Even here, however, Hurston could not foreswear the personal. The initiation rituals she recounted were all rendered in the first person; they are transcribed virtually verbatim in *Mules and Men*. What Hurston adds to this narrative in addition to a heightened emphasis on the personal are the contexts for the relatively small percentage of routines she includes and repeated narrative patterns that bind the two sections of the text.

"Part Two: Hoodoo" begins with temporal and geographical markers ("So I slept a night, and the next morning I headed my toenails toward Louisiana and New Orleans in particular" [193]) that echo earlier patterns; the reference to toenails alludes to conjure practices. The anthropological definition of hoodoo that took up several pages of the article is condensed to one paragraph. Far more important is the definition of hoodoo "the way we tell it"; that is, through a folktale. The tale functions as a bridge between the two parts of the text; moreover its content, which links the spirit with the word, both spoken and written, restates a major theme of *Mules and Men*.[14]

Beginning with a creation myth, the tale focuses on the human quest for the transcendent knowledge which hoodoo represents. According to the tale, the first man who attained even a portion of the knowledge (which is necessarily linked to language, as in "God's power-compelling words") was Moses, and "it took him forty years to learn ten words" (194). Moses, like Big Sweet, achieves an identity between word and deed; he made a book and a nation. In acknowledgment, God presents Moses with the rod that becomes the emblem of his power. The rod is also the figure of the snake that is omnipresent in hoodoo iconography; this association is appropriate because the power that does not come from God Moses learns from Jethro, his Ethiopian father-in-law. Their mentoring relationship is reenacted between Sheba and Solomon. Sheba, the Ethiopian, has power (knowledge) unequal to man; she chooses to make Solomon wise and gives him her talking ring. Solomon then builds himself a room with a secret door and *writes* down the ring-talk in books.

Through this multilayered tale, Hurston establishes the African provenance of hoodoo, its antiquity, and its comparability with Judeo-Christian tradition. As she notes, the Bible is the greatest conjure book of all. Certainly, the Bible is used to legitimize hoodoo for the readers of *Mules and Men*.[15] More important yet, the folktale puts into play the complex connections between hoodoo and the word; that is, between power and language. Those possessing spiritual power gain access to the power of the word. While spiritual power is to some degree a gift, imaged here in the sexual metaphors of rod and ring, those who would possess it fully must seek it. In the tale, as in Hurston's fiction, learning words is a slow and arduous process, though those "in the spirit" may unexpectedly find their tongues unleashed. However wise the words then spoken, the one who gains credit for the wisdom is the one who writes them down.[16]

The gender transpositions between the tale and the surrounding narrative are significant. Zora, readers are encouraged to imagine, has at some point found a room with a secret door and written down the words before us. But, unlike Solomon, she is not claiming the wisdom she is recording as her own. Moreover, it is not gleaned from any one source. Indeed, the diffusion of authority in hoodoo requires the representation of various practitioners. In this respect its depiction extends the communal perspective sustained throughout *Mules and Men*. The creativity and wisdom of the people are never misrepresented as individual property. Still, the question of exploitation that this folktale implicitly raises is answered most profoundly in the last section of the narrative. Zora earns the right to write the words by first seeking the power through which she may invest them with meaning.

Taking great pains to distinguish the sacred beliefs from the "voodoo ritualistic orgies of Broadway and popular fiction," the narrator emphasizes throughout the secrecy with which adherents practice their faith (195). "Hoodoo is private"; it yields its secrets sparingly. To this extent, it is of a piece with all the knowledge revealed in *Mules and Men*. Superficially, Zora is in the same position in relation to the knowledge of her culture that she was in the beginning. But, if she still must struggle to find answers, if she searches for four months and comes up empty, Zora now knows the questions to ask.[17]

Her posture as supplicant is conveyed most compellingly in the representation of her experiences with Luke Turner, a New Orleans practitioner who claims to be the nephew of Marie Leveau. Zora reports that she had studied under five hoodoo doctors before finding Turner, and she introduces the narrative of their association in words informed by the rhythms of ritual. Indeed, from its first paragraph the entire chapter seems written "in the spirit":

> Now I was in New Orleans and I *asked*. They told me Algiers, the part of New Orleans that is across the river to the west. I went there and lived for four months and *asked*. I found women reading cards and doing mail order business in names and insinuations of well known factors in conjure. Nothing worth putting on paper. But they all claimed some knowledge and link with Marie Leveau. From so much of hearing the name I *asked* everywhere for this Leveau and everybody told me differently. But from what they said I was eager to know to the end of the talk. It carried me back across the river into the Vieux Carré. All agreed that she had lived and died in the French quarter of New Orleans. So I went there to *ask*. (200, emphasis added)

The repetition of the verb *ask* not only structures the paragraph, *asking* becomes a metonym for the rite of initiation which is the climax to which the chapter builds. The verb is repeated in succeeding paragraphs. Zora must, for example, make four trips to Luke Turner, asking about Marie Leveau, before he responds to her inquiries. Eventually, he tells how Leveau would seek the spirit herself, then listen "to them that come to ask."

Only after Zora proves her trustworthiness does Turner begin to share the secret knowledge he has been taught by Leveau. Indeed, the narrative dramatizes this event to suggest that the spirit of Leveau accepts Zora as an acolyte; permission comes in the course of Turner's performance of Leveau's curse-prayer. If the talk about secret knowledge is powerful enough to "carry" Zora across the physical river, then the knowledge itself transports Zora to worlds unknown. Or, to put it in secular terms, Zora confronts her "self" in its various dimensions.

As the description of the harrowing initiation makes clear, this Zora has physical strength and mental stamina that are many times greater than those any of the Eatonville homefolk would have attributed to Lucy Hurston's daughter. After nine days of preparation, she arrives at Turner's home with the three snake skins and clean underwear required for the ritual. Naked and stretched out on the skin of the snake that had been Leveau's icon of power, she fasts for three days. "For sixty-nine hours I lay there. I had five psychic experiences and awoke at last with no feeling of hunger, only one of exaltation" (209). On the experiences themselves, the text is silent.

Symbols are then drawn on Zora's back (the lightning symbol, her sign that the spirit would speak to her in storms) and her face (the pair of eyes painted on her cheek, the sign that she could see in more ways than one). A banquet follows the rites of communion, and the initiation climaxes in a damp and dismal swamp with an animal sacrifice. This muck becomes ceremonial ground. A "chant of strange syllables rose. I asked Turner the words, but he replied that in good time I would know what to say. It was not to be taught" (211). The moment in which the petition is answered goes undescribed. But in that silence we can read Zora's possession of the word.

That possession is manifested throughout *Mules and Men,* but nowhere more compellingly than in this chapter. Written "in the spirit," it inscribes the rhythm and passion of the ritual. It serves as well to allegorize the journey of the artist who travels both to the matrix of the culture and to the deepest regions of the self. Having completed this dual journey, she is empowered to tell her story to the world.

The representation of the journey back and the voyage within set forth here is often refigured in contemporary writing by black women. Moreover, like many female personae, Zora locates the authority to speak and create within suppressed and fugitive spiritual traditions. This establishes a pattern followed by, for example, Avey Johnson in *Praisesong for the Widow,* who reenacts the kinds of ritual represented in *Mules and Men.* Analogously, speakers in

Audre Lorde's poems sometimes find sanction through the invocation of the Yoruban Orisha. In *for colored girls*, women improvise rituals from Afro-American vernacular culture to speak of female bonding and self-love.

Whatever the influence of *Mules and Men* on these works, the first revision of the narrative was certainly Hurston's own in *Their Eyes Were Watching God*, a novel widely considered a "mother text" in the tradition of black women's writing. The protagonist Janie Crawford retraces the journey from store porch to jook to muck mapped in *Mules*. Her spiritual progression goes uncharted. But, she is surely not referring to a physical destination alone when she tells her friend: " 'It's uh known fact, Pheoby, you got tuh *go* there tuh *know* there' " (285). Through a process abstracted from ritual, Janie like Zora comes into possession of the word. In its many allusions to its "mother text," the novel distills the vision of female empowerment set forth in *Mules and Men*.

Notes

1. Hurston gives an extended account in *Dust Tracks on a Road*. See also the Hemenway biography.

2. Critics have responded to this ambivalence in various ways. In *Zora Neale Hurston*, Robert Hemenway refers to the narrator as "a self-effacing reporter created . . . to dramatize the process of collecting and make the reader feel part of the scene" (164). Susan Willis argues that Hurston's project in *Mules* as elsewhere was "to mediate two deeply polarized worlds, whose terms include: South/North, black/white, rural/urban, folk tradition/intellectual scholarship" (27). The narrator is the mediating agent. Both critics view the narrator as an essentially static figure. Barbara Johnson argues in contrast that the narrator is constantly shifting her ground and "deconstructing" the terms of reference. In my reading the persona of the narrator gains force throughout the narrative; though in keeping with Hurston's aesthetic, the development is not linear.

3. Darwin T. Turner, introducing the 1970 edition of *Mules*, enumerates its scholarly shortcomings: its lack of "an exhaustive . . . description of the traditions, morés, and living habits of a folk . . . , prescriptions for the[ir] future behavior . . . , suggestions for further studies" and a comparative context for the tales (8). Hemenway highlights the interplay of text and context in his analysis in *Zora Neale Hurston*. In his introduction to *Mules* (1978), Hemenway cites a letter Hurston wrote Franz Boas as the source of her comment on " 'between-story conversation' "; he defends Hurston by pointing to her contention that the " 'conversations and incidents are true.' " He concludes that "Hurston's invention seems to have been limited to condensation and arrangement; she did not invent any folklore for the book" (xxiv–xxv). John Roberts is less certain about the "authenticity of the transcriptions." But, referring to the book's narrative structure, he observes: "It provided her with a unique opportunity to present storytelling context. In the process, she demonstrated a folkloristic sophistication and sensitivity to folklore processes shared by few of her contemporaries" (464).

4. I would speculate that Hurston achieved this understanding through her academic training and fieldwork, but also through her creation of the theatrical productions "From Sun to Sun," "All de Livelong Day," and "Singing Steel," in which she first presented the material she collected.

For a detailed linguistic analysis of "adorned" expression in Hurston's fiction, see Holloway, chapter 5.

5.   An ongoing debate in folklore studies questions the kind of distinction between performance and presentation, public and private speech acts, that Abrahams's terms evoke (see Ferrer). I find the terms useful nevertheless, because they highlight an issue that Hurston's text both raises and resolves.

6.   This doubled thematic pattern has been frequently noted in recent writing by Afro-American women. An arbitrary list of illustrative titles includes Paule Marshall, *Praisesong for the Widow;* Toni Morrison, *Sula;* Ntozake Shange, *for colored girls who have considered suicide when the rainbow is enuf;* and Alice Walker, *The Color Purple.* Here, too, *Mules* functions as a mother text.

7.   This paragraph is informed by my reading of Mae Henderson's "Black Women Writers: Speaking in Tongues," an unpublished paper which sets forth a highly provocative analysis of the discursive dilemma which black women writers confront.

8.   That Big Sweet is so much larger than life makes the correspondence between her androgynous persona and the Fon deity MawuLisa especially striking. The deity combines Mawu (female) and Lisa (male) valences. Mawu, the moon, is cool and gentle; Lisa, the sun, is strong, tough, and fiery. According to Robert Farris Thompson, their union represents a Fon ideal (176). See note 11. In the secular realm, Hurston is proposing Big Sweet as an Afro-American ideal.

9.   As several critics have noted, Walker's novel revises key plot structures, characterizations and metaphors of *Their Eyes Were Watching God;* see for example works cited below by Gates, Henderson, and Sadoff. It is noteworthy that, in her revision of the relationship between Tea Cake and Janie, refigured in that between Shug and Celie, Walker restores the female bonding celebrated in the mother text, *Mules and Men.* Even the name Shug (short for Sugar) suggests an intertextual connection. Notably, Walker's first published reference to Hurston's writing, her incorporation of the curse-prayer in "The Revenge of Hannah Kemhuff," was to *Mules and Men.*

10.   In the following analysis, I measure Big Sweet somewhat differently than I have earlier (see Wall 375–79).

11.   According to the *Standard Dictionary of Folklore, Mythology and Legend,* most students hold that the word *hoodoo* is derived from the Haitian *vodun,* that in turn comes from the identical Dahomean (Fon) word that means deity.

12.   The freedom and creativity hoodoo made available to black women is reenacted in many recent novels. In *Sula,* for example, Ajax's mother is an "evil conjure woman" and the only interesting woman he had ever met in his life.

13.   The value of this power has been called into question often enough, particularly its value vis-à-vis the political—that is, "real"—power of the white slaveowners and their heirs. Levine's statement of the case seems very much in keeping with the premises of Hurston's text: "The whites were neither omnipotent or omniscient; there were things they did not know, forces they could not control, areas in which slaves could act with more knowledge and authority than their masters, ways in which the powers of the whites could be muted if not thwarted entirely" (73–74). These are precisely the areas explored in *Mules and Men.*

14.   By introducing the myth, the text enacts a principle Eliade articulates: "*A rite cannot be performed unless its 'origin' is known, that is, the myth that tells how it was performed for the first time*" (17). As I argue below, the text follows ritualistic patterns in several respects.

15.   The tale contains as well the kernel from which Hurston would develop her 1939 novel *Moses: Man of the Mountain,* in which Moses is at once the Old Testament lawgiver and Afro-American conjure man.

16.   Marjorie Pryse makes the point forcefully when she compares the effect of *Mules and Men* on the black women's literary tradition to that of the Bible on seventeenth-century American Colonial literature: *Mules and Men* "gave her the authority to tell stories because in the act of writing down the old 'lies,' Hurston created a bridge between the 'primitive' authority of folk life and the literary power of written texts. The point is that she *wrote them down,*

thereby breaking the mystique of connection between literary authority and patriarchal power" (11–12).

17. The narrator knows when she must provide answers as well. When her first inquiry about hoodoo in Florida is met with a vigorous denial of any knowledge of " 'dat ole fogeyism,' " Zora responds: " 'Don't fool yourself,' I answered with assurance. 'People can do things to you. I done seen things happen' " (196). The emphatic tone, intensified by the Black English grammar, contrasts sharply with the narrator's demure politeness in the opening chapter. In no time the professed unbeliever being addressed here directs Zora to the local hoodoo doctor.

Works Cited

Abrahams, Roger. "Negotiating Respect: Patterns of Presentation among Black Women." *Journal of American Folklore* 88 (1975): 58–80.

Bauman, Richard. *Story, Performance, and Event: Contextual Studies of Oral Language.* Cambridge: Cambridge UP, 1986.

Blassingame, John. *The Slave Community.* New York: Oxford UP, 1973.

Eliade, Mircea. *Myth and Reality.* New York: Harper Colophon, 1975.

Ferrer, Claire R. "Women and Folklore: Images and Genres." *Women and Folklore.* ed. Ferrer. Austin: American Folklore Society, 1975. vii-xvii.

Gates, Henry Louis, Jr. *The Signifying Monkey: A Theory of Afro-Literary Criticism.* New York: Oxford UP, 1988.

Hayes, Frank L. "Campaigns Here for Negro Art in Natural State." *Chicago Daily News* 16 Nov. 1934.

Hemenway, Robert. Introduction. *Mules and Men.* By Zora Neale Hurston. Bloomington: Indiana UP, 1978. xi-xxviii.

———. *Zora Neale Hurston: A Literary Biography.* Urbana: U of Illinois P, 1977.

Henderson, Mae G. "The Color Purple: Revisions and Redefinitions." *Sage* 2 (Spring 1985): 14–18.

Holloway, Karla. *The Character of the Word.* Westport: Greenwood, 1987.

Hurston, Zora Neale. "Characteristics of Negro Expression." *The Sanctified Church.* Berkeley: Turtle Island, 1981. 49–68.

———. *Dust Tracks on a Road.* 2nd ed. Urbana: U of Illinois P, 1984.

———. "Hoodoo in America." *Journal of American Folklore* 44 (1931): 317–417.

———. *Mules and Men.* 1935. Bloomington: Indiana UP, 1978.

———. *Their Eyes Were Watching God.* 1937. Urbana: U of Illinois P, 1978.

Johnson, Barbara. "Thresholds of Difference: Structures of Address in Zora Neale Hurston." *"Race," Writing, and Difference.* ed. Henry Louis Gates, Jr. Chicago: U of Chicago P, 1986. 317–28.

Levine, Lawrence W. *Black Culture and Black Consciousness: Afro-American Folk Thought from Slavery to Freedom.* New York: Oxford UP, 1977.

Pryse Marjorie. "Zora Neale Hurston, Alice Walker, and the 'Ancient Power' of Black Women." *Conjuring: Black Women, Fiction, and Literary Tradition.* ed. Pryse and Hortense Spillers. Bloomington: Indiana UP, 1985. 1–24.

Roberts, John. Rev. of *Mules and Men* and *Their Eyes Were Watching God* by Zora Neale Hurston. *Journal of American Folklore* 93 (1980): 463–66.

Sadoff, Diane F. "Black Matrilineage: The Case of Alice Walker and Zora Neale Hurston." *Signs* 11 (Autumn 1985): 4–26.

Standard Dictionary of Folklore, Mythology and Legend. New York: Funk, 1972.

Thompson, Robert Farris. *Flash of the Spirit: African and Afro-American Art & Philosophy.* New York: Vintage, 1984.

Turner, Darwin T. Introduction. *Mules and Men.* By Zora Neale Hurston. New York: Harper, 1970. 6–15.

Walker, Alice. *The Color Purple.* New York: Harcourt, 1982.

Wall, Cheryl A. "Zora Neale Hurston: Changing Her Own Words." *American Novelists Revisited: Essays in Feminist Criticism.* ed. Fritz Fleischmann. Boston: Hall, 1982. 371–93.

Williams, Sherley Anne. Foreword. *Their Eyes Were Watching God.* By Zora Neale Hurston. Urbana: U of Illinois P, 1978. v–xv.

Willis, Susan. *Specifying: Black Women Writing the American Experience.* Madison: U of Wisconsin P, 1987.

THEIR EYES WERE WATCHING GOD
(1937)

◆

Vibrant Book Full of Nature and Salt
[Review of *Their Eyes Were Watching God*]

SHEILA HIBBEN

Somewhere in Zora Neale Hurston's book somebody is talking tall about Big John the Conqueror. "Nature and salt, dats what makes a strong man like Big John the Conqueror. He was a man wid salt in him," says this somebody. "He could give uh flavor to anything." Well, that's just what Zora Hurston can give to her writing and when a book has Nature and salt, it's got a lot.

Not that Miss Hurston has to depend on wit and feeling in "Their Eyes Were Watching God." Here is an author who writes with her head as well as with her heart, and at a time when there seems to be some principle of physics set dead against the appearance of novelists who give out a cheerful warmth and at the same time write with intelligence. You have to be as tired as I am of writers who offer to do as much for folks as Atlas, Joan of Arc, Faith, Hope and Charity, Numerology, NBC and Q.E.D. to be as pleased as I am with Zora Hurston's lovely book—sensitive book I might have said, if the publishers' blurb writers had not taken over that adjective for their own.

Readers of "Jonah's Gourd Vine" and "Mules and Men" are familiar with Miss Hurston's vibrant Negro lingo with its guitar twang of poetry, and its deep, vivid humor. If in "Their Eyes Were Watching God" the flowers of the sweet speech of black people are not quite so full blown and striking as in those earlier books, on the other hand, the sap flows more freely, and the roots touch deeper levels of human life. The author has definitely crossed over from the limbo of folklore into the realm of the conventional narrative.

As a great many novelists—good and bad—ought to know by this time, it is awfully easy to write nonsense about Negroes. That Miss Hurston can write of them with simple tenderness, so that her story is filled with the ache of her own people, is, I think, due to the fact that she is not too preoccupied with the current fetish of the primitive. In a rich prose (which has, at the same time, a sort of nervous sensibility) she tells the tale of a girl who "wanted things sweet with mah marriage, lak when you sit under a pear tree and think." Janie did not get sweetness when her Grandma married her to

Reprinted from *New York Herald Tribune Books* (26 September 1937): 2.

73

Mister Killicks with his sixty acres of West Florida land, and his sagging belly, and his toenails that looked like mules' foots; and she didn't get it when she ran off with Joe Starks and got to be the Mayor's wife, and sat on her own store porch. But when Tea Cake came along with his trampish clothes and his easy ways and his nice grin that made even a middle-aged woman like Janie sort of wishful the minute she sets eyes on him, he handed her the keys of the kingdom, and their life together (what there was of it) was rapture and fun and tenderness and understanding—the perfect relationship of man and woman, whether they be black or white.

If I tried to tell you the plot of "Their Eyes Were Watching God" (an inept enough title, to my mind) I would only make a mess of it, so dependent is the story upon Miss Hurston's warm vibrant touch. There are homely, unforgettable phrases of colored people (you know, all right, that a man wasn't fooling if he threatened to kill you cemetery daid); there is a gigantic and magnificent picture of a hurricane in the Everglades country of Florida; and there is a flashing, gleaming riot of black people, with a limitless sense of humor, and a wild, strange sadness. There is also death—"not the death of the sick and ailing with friends at the pillow and at the feet," but "the sudden dead, their eyes flung wide open in judgement." Mostly, though, there is life—a swarming, passionate life, and in spite of the Tea Cake's tragic end and the crumbling of Janie's happiness, there is a sense of triumph and glory when the tale is done.

Between Laughter and Tears
[Review of *Their Eyes Were Watching God*]

RICHARD WRIGHT

It is difficult to evaluate Waters Turpin's *These Low Grounds*, and Zora Hurston's *Their Eyes Were Watching God*. This is not because there is an esoteric meaning hidden or implied in either of the two novels; but rather because neither of the two novels has a basic idea or theme that lends itself to significant interpretation. Miss Hurston seems to have no desire whatever to move in the direction of serious fiction. With Mr. Turpin the case is different; the desire and motive are present, but his "saga" of four generations of Negro life seems to have been swamped by the subject matter.

These Low Grounds represents, I believe, the first attempt of a Negro writer to encompass in fiction the rise of the Negro from slavery to the present. The greater part of the novel is laid on the eastern shore of Maryland, where Carrie, upon the death of her slave mother, is left to grow up in a whorehouse. After several fitful efforts to escape her lot, Carrie finally marries a visiting farmer, Prince, with whom she leads a life of household drudgery. Having helped Prince become the leading Negro farmer in the county, Carrie rebels against his infidelities and domination and, taking her two young daughters, runs away. Years later Prince discovers her and persuades her to return home. As she is about to make the journey, she is murdered by Grundy, her drunken and jealous lover. The two daughters return to the farm; Blanche remains with her father, but Martha flees north to escape the shame of pregnancy when her lover is killed in an accident. Martha's subsequent career on the stage enables her to send her son, Jimmy-Lew, to college to become a teacher. The novel closes with a disillusioned Jimmy-Lew comforted by his wife because of his bitterness over the harsh and unfair conditions of southern life.

The first half of the book is interesting, for Turpin deals with a subject which he knows intimately. Those sections depicting post-war Negro life in the North do not ring true or full; in fact, toward the conclusion the book grows embarrassingly sketchy, resolving nothing.

Reprinted from *New Masses* (5 October 1937): 22, 25.

Oddly enough, Turpin seems to have viewed those parts of his novel which deal with the Modern Negro through the eyes and consciousness of one emotionally alien to the scene. Many of the characters—Carrie, Prince, Martha—are splendid social types; but rarely do they become human beings. It seems that Turpin drew these types from intellectual conviction, but lacked the artistic strength to make us feel the living quality of their experiences. It seems to me, he should strive to avoid the bane of sheer competency. He deals with great characters and a great subject matter; what is lacking is a great theme and a great passion.

Their Eyes Were Watching God is the story of Zora Neale Hurston's Janie who, at sixteen, married a grubbing farmer at the anxious instigation of her slave-born grandmother. The romantic Janie, in the highly-charged language of Miss Hurston, longed to be a pear tree in blossom and have a "dust-bearing bee sink into the sanctum of a bloom; the thousand sister-calyxes arch to meet the love embrace." Restless, she fled from her farmer husband and married Jody, an up-and-coming Negro business man who, in the end, proved to be no better than her first husband. After twenty years of clerking for her self-made Jody, Janie found herself a frustrated widow of forty with a small fortune on her hands. Tea Cake, "from in and through Georgia," drifted along and, despite his youth, Janie took him. For more than two years they lived happily; but Tea Cake was bitten by a mad dog and was infected with rabies. One night in a canine rage, Tea Cake tried to murder Janie, thereby forcing her to shoot the only man she had ever loved.

Miss Hurston can write; but her prose is cloaked in that facile sensuality that has dogged Negro expression since the days of Phillis Wheatley. Her dialogue manages to catch the psychological movements of the Negro folk-mind in their pure simplicity, but that's as far as it goes.

Miss Hurston *voluntarily* continues in her novel the tradition which was *forced* upon the Negro in the theater, that is, the minstrel technique that makes the "white folks" laugh. Her characters eat and laugh and cry and work and kill; they swing like a pendulum eternally in that safe and narrow orbit in which America likes to see the Negro live: between laughter and tears.

Turpin's faults as a writer are those of an honest man trying desperately to say something; but Zora Neale Hurston lacks even that excuse. The sensory sweep of her novel carries no theme, no message, no thought. In the main, her novel is not addressed to the Negro, but to a white audience whose chauvinistic tastes she knows how to satisfy. She exploits that phase of Negro life which is "quaint," the phase which evokes a piteous smile on the lips of the "superior" race.

You Can't Hear Their Voices
[Review of *Their Eyes Were Watching God*]

OTIS FERGUSON

It isn't that this novel is bad, but that it deserves to be better. In execution it is too complex and wordily pretty, even dull—yet its conception of these simple Florida Negroes is unaffected and really beautiful. Its story comes mostly through the person of Janie, a mulatto girl carefully married off to a proper fellow whom she ran away from shortly because that wasn't love and living as she hoped it would be. And her second husband, though he built a town and promoted for himself a main place in its life, cooped her up and smothered her with rectitude until he died, leaving her wiser with middle age, and still handsome.

Through these chapters there has been some very shrewd picturing of Negro life in its naturally creative and unself-conscious grace (the book is absolutely free of Uncle Toms, absolutely unlimbered of the clumsy formality, defiance and apology of a Minority Cause). And when Tea Cake swaggers in with his banter and music and rolling bones and fierce tender loyalty, there is a lot more picturing of what we would never have known: Darktown and the work on the Everglades muck, the singing and boasting and play-acting, people living the good life but, in the absence of the sour and pretentious and proper, seeming to live it in a different world. It is the time of the Big Blow in Florida, and though Tea Cake and Janie fought through it, the aftermath left the man with hydrophobia, and she had to kill him like a dog. Janie went back to her town after that, her late years to be mellowed with the knowledge of how wide life can be.

If this isn't as grand as it should be, the breakdown comes in the conflict between the true vision and its overliterary expression. Crises of feeling are rushed over too quickly for them to catch hold, and then presently we are in a tangle of lush exposition and overblown symbols; action is described and characters are talked about, and everything is more heard than seen. The speech is founded in observation and sometimes wonderfully so, a gold mine of traditional sayings. "Don't come to *me* with your hair blowing back," someone says. Or, "My old woman . . . get her good and mad and she'll wade

Reprinted from *The New Republic* (13 October 1937): 276.

through solid rock up to her hip pockets"; "She ain't a fact and neither do she make a good story when you tell about her." Or such phrases in their proper place as "Well all right then," and "Got the world in a jug." Or such vivid-simple picture making as a comment on great wind and thunder: "Big Massa draw him a chair upstairs." Or illustrations from natural life, as in the case of the old girl who said you didn't have to worry about her blabbing; she was like a chicken—"Chicken drink water but he don't pee-pee."

But although the spoken word is remembered, it is not passed on. Dialect is really sloppy, in fact. Suggestion of speech difference is a difficult art, and none should practise it who can't grasp its first rule—that the key to difference must be indicated by the signature of a different rhythm and by the delicate tampering with an occasional main word. To let the really important words stand as in Webster and then consistently misspell no more than an aspiration in any tongue, is to set up a mood of Eddie Cantor in blackface. The reader's eye is caught by distortions of the inconsequential, until a sentence in the supposedly vernacular reads with about this emphasis: "DAT WUZ UH might fine thing FUH you TUH do.' "

And so all this conflict between the real life we want to read about and the superwordy, flabby lyric discipline we are so sick of leaves a good story where it never should have been potentially: in the gray category of neuter gender, declension indefinite.

Power, Judgment, and Narrative in a Work of Zora Neale Hurston: Feminist Cultural Studies

RACHEL BLAU DUPLESSIS

The first time we see the hero/ine of *Their Eyes Were Watching God,* she is sauntering down a road, the knowing subject of gossiping judgment. Janie is an expressively sexual woman (her buttocks and "pugnacious breasts" are immediately mentioned). She is black, but her "great rope of black hair" operates as a marker of her racial mix, and an evocation of the internal color lines in the African-American community.[1] She is all of forty—too old, according to her neighbors, collectively termed "Mouth-Almighty," to change, adventure, or express sexuality. And finally, her overalls are a nice bit of cross-dressing, signifying equality and sexuality in gender terms, and in class terms signifying her double class status as property (petty-bourgeois— local notable) annealed to "poverty" (agricultural day worker). Janie can be seen from the very first moments of the novel to be made of signs, like "Alphabet," her childhood nickname. These signs of Janie are constructed by Hurston to be conflictual and heterogeneous in the array of race, gender role, age, class, and sexual markers.[2] However, as the early incident of the photograph pointedly tells, the multiplicity and plurality of "Alphabet" are focused suddenly: "Aw, aw! Ah'm colored!" (9). The paradox of Janie—her fascination—is Hurston's narrating Janie's efforts to spell her life with more than that one word "colored," while necessarily, her life is focused by the social, economic, and cultural meanings of blackness. Race is first, or primary, yet at the same time race exists among many social determinants. Analyzing the narrative and textual interplay and effects of these multiple determinants is the task of feminist cultural studies.

Janie is in an incessant dialogue with the meanings of "colored," of which she is not in control. To construct Janie's dialogue, Hurston has treated

Reprinted with permission from *New Essays on Their Eyes Were Watching God,*" ed. Michael Awkward (Cambridge: Cambridge University Press, 1990): 95–123.

many of these social determinants (such as class, sexuality, and gender role) as if they were matters of choice and risk for her character, not fixed and immobilized. Hurston's presumption of Janie's choice in coping with social determinants is an assumption she also makes in her autobiography, *Dust Tracks on a Road.* There her basic attitude is that my race is part of the hand I have been dealt; now I will play it. Race is something with which to be strategic. Her race is not "a low-down dirty deal"; she is not, as she tersely informs us, either a self-pitying or a "tragically colored" person.[3] Her scathing critique of the unifying fervors of Race Pride, Race Consciousness, and Race Solidarity, and her scathing contempt for anti-Negro racial prejudice match each other. She wants an end to binary thinking about race. She is in favor of "seeking individual capabilities and depths," a proposal that occurs upon her nonetheless inescapable material ground of racially situated rural poverty, early bereavement, family scattering and anger, and scrabbling for education and employment.[4]

Hurston wants to analyze race without being reduced to race. In the title "How It Feels To Be Colored Me," she makes a distinction between "it" and "me"; by saying that she is not "it," she implies that her ego, her "me" is informed by, yet not reduced to her race. Yet "colored me" is in the object case, not the subject form, suggesting the impact of objectification on her in spite of herself. To echo an image Hurston uses in the novel, there is an "inside" and an "outside" to Hurston's rhetorical choice, and although she uses this image of unmasking (an "I will tell you how it feels"), still the word "it" does mask things. By saying "I have no separate feelings about being an American citizen and colored," she provides a critical reply to DuBois's influential analysis of African-Americans' double consciousness. Yet sometimes she insists that she feels "*so* colored," thus constitutively African-American; at other times she implies she is just one among many differently hued human "bags" with their diversified contents, separating one's outside color and one's real insides.[5]

Because Janie is constructed of dialogic play among multiple social factors, Hurston's hero/ine provokes a critic toward this feminist imperative: the critical analysis of multiple social determinants in their narrative meanings. Gynocriticism—the study of women writers—has been in a divided state virtually since it was first defined. If it is gynocentrist and polarizing in its assumptions (as in reasserting cultural stereotypes, fixed definitions of gender behavior, wars between the sexes, or static, transhistorical gender categories), it will be writing a story of dominance versus otherness which seems finally to have a religious plot of a victim transformed by celebratory glorification. But there has always been a gynocriticism emphasizing the cultural analysis of texts. Still, in Elaine Showalter's summarizing statement in "Feminist Criticism in the Wilderness," one is engaged with a special kind of fruitful tension. Showalter calls for feminist criticism as cultural studies; understanding "differences between women as writers: class, race, nationality, and history are literary determinants as significant as gender."[6] Yet Showalter goes on immediately to propose that in this ensemble of practices, gender is primary, and "women's culture" still has a "binding force." Several similar formulations follow, each using slightly different metaphors. Showalter sees gender as the most constitutive among multiple strata, and sees other factors as intersections on a field primarily formed by gender. How can one both hold to gender—as a feminist critic—and release it to function in a network or ensemble of factors that is not controlled by a more privileged "binding" element? For feminist criticism is historically well placed to contribute to a criticism of social determinants in their relation to representation and ideology—in short, cultural studies.[7] But to do so one has to situate the feminism most comfortably in the critic, and be agnostic about whether a specific text or author makes gender primary. Feminist cultural studies are those discussions of social ensembles made in specific by a *feminist* critic who encourages, as Nancy Miller does, one particular task of overreading.[8] To have isolated gender solely and totally was a practice necessary for the origins of feminist criticism. But now, the impact and meanings of gender must be explored contextually. Feminist cultural studies will produce analyses of the multiple social forces at issue in cultural activity, especially as those are seen textually, in narrative and image.

Three necessary engagements enable this kind of criticism. First, following Lillian Robinson, we must reaffirm and repractice a break with kinds of social privilege expressed in (or as) "literary criticism," especially the privilege of disinterested scrutiny of something other, in which we claim we are not implicated. For example, taking the social determinants of race, gender, class, and sexualities, a critic must deeply acknowledge that race is not exclusive to blacks (or other "minorities"); gender is not exclusive to women; class is not exclusive to working people; sexualities are not limited to gays, lesbians, and bisexuals.[9] That is, to look only at the marked group's markers is to replay certain ideological polarizations by which powerholders (women among them) never question themselves as markable, or see themselves as speaking socially inflected, ideological texts.

A white critic looking at Hurston could see her Negroness as marked, and will want to elaborate her attitudes toward that race in isolation from all other factors, including the critic's own assumptions about blackness and whiteness. But Hurston has a decided racial bifocality. The narrative memories and patterns of *Dust Tracks* show Hurston being (and narrating herself as) a participant in both black and white worlds, show the degree to which she was equally touched by black and white people, the degree to which both black and white were powerful generative forces in her life. The (mainly) positive connections to whites which Hurston chooses to narrate (as I, a white person, see this) began at Hurston's birth, for she was "grannied" by a white man (*DT* 29–30), who remained friendly through her childhood. He instructed her, "Don't be a nigger." She thus learned that the word "nigger" could sometimes mean class and values, not race (*DT* 41).[10] Her paean to friendship is a perfectly even-handed tribute in which she treats both white and black: Fannie Hurst and Ethel Waters. It is a chapter significantly titled "Two Women in Particular" and set after the "My People! My People!" agglomeration, as if to prove that it was always the specificity of individuals that mattered and not their race (*DT* 238–48). About slavery she pointedly notes bifurcated responsibility: "My people had *sold* me and the white people had bought me" (*DT* 200). And the final paragraph of her autobiography is a beneficent extension of herself as a model world-citizen, pleasantly inviting high and low, black and white: "Let us all be kissing-friends" (*DT* 286). Hurston might have been narrating a higher degree of racial cooperation than one might expect in America, narrating her version of social progress, narrating an interpretation of her genius transcending race.

In a feminist program of cultural studies, each social determinant must be seen multifocally, conflictually, and over time. In a challenge toward feminist criticism to work with multiple systems of social difference to examine how race, class, and gender constitute themselves in interaction and dialogue, the critic Cora Kaplan insists that none of the "social determinants" is itself unitary and unconflictual, and that all are the results of ongoing discursive practices as well as ongoing social relations.[11] Hurston offers clear evidence, for she had a very complex and conflictual picture of her race. Hurston sees "Negroness" first as a material fact of course involving marked social prejudice which it was in her interest and in her capacity to transcend. "It would be against all nature for all the Negroes to be either at the bottom, top, or in between. It has never happened with anybody else, so why with us? No, we will go where the internal drive carries us like everybody else. It is up to the individual. If you haven't got it, you can't show it. If you have got it, you can't hide it" (*DT* 237). Hurston offers this "genius theory" in defiance of the invisible shackles of institutionalized race and economic prejudice. Second, Hurston sees her race as a determinant that itself could be overruled by class and economic self-interest. She discusses the attempt of a black man to cross the Jim Crow color line in a black-owned and black-run barber shop in which Hurston was a manicurist, a shop designed to serve whites only. He gets thrown out by the black owner and workers. She says she "realized I was giving sanction to Jim Crow, which theoretically, I was supposed to resist." But she concludes that these actions exemplified economic self-interest (*DT* 162–65). Third, Hurston sees her race as a cultural heritage it was her destiny and conscious glory to embody. She repeatedly speaks of the folk sources of her art, and, in an often-cited, succinct credo, said about her specific relation with her patron, but really all her art: "I must tell the tales, sing the songs, do the dances, and repeat the raucous sayings and doings of the Negro farthest down" (*DT* 177). This aesthetic position is a conscious repudiation of the "better-thinking Negro" who "wanted nothing to do with anything frankly Negroid. . . . The Spirituals, the Blues, *any* definitely Negroid thing was just not done" (*DT* 233). Fourth, Hurston sees race as a falsely universalizing category: "There is no *The Negro* here" (*DT* 237). In the course of her remarkable chapter on the class divisions in the Negro community ("My People! My People!"), Hurston remarks, "Light came to me when I realized that I did not have to consider any racial group as a whole" (*DT* 235).[12] To try to say how Hurston regarded her race is hardly to propose a simple answer.

To try to say how the whites around her saw her race is also to propose a conflictual ensemble of white views of blackness. The white person who most decisively influenced her during the period before she wrote *Their Eyes Were Watching God* was the patron who also patronized her, and who may have passively discouraged her from writing the novel. Mrs. Mason took a specific kind of pleasure in all her black friends: She liked them to manifest what she "knew" as the deep and essential structure of their being: primitiveness. This concept seems to be a repeated concern in white vanguardist artistic and social communities (Lawrence comes to mind). To the degree that this a priori assumption is an awkward way of stating an interest in African survivals in the diaspora, it is a plausible hypothesis about black culture in the Americas. This still shows how important positional difference is to the articulation of ideas—for it is one thing for African-American writers to assume the "primitive and intuitive" as a badge of pride and common identity, and it is quite another—indeed, a form of colonization—for a white person to insist that blacks manifest these traits above all others. And to the degree that Mason's insistence that the primitive was the sole black authenticity "savagely" stereotypes heterogeneousness and compromises the individuality of African-Americans, we can only call her interest a kind of racism.[13]

Finally, feminist cultural studies would attempt to isolate crucial moments when a reader understands the interplay of social contexts and narrative texts. For example, it might be plausible to see Hurston's multiple occasions for making stories (orally in "personal performance," in short stories, in drama, in novels, in autobiography) as a construction of author as a tribal teller of tales. She did not especially alter the stories told, but she did alter the audiences to which and the narrative contexts in which the stories occurred. The multiple tellings are then replicas of the folklore situation, as if different "versions" of a tale could occur, none final, settled, or fixed despite being in a given work of art.[14] This writing tactic across her career challenges the boundaries of a work of art, and is thus a strategy of the African-American "deformation of mastery" by at once making a finished (bounded) work and redissolving its materials into a folk pool. Her tactic is also, arguably, a critique of hegemonic tactics of story-making by a version of the "delegitimation" characteristic of the gendered poetics of critique. Specifically African-American and feminist critical practices shed related cross-lights on her art.[15]

Feminist cultural studies would foreground the interplay of as many social determinants as can be justly, and imaginatively, seen first in the text—in narrative choices, structures, systems, outcomes, and tropes—and second, in the web of circumstances surrounding a text, especially its fabrication and its reception.[16] This kind of critical agenda leads finally to those textual moments when multiple social determinants seem to have concrete impact on narrative materials.

Their Eyes Were Watching God is structured in such a way as to reserve judgment to or for the black community, and most particularly to whomever might be construed as "the Negro farthest down" in any situation (*DT* 177). The most melodramatic and satisfying moment occurs in the notable confrontation of Joe by Janie in an exchange that ends with her decisive remark, "You look lak de change uh life" (75). In this novel, any kind of bullying is undercut by whoever is a "cut under": Sop-de-Bottom and Tea Cake undercut Mis Turner; Janie undercuts Joe; mules undercut men.

But this active pattern occurs not only in local scenes. It is the motor that runs the whole narrative structure with its framing of the quest and romance plots. The undercutting in particular accounts for significant moments when Janie's speech is depicted by Hurston but indirectly, or "silently"—as in the courtroom scene. Hurston achieves this appropriation of judgment to "the Negro furthest down" even though whites do have, and must be depicted as having, more political, legal, and extralegal powers of judgment, and even though black judgment (the wisdom of the community or its members) often runs strongly against Janie. The trial scene is the main place in which race and gender (as well as class and sexuality)—an ensemble of social forces—show intense cross-purposes and mutual conflicts in their narrative impact.

One must begin thinking through the trial scene by recalling that after the hurricane Tea Cake and Janie decide to return to the muck, on the principle, laughingly discussed, that the whites who know you are better than the whites who don't because of the structure of prejudice brought down to its basic component—prejudgment: "De ones de white man know is nice colored folks. De ones he don't know is bad niggers" (164). Tea Cake has just slid away from a press gang burying the dead. Soon after, his symptoms of rabies become unmistakable, Janie has a foreshadowing moment: "Ah loves him fit tuh kill" (168). The scene of the shooting is very carefully structured by Hurston, in every detail exculpatory: Tea Cake's mind gone paranoid, his pistol already loaded to try to kill her, and Janie shifting the bullets in the chambers in self-protection; her rifle put at readiness; the clear aggression of the rabid man, his three "false shots" (the three blank chambers), her warnings and attempts to stop him, and the final simultaneous and mutual shots, where Janie—as has been carefully noted before—is a better shot than he. He dies in the position of biting her.

This careful choreography of realistic, foregrounded dialogue and precisely delineated action is immediately followed by the trial scene, a blurry, dreamlike, bizarre scene, imprecise in inception ("she must be tried that same day" is to the highest degree unlikely), choral and diffuse by its end. White men are the jury and judges, the prosecuting attorney and the defense attorney. They are all strangers (the word "strange" recurs, too, and the tone of the indirect narrative is estranged). They "didn't know a thing about people like Tea Cake and her" (274)—Hurston's innocent-voiced irony about a "jury of one's peers." These strange, stranger whites have little interest in the issues, but they have the power to define fact and procedure: to "pass on what happened" and "as to whether things were done right or not."

The main interests of the white men are served by their intense blast at one of Tea Cake's angry friends. For his attempt to intervene in the "white man's procedures" and to use "the only real weapon left to weak folks," the "only killing tool they are allowed to use in the presence of white folks"—the power of speech (which is described in gunlike terms: "tongues cocked and loaded," 176)—Sop-de-Bottom is silenced and threatened with the law. The interest of white men in this trial is to contain and disempower the rage of the black male community. However, white men are also depicted as being brought to a realization of the deep meaning of the marriage of Tea Cake and Janie by the power of Janie's own testimony: that is, they are forced to acknowledge the sexual-relational feelings (the "humanity") of their social, and racial, "inferiors." The trial is a conversion experience for whites in their crediting part of the experience of blacks: they appreciate romance, but not forms of political outrage. My response (as a white critic) is that whites have gotten off easier than is plausible by virtue of the commanding stature with which Hurston has invested her hero/ine, but also (possibly) because of Hurston's own charitable asocial attitude toward the constitutive nature of prejudice which allows her to depict Janie as a superior force who can (as Hurston argues for herself in her autobiography) transcend racism.

The white women are depicted in a double way at the trial. There were a handful present, almost the number of another jury, all with "the pinky color that comes of good food"—pointedly, "nobody's poor white folks" (176). Hurston has Janie yearn for the understanding of these middle-class women, and wish she could tell her story to them "instead of those menfolks" (176). Sexuality and gender appeals here to override class and race. "Love" as a story can translate across class and racial barriers. Hurston is at one with conventional ideology in her emphasis on love conquering all. Or almost all. The white women applaud when the black (male) community is controlled; yet when the verdict of not guilty is rendered, the white women, with happy sentimentality, "cried and stood around her like a protecting wall" (179). These women as women identify with the woman's story of romantic tragedy, no matter the race and class of the protagonists, but identify with their race interests against the African-American males.

Black males—for no black women are *said* to be present except Janie—have the most volatile role. They are fiercely disgruntled that a woman has killed a man, their friend. They repeat, and partially invent, a false story about her adulterous disloyalty, and speak generalizations about the relation of black men and women—even and almost speaking for black women: "No nigger woman ain't never been treated no better [than Janie]" (177). They are also bitter that a woman who "look lak her" has used (as they see it) her gender and color privilege (as looking rather more white than they) to avoid justice. They are ironic on the subject of the cheapness of their lives relative to their race: "[L]ong as she don't shoot no white man she kin kill jus' as many niggers as she please" (179).

Indeed, their conclusion answers Nanny's mule trope at the beginning of the book. Nanny had outlined a stark power hierarchy: "So de white man throw down de load and tell de nigger man tuh pick it up. He pick it up because he have to, bot he don't tote it. He hand it to his womenfolks. De nigger woman is de mule uh de world so fur as Ah can see. Ah been prayin' fuh it tuh be different wid you" (14). In contrast, the black men say, " '[U]h white man and uh nigger woman is de freest thing on earth. Dey do as dey please' " (180). If black women see black women as mules, but black men see black women as free, simple subtraction proposes that the black men are then "de mule(s) uh de world." It is clear to Hurston that their race does not necessarily unify black men and women; they may have different interpretations of their oppression, seeing it distinguished by gender. In the men's terms, a black woman has been elevated into utter powerfulness by killing a black man. It is a disturbing allegation, and shows a bitter conflict of race and gender played out in the black community.

In a sense, the trial scenes multiply. Hurston depicts one trial by white men's hegemonic laws, and one by black men's disgruntled postmortem which Janie overhears from a boarding house room. The white women are a sprinkling of powdered sugar over this confrontation. The black men are wrong, though for some of the right reasons: The political privileges of the white race, of the professional (doctoring, lawyering, judging) class, and of light-colored blacks do exist. The lower-class black men are being done out of their self-proclaimed substitute: their gender privilege, which can include rights of possession, and sexual arousals enforced by light wife-beating and mutual fighting (140, 131–32).[17] And then the white men and women are right for possibly the wrong reasons. Being fascinated by the "whiteness" of this black woman, and by her "romance," but also wanting to put black men in their place, they judge her not guilty. This play of multiple social forces, here visible in the cross-purposed agendas of the two "juries," has the effect of isolating black woman at the intersection point where race, gender, and class and the hegemonic story of romance meet.

The trial of Janie as a black woman does not, however, end with that one complex scene. The whole narrative—Janie's account to her friend Pheoby— is like a trial. The beginning of the novel announces that Janie is being tried by her rural community and condemned without being a "witness" in her behalf, without being asked to testify. The choral collections of folk construct power for themselves through judgment talk, an act that reclaims their humanity despite their being treated as beasts. They scapegoat Janie so they won't themselves be "mules." "Mules and other brutes had occupied their skins. But now the sun and the bossman were gone, so the skins felt powerful and human. They became lords of sounds and lesser things. They passed nations through their mouths. They sat in judgment" (1–2). This rural gossip, with its combination of paralysis and cruelty (depicted at the beginning in the voices of named black women—Pearl Stone, Lulu Moss, Mrs. Sumpkins—and nameless black men), functionally compensates for the speakers' low racial and economic status; at the same time folk tales/folk talk are extremely vital cultural creations. So this folk talk is presented bifocally by Hurston. It is ennobled by the Biblical and ritualized parallelism of the rhetoric in which she presents these gossips, and folk talk is made inadequate by its sour opposition to Janie's value. Janie, then, undergoes a formal trial by the white community, a second informal trial by overhearing black men's bitter aphorisms on her case (179–80), and a third trial by her community of origin. The book involves three trials, one by white people's roles, another by black men's rules, a third by the roles of "Mouth-Almighty" (5)—her black working-class rural community. However, the trial of an autonomous black woman (a black woman who acts equal to anything) cannot play by any of these sets of rules; whatever the judgments rendered, all the trials are inadequate at root. Yet because of the black woman's relative powerlessness, her construction of her own trial by her own rules must be deferred until all of the other trials are finished.

In constructing her story in this way—framed thus, and with key moments of undepicted speech to persons who are only partially equipped to judge (although they have various legal and traditional powers of judgment)—Hurston makes the whole story a "retrial," with the proper jury and judge (a black woman—Pheoby), and the proper witnesses and defense lawyer (all Janie herself; note how in political trials, "criminals" often choose to act as their own lawyers). These trials are temporally lively in the narrative choices Hurston makes. The black female trial (Pheoby and Janie) succeeds higher-class white male and female, lower-class black male, and black community trials chronologically, but envelops them narratively. Therefore, Janie's own self-testamentary trial claims final power and final appeal.

To investigate the whole book as a trial, we must begin with Pheoby.[18] Her very name deserves some comment: It alludes to Diana or Artemis, as luminously bright—but a moon reflecting Janie's sun, for, as Hurston remarks of Janie, "the light in her hand was like a spark of sun-stuff washing her face in fire" (183).[19] A phoebe is also a small dull-colored bird, common in the eastern United States, and distinguished by "its persistent tail-wagging habit."[20] Not only a punning allusion within the book ["you switches a mean fanny round in a kitchen," says Janie to Pheoby (5)], this is also a punning allusion to the power of tale-wagging or storytelling, for Pheoby is invited by Janie to "tell 'em [the gossiping neighbors] what Ah say if you wants to" (6).

But Pheoby's first role is to be the jury of her peers which Janie had long sought for a proper (a telling) judgment of her story. As well she is the next (though undepicted) storyteller or tale-wagger: In a striking image of doubled power, Janie remarks: "[M]ah tongue is in mah friend's mouf" (17, cf. *DT* 245), a phrase that means we understand each other so well you could speak for me.

But talk is only one part of power; at novel's end, Janie criticizes those who talk without action: "[L]istenin' tuh dat kind uh talk is jus' lak openin' yo' mouth and lettin' de moon [cf. Phoebe!] shine down yo' throat" (183). Pheoby is not one of the actionless—at least according to her self-proclaimed growth and her vow to make Sam take her fishing. But insofar as tales are substitutes for action, the full weight of Janie's final judgment—for she is judge as well as criminal and lawyer—is levied against that displacement. "Talk" in the deep narrative ideology of this novel can be seen bifocally—as folk power, activated knowledge, and judgment possibly motivating action, or as the powerless substitution for both knowledge and action. This bifocal vision of the "talk" of the porch-sitters is a replica of Hurston's contradictory and subtle notions of race: It is a source of power; yet some use it as a shoddy excuse for powerlessness. Thus Janie's silence, insofar as it was filled with "finding out about livin" autonomously, with learning the necessity "tuh *go* there to *know* there," and with "going tuh God" (183)—a metaphor for extremes of death, love, and suffering—Janie's thinking silence (keeping inside and outside distinct, having "a host of thoughts" not yet to be expressed, as in the passage on 112–13) is a source of knowledge depicted as equal to her tale wagging.[21]

There are, as Michael Awkward shows, long passages of—long years of—a protesting silence, punctuated with Janie's tart and decisive speech; but these passages—involving gender and sexual silence with her husband, alias "big voice" (43, 75), class silence with the porch-sitting folk—are now "spoken" by Janie. The novel constructs the female hero as narrating her own silences; she is unsilencing them in the specific context of testifying to Pheoby. To appreciate this narrative strategy, I want to look closely at several incidents of what is called undepicted speech. These are moments when Hurston says that Janie spoke, but Janie's speaking is not rendered in Janie's voice when it occurs. The primary moments are on the muck, in the courtroom scene, and with Eatonville's "Mouth-Almighty." On the muck, in the context of all men, the narrative informs us: "The men held big arguments here like they used to do on the store porch. Only here, she could listen and laugh and even talk some herself if she wanted to. She got so she could tell big stories herself from listening to the rest" (127–28). In the courtroom scene (278), Hurston gives a lot of interior motives and notions that Janie was trying to communicate, but about her telling, Hurston simply says: "She just sat there and told and when she was through she hushed" (178). The implication is that her words had a terrific impact. A third important moment of undepicted speech occurs as the ostracized Janie returns to her community's judgment, characterized as "mass cruelty" (2) by Hurston: "When she got to where they were she turned her face on the bander log and spoke. . . . Her speech was pleasant enough, but she kept walking straight on to her gate" (2). All these undepicted speeches function to "save up" Janie's talk until she has a chosen place and time and audience.

There is a vital ideological meaning for undepicted speech as a narrative strategy. Undepicted speech is Hurston's narrative resolution of conflictual social determinants of race, class, and gender. In a response to the courtroom situation, Hurston depicts Janie actually speaking her tale in and for the black community only, even though the white community is depicted as allowed to hear, and is even seen rendering a better judgment. Thus with the undepicted speech in the courtroom scene, Janie "tells" her tale to whites, but she will later really speak her love story and life narrative to a black person. Hurston thus resolves a tension about power and powerlessness (as it intersects with race), offering Janie's speech back to "the Negro farthest down." But not all these African-Americans appreciate Janie. Because of her explorations of social class and of sexual freedom, they bully her. So Hurston must arrange for this speech to "go" to a black person or persons untainted by authoritarian gossip, for rural "Mouth-Almighty" here brooks comparison with Joe Starks's mercantilist "I God" as a parallel misuse of power, authority, and voice. Janie disparages the community that will not listen (listening, the kind of intimate empathetic listening that Pheoby does, is a requisite for good talk). The porch-sitters who judge her are unlistening talkers already scripting a narrative for her whether or not they have all, or even any, of the proper information (see 5–7). Therefore Hurston will locate Janie's telling to and for one black woman alone, which solves the issue of unlistening community by selecting a listening individual who can represent "the Negro farthest down": a black woman.[22] Hurston chooses a woman listener, which recalls Janie's desire, in the courtroom scene, to speak to white women rather than white men. Similarly, Hurston will make race a factor that intersects with "class" or values of curiosity, mobility, and change by choosing a person (Pheoby) who has separated herself from the porch-sitters. In proposing these moments of undepicted speech, Hurston disassembles three significant groups (race, class, gender), and makes, through narrative choices, subtle distinctions, subtle judgments among them.

II

This novel's title, although clearly generated at one moment in the work, is mysterious in its meaning, not easily glossed in relation to the body of the novel as a whole. Yet even before Pheoby moves toward Janie's house with a covered bowl of mulatto rice, the absolute beginning of the book begins playing with title materials and meanings by opening issues about words and the Word in relation to gender and racial power. The third paragraph starts with a revisionary articulation of Biblical rhetoric "So the beginning of this was a woman" in the place of, taking the world-creating place of Word or God. This woman has seen the "sudden death, their eyes flung wide open in judgment" (1)—making both an allusion to those drowned in the flood, and a prefiguration of the theme of judgment. "Their eyes" is, of course, one portion of the title and a reference to it. All of the moments of special metaphors in the title and elsewhere bear some relation to the multiple social determinants that are narratively active in the novel.

"The sun was gone . . ." (1) and the story begins, at the end of which night, a new sun emerges, and that sun is a woman. Indeed, she appropriates the horizon "from around the waist of the world" for her own garment and gives Tea Cake "the sun for a shawl" (183). Given the cosmic imagery of the ending—the "fishing for life" (which relocates the different episodes of pleasure, leisure, and fishing in this book)—one might say that the progress or education of the novel is about a black woman who changes from being a mule to being a sun.[23] And being a "sun" is, as Henry Louis Gates points out with a significant citation from *Mules and Men,* related to the ability to "seek out de inside meanin' of words."[24] How do the "inside meanin'[s] of words" act within the novel? How is language susceptible to analysis by feminist cultural studies?

The separation of animal from human by the related acts of talking and judgment is made especially crucial to that being called, in Nanny's monologue, "de mule uh de world" (14): woman. The "Nanny" section of the novel unfolds itself as a doomed dialectic between sexual pleasure and racial prejudice which issues in the enforcing of gender and class protection. Social decency, straight paths, reductions of impulse all are the desired end: Janie, her Nanny decrees, must "marry protection" (14). Protection ironically takes the form of a man; self-sufficiency is not and cannot be a thought, although Nanny herself has, within racial parameters (and with the help of Mrs. Washburn), achieved it. Choice does not enter; but Janie makes a rudimentary sexual-gender resistance to graceless Logan Killicks and his dim rural life (i.e., to class and to race construed in a limited, servile way). In fact, allegorically speaking, this marriage is an image for slavery.[25] It is significant that as she leaves the marriage, Janie was about to become Killicks's third mule and be put behind a plow. The kind of economic "protection" offered by the first marriage is explicitly tabulated by Tea Cake much later in the novel as inadequate. Thinking that Janie might need protection (autonomy) from "some trashy rascal" (124), Tea Cake teaches Janie how to shoot. She thereupon becomes a dazzling shot; self-sufficient in this precise way, she is able to protect herself against a most unpredictable and tragic assault, ironically by Tea Cake himself.

Protection as Nanny construes it—gender and class based—is in the most articulate contradiction to sexualities. And Hurston does not stint in our understanding of this by her lavishly sensual and orgasmic description of the pear tree, Janie's own articulation of her desire.[26] But that desire, as Nanny then tells, if not innocent and naive, must be informed and infused with the history and genealogy of race told in another tree metaphor: by virtue of slavery, "us colored folk is branches without roots." Under slavery, political power for real social interaction is eradicated: "It sho wasn't mah will for things to happen lak they did" (15), says Nanny. Note the emphasis, even in her utter powerlessness, on bringing things about, making things happen.

What follows is an open-ended narrative of severe sexual as well as socioeconomic bondage for black women. The colonial and class relations working together make of Nanny at once "a work-ox and a brood-sow" (15). The doubling of the animal image makes monstrous the situation, though not the person. Nanny was the favored slave, and bore her master's children; deprived of his protection during his absence in the Civil War, she is threatened by the master's wife in such drastic ways that she flees, despite having just been brought to childbed, of a daughter, Janie's mother.[27] That daughter, Leafy (a name in poignant relation to the tree metaphor), was raped at seventeen by her school teacher—a kind of class betrayal, for, as Nanny says, "Ah was 'spectin' to make a school teacher out of her" (36). She never recovered and became troubled and promiscuous. With that racially and socially inflected sexual history as Janie's matrilineage, it is significant that one could read the novel as a quest for autonomous, pleasurable sexual choice—the lessons of Tea Cake cut deeply into the seared and sere terrain of the post-slavery generations of black womanhood.

Despite being severely repudiated by Janie ["she hated her grandmother" (85)], Nanny is given a profound narrative and textual function by Hurston. She is the prophet—without honor perhaps, but serving the function of textual prophet. For Nanny's words are predictive and come true later in the novel.[28] The creative word, the word acting in time, the word able to bring events into being, is a mighty powerful word. Nanny says the word, and then the word is made flesh and narrative in Janie, who is called, in her incipient state, her grandmother's "text" (16). One might say that Hurston compensates Nanny for typical historical losses in slavery and Reconstruction by endowing her with the power of the word.

For instance, Nanny says, "Ah can't die easy thinkin' maybe de menfolks white or black is makin' a spit cup outa you" (19). The sexual vulnerabilities of both grandmother and mother are recapitulated here. That spit cup is suggestively literalized in the Joe Starks section, for he has provided the most up-to-date spittoons his town has ever seen, and the commentary, sotto voce, is made through this text by Hurston—but it's still a spit cup after all; it's a spittoon like the ones whites use in a "bank up there in Atlanta" (44) and it "made the rest of them feel that they had been taken advantage of" (45). This spittoon condenses Joe Starks's class superiority (indeed, his structural "whiteness") and his sexual reductionism in one image.

Probably the most striking metaphor literalized in the text is "de mule uh de world," for the mule as well as spittoon is the sign under which Janie's marriage to Joe Starks unfolds. With Nanny's mule soliloquy as groundwork, the choral comments of the male community pass from Jody and "dat chastisin' feelin' he totes" (46) to the mule. Indeed the men are called "muletalkers" and the mule is the subject—one might say the allegory—they propose. Chapters 6 and 7 contain the climactic analysis and disintegration of Joe and Janie's relationship, interwoven with the fate of the mule. The mule is any and all "underclasses": deprived, overworked, starved; it is the butt of jokes; it is stubborn and ornery to its master, with ways of resistance that are deeply appreciated by the talkers. Indeed: "Everybody indulged in mule talk," says Hurston with devastating clarity. "He was next to the Mayor in prominence and made better talking" (50). The figure of the mule summarizes power relations of class, race, and gender: the porch-sitters to Joe, all blacks to whites, and Janie herself to Joe, who, although she had "thought up good stories on the mule," was forbidden to say them. This is the symbol of all the silencings Joe imposes on Janie throughout their marriage, and has been seen as such by most critics of the novel.

Janie's bitter empathy for the mule, expressed in words overheard by Joe, precipitates the striking event of its "emancipation," with its multiple social meanings. "People ought to have some regard for helpless things" (54) is her comment to herself, and it clearly figures her own sense of gender entrapment speechlessness. Joe responds by purchasing the mule—"Ah bought dat varmint tuh let 'im rest" (54)—a moment of social largesse that can be construed in class terms, as a sign of his superiority to the folks who must work a mule—and themselves—to death. Janie's moving, eloquent response to the "free mule" (55) figures the moment with touching irony as if Starks were the Great Emancipator—a white king who frees the Negroes, in racial noblesse oblige. But Janie's brief speech in Starks's honor precipitates a group realization that "[yo]' wife is uh born orator, Starks. Us never knowed dat befo' "—and foreshadows Janie's devastating assumption of speech in the next chapter. So the mule is an actor in Janie's realization and emancipation.[29]

This is nowhere as clearly seen as in Janie's exclusion from the folk festival made of the mule's funeral. At the ideological center of the novel, the figurative "mule uh de world" (a black woman) has been literalized (as a mule), and has become a condensed figure for black, rural, female resistance, and for folk-pleasures in the parody of power. The power of the mule carnival infuses Janie, who then vocally and publicly doubts her husband's potency, power, and "big voice" (75). This accusation punctures his sexual, political, and even economic power. It is the revenge of the mule.

In the Tea Cake section, Hurston continues to explore the ways in which words and tropes reveal the multiple forces she has at stake in the novel. Tea Cake and Janie marry after a sporty and sexually luxuriant courtship, but class remains an issue. "Jody classed me off" (107), says Janie explaining to Tea Cake that this was not her choice or her desire. But Tea Cake is self-conscious about falling in love with a woman of a better class (more proper-tied), for he is a day worker, and doesn't hang around with "no high muckty mucks" (118); no one will be surprised to see the literalized Muck of the Lake Okechobee region here verbally prefigured. Janie sees her social class as a burden of internalized repression, preventing her from enacting various desires. She says: "Ah wants tuh utilize mahself all over" (107), a phrase with evident sexual but also social resonance: to know all classes and peoples.

She wants to saturate herself in her people to see, feel, and experience what they are—and what she is. And Tea Cake is "the people."[30] Tea Cake leads, for the most part, a high risk, improvident, charmed and charming life; like the blues he sings, he is "made and used right on the spot" (125). He is one who will "cherish de game" (91), a resonant phrase about risk, love, courtship—and the joie de vivre of the character. He is the very opposite of the bourgeois virtues of Joe ["positions and possessions" (47)], and, if anyone cares to remember him, the rural plod of Killicks. He is playful and urbane (indeed urban in certain of his skills, despite his rural worker status). Hence Janie has, among her three husbands, traveled through an array of available social classes. And Hurston's narrative tests each class for its possibilities of satisfying a woman's life—that is, she tests social class by gender criteria. Reckless gambling artists come out best. Tea Cake gambles with fate; he is, indeed, a gambler, and that gaming quality is a trope for existential risks ultimately respected by Hurston. In fact, she has put some of that in her title, for a roll of the dice during the storm does not abolish chance, but only accentuates it. And in that spirit, the eyes of the gamblers, male and female, watch God.

Janie has, by Tea Cake's actual sincerity, avoided the fate of poor Mis Tyler, taken for the proverbial ride by a young gigolo; this story of her sexual and gender trap is threateningly interwoven throughout the account of their early marriage. Hurston then constructs, with great cunning, a second trap built of the crosscurrents of class and race, with a tricky admixture of gender and sexuality.[31] The long and subtle treatment of Mrs. Turner (Chapters 16 and 17), and the relationship of the names Mis Tyler and Mrs. Turner, indicate that there is some link between the incidents.

Color (and Caucasian features) within race has always been a painful part of African-American heritage—indeed, as part of a worldwide system of racism which has its roots in economic and imperial domination. Ideas of female beauty coincide with, and support, the political hegemonies of dominant race, class, and sexual choice. The section focusing on Mrs. Turner, which is long, repetitive, and interestingly polemical, is a confrontation with the temptation to "class off" to "lighten up" the race (135) by a kind of eugenicist choice of sexual partner, and to try to put distance of manner as well of skin tone and "features" (thin lips, flat buttocks, narrow or pointed nose) between oneself and other blacks.[32] Although African-American, Mrs. Turner is a racist against Negroes: "Ah can't stand black niggers. Ah don't blame de white folks from hatin' 'em 'cause Ah can't stand 'em mahself" (135). Mrs. Turner is described as a "milky sort" (133), her color light, but also a kind of cow sporting her own rabid opinions ["screaming in fanatical earnestness" (136), in Hurston's judgmental phrase]. Tea Cake overhears her; his comment, "Ah been heah uh long time listenin' to dat heifer run me down tuh de dawgs . . ." (137), is a prophetic image literalized in the flood scene in which a confused cow and a vicious dog in combination are the proximate cause of Tea Cake's irrevocable wound. A rabid dog sitting on a burdened, bewildered beast seems to be Hurston's deep allegorical comment on the system of race-inflected social stratification.

Mrs. Turner identifies Janie as an appropriate companion for no quality but her "whiteness," and would see dark Tea Cake as a husband worthy of Janie only if he would cover his darkness with "plenty money" (134). Janie does not say much to Mrs. Turner's monologues—the two are not equally fanatical. But what she says is to the point: "We'se uh mingled people and all of us got black kinfolks as well as yaller kinfolks. How come you so against black?" (135). Mrs. Turner blames the darkness of certain blacks for the existence of racism: "If it wuzn't for so many black folks it wouldn't be no race problem. De white folks would take us [i.e., people of her approximate color] in wid dem. De black ones is holdin' us back" (135). The debate about "Booker T." occurs in this context. There is cultural irony when Mrs. Turner calls him "uh white folks' nigger" (136).[33] Janie claims not to have thought much about this subject, but produces the opinion that class is a greater determinant than race for blacks' position: "Ah don't figger dey [whites] even gointuh want us for comp'ny. We'se too poor" (135).

There are other, subtle ways in which pure racial polarization is disavowed while race is factored in as a deeply structuring social determinant. The plot against Mrs. Turner's restaurant begins with a boycott: "Since she hate black folks so, she don't need our money in her ol' eatin' place. Ah'll pass de word along. We kin go tuh dat white man's place and git good treatment" (137). Of course, the protest ends in an ironically complicit and staged incident, in which Tea Cake, chivalrously defending Mrs. Turner's "niceness" from "dumb niggers" (142), wreaks, with their help, the proper amount of destruction to drive Mrs. Turner back to "civilization." In fact, using sequence tellingly, Hurston opens the next chapter with an exact and political contrast—a scene of what one might call Pan-Africanism, or alliances across the diaspora—the brief mention of the befriending of the Bahamans by Janie and Tea Cake, which brings their dance and music into fruitful relation with the American blacks. Nationality of itself, color of itself, does not necessarily make prejudicial difference, but constructs *appreciable* difference—differences and specificities that one can appreciate (as the Bahamans bring their music into the "mingling" or as a white man's restaurant is more welcoming than one run by a prejudiced black woman). In her text here, Hurston credits, without showing social or rhetorical stress, those (few) whites who get along with blacks.[34] The white doctor "who had been around so long that he was part of the muck" (167) is able quickly to listen to Tea Cake and Janie's stories, diagnose him, promise to try against fact to save him, and finally, after the death, to bear a "good thought" (7)—honest witness—in Janie's favor.

Race, class, and color within race rise in structural and figural importance in the latter part of the book, building toward, and away from, the hurricane. The coming of the storm is foretold by Native American Seminoles, who can read natural signs. Janie does not leave the low ground, the muck, because she does not believe the best judgment of the Seminoles, but rather, lightly, listens to and believes a loosely structured identification with whites and white values. The Seminole message is heard, but denigrated and denied, and the final point in favor of staying on the low ground is that "Indians are dumb anyhow, always were" (147). Hurston makes a dramatic irony of this racial prejudice, and its unthinking faith in the white man and the "boss-man's" (150) ability not to let nature overwhelm them—a gross misjudgment of natural and political powers. It is a key moment when the inability to credit the Seminoles' way of "seeking de inside meanin' " of signs, the denial of the interpreting ability of a nondominant group, means disaster.

As the storm worsens and all chances to drive away from the flooding lake have been lost, Hurston locates the dramatic revelation of her title: "The time was past for asking the white folks what to look for through that door. Six eyes were questioning *God*" (151).[35] Blacks' unthinking dependence on or internalization of white judgment, "readings," or interpretations is abruptly, startlingly addressed. The contrast of white power as a form of political idolatry and fate's (God's) power is the most particularly striking in this version of the title sentence. Overt white power, narratively absent from most of the work, is still constitutive in a racial caste society; to the degree that blacks believe in this power, their interpretative capacities are controlled.

When Hurston says two pages later, "They seemed to be staring at the dark, but their eyes were watching God" (151), the title is totally present in this citation. In it there is an image of reading, reading through, or piercing the darkness (obviously the natural darkness of the storm, but also possibly blackness) to universals of fate. The characters are trying to read their own fortunes. They seemed to be seeing only the dark, or "being in the dark," but their understanding looked through blackness (or darkness) to something more primary. Here an image encompassing race (blackness) seems to give way to universals of awe. Race is transcended.

There are a number of substitutions for God made in this book, usually in the form of big talkers—"Mouth-Almighty" of the rural folk, and "I God" for Joe Starks's comic blasphemous condensation of political and economic power. Mrs. Turner's "color-struck" state, presented as the worship of a (lower case) god, the idol of whiteness, is just one more moment of idolatry. But Hurston is subtle; to some degree all blacks in the book are capable of this kind of idolatry; it is not only externalized in a dismissible character or two, but it also increasingly delimits the choices and judgments of the various and collective heroes. Although in the overlay of meanings clustered in the pages that announce the title, Hurston shifts meaning from race to fate itself, yet still she makes clear that there is no fate in this book uninflected by race.[36] Hence the title is contradictory in its impact. It talks about fate and race at once, and a single meaning cannot be settled one way or the other.

Dramas of race occur in a telling scene when Tea Cake is pressed into service in Palm Beach by two authoritative white men with rifles. The sullen, racially mixed crew is instructed to "examine" the rotting bodies to ascertain which storm victims are white and which are black so they may be differentially buried, the one in coffins, the other in mass graves. However, it is graphically stated, "[D]e shape dey's in[,] can't tell whether dey's white or black" (165). What use is color to ultimate facts: death, fate? Meantime, these dead bodies are described as "watching, trying to see beyond seeing" (162), yet another version of the title phrase. "Watching," then, becomes a way of seeing which gets beyond seeing normally; "normally" here involves seeing difference, especially racial difference. In this use, it appears that Hurston's title is an encoded critique of the color line (whether managed or evoked by white or black) and especially of white power. The human knowledge that the staring dead have is richer and deeper than the mere political prejudices of the whites.

But let me give Tea Cake the final, ambiguous word—ambiguous in its racial notions, and so fully in character and voice that it is hard to decipher: "They's mighty particular how dese dead folks goes tuh judgment . . . Look lak dey think God don't know nothin' 'bout de Jim Crow law" (163). These two statements cut two ways. The first may suggest that God Himself doesn't care about men's laws and exterior differences in judging those brought before Him. (And He is reputed not to.) The second sentence says that these white men are overly scrupulous in preparing segregated facilities for the dead, since God is clearly capable of making Jim Crow separations if He wants to, and even from masses of dead human material buried jointly in one grave. If omnipotent means anything, it certainly means the power to individualize and make distinctions among the putrescent mass. They are acting as if God were a dummy. (And He is reputed not to be.) One sentence mocks white political pretension, whereas the other suggests casually that racial prejudice might have divine approval. In this novel, "God" is evoked mainly as cosmic critique of the lunacies of racist politics; the use of God in the title is an "inside meanin' " that suspects the normative politics of race and power. And thus one might watch Him with awe. But He also might be an image for the implacability of political power, as experienced by African-Americans; God might indeed know too much about the Jim Crow laws. One might then watch Him warily, bifocally. Even in her denials that race matters, and her invocations of cosmic or color-blind standards, Zora Neale Hurston makes it matter.

Notes

1. Janie's lightness of skin tone is commented upon at several junctures. Mary Helen Washington remarks that descriptions of Janie draw upon discourses of the "mulatto novel" and its conventions of romance. *Invented Lives: Narratives of Black Women 1860–1960*, ed. Mary Helen Washington (Garden City: Anchor Press, 1987), p. 250. Hurston made this choice despite her insistence that "before being tampered with" by white cultural values (and Northern values), darker Negro women were not disparaged by the folk. Hurston, "Characteristics of Negro Expression," in Nathan Irvin Huggins, *Voices from the Harlem Renaissance* (New York: Oxford University Press, 1976), pp. 233–5.

2. There are a variety of provocative readings of this briefly mentioned, but textually foregrounded, nickname. Among them, Houston A. Baker, Jr., says that the nickname indicates the "marginally situated" Afro-American who has "the possibility of all names." *(Blues. Ideology and Afro-American Literature* [Chicago: University of Chicago Press, 1984], p.59); and Henry Louis Gates, Jr., says that Janie is a "nameless child" (*The Signifying Monkey* [New York: Oxford University Press, 1988], p.185).

3. Hurston, "How It Feels To Be Colored Me" (1928), in *I Love Myself When I am Laughing . . .: A Zora Neale Hurston Reader*, ed. Alice Walker (New York: The Feminist Press, 1979), p.153.

4. Hurston, *Dust Tracks on a Road: An Autobiography* (1942), second edition, including previously unpublished chapters (Urbana: University of Illinois Press, 1984), p.330. Subsequently cited as *DT* in text, where needed for clarity. One will not easily forget, among other telling symbolic incidents about the irregular acquisition of education and a relationship to culture, Hurston finding a copy of the *Complete Milton* in the garbage.

5. In *A World of Difference* (Baltimore: Johns Hopkins University Press, 1987), Barbara Johnson discusses this essay: "Far from answering the question of 'how it feels to be colored me,' she deconstructs the very grounds of an answer, replying, 'Compared to what? As of when? Who is asking? In what context? For what purpose? With what interests and presuppositions?' " (178).

6. The essay dates from 1981, in *The New Feminist Criticism*. ed. Elaine Showalter (New York: Pantheon, 1985), p. 260.

7. In Terry Eagleton's succinct formulation: "[T]he field of discursive practices in society as a whole, [with] particular interest . . . in grasping such practices as forms of power and performance." *Literary Theory: An Introduction* (Minneapolis: The University of Minnesota Press, 1983), p. 205.

8. Nancy Miller, "Arachnologies," in her *Subject to Change: Reading Feminist Writing* (New York: Columbia University Press, 1988), pp. 83–90.

9. Lillian Robinson, "Feminist Criticism: How Do We Know When We've Won?" in *Feminist Issues in Literary Scholarship*, ed. Shari Benstock (Bloomington: Indiana University Press, 1987), p. 147.

10. She even footnotes her use of the term thus: "The word Nigger used in this sense does not mean race. It means a weak, contemptible person of any race." She of course begs the question of the origin of this particular synonym for "contemptible" (*DT* 41).

11. Cora Kaplan, "Pandora's Box: Subjectivity, Class and Sexuality in Socialist Feminist Criticism," in her *Sea Changes: Culture and Feminism* (London: Verso, 1986), pp. 147–176.

12. There may be other of her attitudes, but this gives some of the range. (I cannot here "specify texts, politics, movements" with which these statements are in dialogue, to cite Cora Kaplan, "Keeping the Color in *The Color Purple*" (184), but I would like to note the necessity of doing so.)

13. Robert E. Hemenway, *Zora Neale Hurston: A Literary Biography* (Urbana: University of Illinois Press, 1977), pp. 106–8.

14. Part of Susan Friedman's idea about palimpsest and version, seeing author-repeated stories "as part of an endless web of intertexts": Friedman, "Return of the Repressed in H.D.'s Madrigal Cycle," in *Signets: Reading H.D.*, ed. S. Friedman and R. B. DuPlessis (Madison: University of Wisconsin Press, 1990).

15. Houston A. Baker, Jr., *Modernism and the Harlem Renaissance* (Chicago: The University of Chicago Press, 1987), is the source of this key phrase. He argues that there are two potentially intersecting strategies of Afro-American modernism. The first is "mastery of form"—a "minstrel" mimicry of surface exactness parallel to "white" art as a kind of mask under which folk "sounds" can be given room. The second is "deformation of mastery"—a strategy of display, advertising the engagement of hegemonic cultural training with folk materials to prepare some fusion of class and mass. Baker, passim, pp. 15–81. For "displacement" and "delegitimation" see DuPlessis, *Writing Beyond the Ending: Narrative Strategies of Twentieth-Century Women Writers* (Bloomington: Indiana University Press, 1985). Both are tactics making critiques of conventional story or narrative, but extended to mean tactics criticizing accepted (hegemonic) modes, manners, and conventions of storytelling.

16. I will not treat reception at all, but production is a point of great interest. For any text has to be made, and the conditions of its making are a tremendous site for feminist investigation, as Virginia Woolf, Tillie Olsen, and Adrienne Rich have all shown in their generative, analytic essays. The forces at work in Hurston's production, including a kind of scholarly sharecropping, have been strikingly and forcefully presented by Robert E. Hemenway.

17. Hurston also constructs a reconciliation between Tea Cake's friends and Janie at the funeral; they knew they were wrong about Janie, and run another of the Turners off the muck as a scapegoat for their feelings of betrayal. But this reconciliation is understated, for it is not part of the political balance sheet Hurston is drawing.

18. This point about the centrality of the trials is similar to a work by Carla Kaplan (Yale University), which I heard after writing this paper; her provisional title is "Negotiating Distance: Zora Neale Hurston and Juridical Narratives."

19. *Dust Tracks* tells us that Hurston lived under the maternal injunction " 'Jump at de sun' " (21).

20. Roger Tory Peterson, *A Field Guide to the Birds* (Boston: Houghton Mifflin, 1934), p. 109, *Soyornis phoebe:* "This grey tail-wagger has a weakness for small bridges. . . . This lack of wing-bars, its upright posture, and its persistent tail-wagging are all good points [to facilitate identification]."

21. This comment is meant to enter an ongoing debate about speech and silence in this novel. Feminist analysis has valorized the assumption of voice that characterizes Janie as hero (cf. B. Johnson). African-American critics Robert Stepto and, in reluctant agreement, Mary Helen Washington, have suggested that Janie does not finally achieve a voice. Washington notes that Janie's final comments make "an implicit criticism of the culture that celebrates orality to the exclusion of inner growth" (*Invented Lives*, 247). I have echoed that here. Michael Awkward argues, against Stepto, that part of the point of the novel is Janie's learning to "dislike talk for talk's sake" (59), that Janie exhibits differing relations to talk and action in the course of the novel, and that Janie has learned both "her own voice's authenticating power" and the value of community; hence Hurston offers a narrative strategy that "represents collec-

tive interaction rather than individual dictation." See *Inspiriting Influences: Tradition, Revision, and Afro-American Women's Novels* (New York: Columbia University Press, 1989), pp. 53–55.

22. Hurston's pattern of preferring an individual figure as more satisfying than a stereotyped group is visible throughout *Dust Tracks*.

23. Susan Willis, *Specifying: Black Women Writing the American Experience* (Madison: The University of Wisconsin Press, 1987) offers this clarification: "[I]n the black cultural tradition, 'goin' fishin',' fish tales and fish fries commonly suggest 'time off' and the procuring of food by alternative economic means" (p. 9).

24. After a person cites some proverbs, he says, "They all got a hidden meanin', jus' like de Bible. Everybody can't understand what they mean. Most people is thin-brained. They's born wid they feet under de moon. Some folks is born wid they feet on the sun and they kin seek out de inside meanin' of words." *Mules and Men* (Bloomington: Indiana University Press, 1935; reprint, 1963), p. 135. Gates is speaking of signifyin(g) as a skill in interpreting the figurative, pp. 205–6.

25. And Michael Awkward points to the *Starks* marriage as slavery; putting these two together, one might then see *Bildung* in this novel as deeply related to and figuring Emancipation, and this despite Hurston's presenting slavery, in *Dust Tracks*, as having occurred in the past and being of no particular concern to her.

26. Later matured, beyond this tree of heterosexual romance to the tree of life where "[d]awn and doom was in the branches" (20). A rich and complete tracing of this tree metaphor is found in Gates, *Signifying Monkey*.

27. Houston Baker offers the most succinct reminder: Under slavery "the owner's sexual gratification (forcefully achieved) was also his profit," for his children were also his property. See *Blues*, p. 57.

28. Both Tea Cake and Janie have at least one such prophetic moment; Nanny has several. Many of her words are brought into action.

29. Early in the Starks section, upon the couple's arrival in Eatonville, Janie is asked for a brief speech, a suggestion abruptly cut off by Joe. Not only a prefiguration of the silencing of the bourgeois woman ["she's uh woman and her place is in de home" (69)], it also suggests that the folk have an easier and more tolerant relationship to female speech.

30. So much so that I argued in *Writing Beyond the Ending* that their relationship was less romance for its own sake than the expression of a quest for community.

31. Tea Cake, first in jest and then in desperate seriousness, attempts to suspect that Janie is going to desert him for Mrs. Turner's brother.

32. Indeed, Missy Dehn Kubitschek points out that "[e]ach community in the novel— that of Nanny, Eatonville, and Belle Glade—contains a black character or a group of black characters who have internalized white values." " 'Tuh de Horizon and Back': The Female Quest," *Modern Critical Interpretations: Their Eyes Were Watching God*, ed. Harold Bloom (New York: Chelsea House, 1987), p. 31.

33. There could be more to say about this glancing allusion to Booker T. Washington. As a partial context, Hurston's opinion, in *Dust Tracks*, was that Washington was wrongfully considered a pariah by upwardly mobile African-Americans for "advocating industrial education"—a reminder of lower class and racial status which certain blacks tried to ignore; p. 233.

34. *Dust Tracks* makes the same point about black and white in a more overt and staged fashion, as I have indicated above.

35. Janie and Tea Cake have been joined by a friend, hence the six eyes.

36. See, for example: "[W]hite folks had preempted that point of elevation and there was no more room" (243) for others in their escape from the flood.

" '. . . Ah said Ah'd save de text for you' ": Recontextualizing the Sermon to Tell (Her)story in Zora Neale Hurston's *Their Eyes Were Watching God*

DOLAN HUBBARD

> If you want to find Jesus, go in de wilderness
> Go in de wilderness, go in de wilderness.
> Mournin' brudder, go in de wilderness
> I wait upon de Lord.
>
> (qtd. in Dixon 13)

Zora Neale Hurston writes in *Their Eyes Were Watching God* (1937) from the interiority of black culture. The fact that she sees religion as a mode of making sense of the experiences of a black tradition makes *Their Eyes Were Watching God* a strong, assertive statement. In contrast, many of the novels of the 1920's and '30's view blackness as a pathology. Van Vechten's *Nigger Heaven* and McKay's *Home to Harlem,* for example, emphasize the exotic primitive, while Fauset's *There Is Confusion* and Larsen's *Passing* emphasize assimilation. For this reason, *Their Eyes Were Watching God,* along with Hurston's work as an anthropologist and folklorist, bears witness to the desire of black people to argue, live, love, and die in a place of their own creation and to center themselves in a universe independent of the tyranny of manmade states of oppression. That she set her novel of romantic love in Eatonville, Florida, one of the first all-black towns in the United States, is itself a religious expression. Hurston, thus, challenges black writers to enter the mainstream of American society on their own terms, which means to accept and promote the integrity of black culture. To the extent that she externalizes through language the values of black culture, Hurston saves the text.

The power of Hurston in *Their Eyes Were Watching God* centers on her ability to fix extant cultural values in language and in the work of art. Like the preacher, Hurston's artistic gift "consists in discovering the not-yet-

Reprinted from *African American Review* 27(1993): 167–79. © 1993 Indiana State University. Reprinted by permission of the publisher.

discovered subsistent values and meanings that make up [her text's] object in the creative act which is the revelation of that object in and through the language (Vivas 1073–74; Fontenot 38–41). In other words, *Their Eyes Were Watching God* brings the meanings and values of the culture to its participants' attention. The narrative performs a normative function, since the participants espouse the values and meanings which the narrative reveals.

The end product of Hurston's vision is to create a new black woman, through a critique of the past. In looking back, Janie also looks forward to the day when American women of African descent will no longer be the mules of the world. Using familiar Bible-based tropes and metaphors, Hurston drives to the heart of a series of related questions: What does it mean to be black and female in America? What are the terms of definition for women outside the traditional hierarchies? Is female state negated without a male defining principle? And she raises these questions to reveal to the black community the one face it can never see—its own.

Although Hurston's narrative focuses on the emergence of a female self in a male-dominated world, she tells her magnificent story of romantic love against the background of church and extrachurch modes of expression. Understanding this fact helps to explain those sections of the narrative that have been said to have no meaning beyond their entertainment value (Hemenway 218). Hurston knew that the religious life of Americans of African descent manifests itself in all spheres of this life. The extrachurch modes of expression possess great critical and creative powers that have often touched deeper religious issues regarding the true situation of black communities than those of the institutional black church. These church and extrachurch modes of expressions may be seen in the novel's narrative structure, in the texture of Hurston's language and imagery, and in the manner in which her language itself is alive with history and historical struggle in order to convey the story of the emergence of a female self in a male-dominated world.

Divided into three sections that correspond roughly to modes of religious expression, *Their Eyes Were Watching God* celebrates the art of the community in such a manner that "the harsh edges of life in a Jim Crow South seldom come into view" (Hemenway 218). Section one has a spiritual orientation and covers the time of Janie's marriage to Logan Killicks (which sets in motion the initial tension in the novel—that between Janie and her grandmother over what a woman ought to be and do); section two focuses on the richness and diversity of the styles of life in the black community (black peoples' will to adorn and our sense of drama are daily put on display on Joe Starks's storefront porch); and section three, which focuses on the blues impulse, covers Janie's life with Tea Cake in the Everglades (and provides movement toward the resolution of the tension that has sent Janie to the horizon and back). Given Janie's history, an overarching question that unifies these sections is: What rescues Janie from becoming a full-fledged blues figure—and is Hurston ambivalent about this?

Their Eyes Were Watching God is a story within a story, deeply influenced by the power of language and myth in and out of the homiletical mode. The received language "dictates" that *Their Eyes Were Watching God*, though set in Florida, must occur outside of a specific time and place. (This strategy receives its fullest deployment in James Baldwin's *Go Tell It on the Mountain*.) By placing her narrative in the context of the Christian journey, itself a romance, Hurston overrides reader expectation that the protagonist should marry her black prince charming and live happily ever after. Having returned from the horizon, Janie Crawford represents the mature voice of experience and wisdom as she retrospectively tells her story to one who is, from an experiential point of view, a novice. Janie intends to convert Pheoby and the reader/participant. Her first move in her conversion narrative is to revise the patriarchal vision of seeing the world through a male dialectic.

Janie's story, as sermon and testimony, merges the material with the spiritual world. This constitutes the "unsaid" in the novel's arrestingly powerful opening scene:

> Ships at a distance have every man's wish on board. For some they come in with the tide. For others they sail forever on the horizon, never out of sight, never landing until the Watcher turns his eyes away in resignation, his dreams mocked to death by Time. That is the life of men.
>
> Now, women forget all those things they don't want to remember, and remember everything they don't want to forget. The dream is the truth. Then they act and do things accordingly. (1)

Hurston presents us with the classical Biblical picture of the looker standing before the horizon and wondering if she and the horizon shall ever meet. The looker sees a picture that is both in time and timeless, finite and infinite. The ships on the horizon are emblematic of the dreams of the person standing on shore. This timeless picture speaks of a person's desire to be related to God, the ultimate Other—"a need in the moment of existence to belong, to be related to a beginning and to an end" (Kermode 4).

As her story unfolds, we come to realize that the naïve, sixteen-year-old Janie, as the Looker, stands before the horizon (the pear tree in bloom) as one whose spiritual loyalties are "completely divided, as [i]s, without question, her mind" (Walker 236). Her spiritual loyalties are divided because she has not yet earned the unspeakable intimacy that binds the community of faith. In contrast to her grandmother, Janie lacks the faith-knowledge that comes from a firsthand experience with the Holy Spirit. Faith-knowledge does not rely on the evidence of the senses but is, in the scriptural phrase, "the evidence of things not seen"—that is, not presented to sense-perception—and it would lose its essential nature and be transformed into a mere sorry empirical knowledge if it relied on any other evidence than "the witness of the Holy Spirit" (Otto 228), which is not that of sense-experience. Sustained by her faith-knowledge born in the midnight of despair of the slave experience, Nanny, a recognizable figure in the black community, breaks the pervasive silence of her sixteen-year "silent worship," as she passionately tells Janie of her dream. Her sermonic monologue, one of the most moving scenes in all of black American literature, serves to order experience. Janie's life is the sermon, as Nanny makes clear:

> "Ah wanted to preach a great sermon about colored women sittin' on high, but they wasn't no pulpit for me. Freedom found me wid a baby daughter in mah arms, so [on my knees] Ah said [to my God] Ah'd take a broom and a cookpot and throw up a highway through de wilderness for her. She would expound what Ah felt. But somehow she got lost offa de highway and next thing Ah knowed here you was in de world. So whilst Ah was tendin' you of nights Ah said Ah'd save de text for you." (15–16)

The text that Nanny saves is the cultural genealogy of black America in general and the black woman in particular. This believable, manageable fiction centers on an interpretation of history that is consistent with a Judeo-Christian view that emphasizes patience, humility, and good nature. Created by blacks in the face of limited options, this interpretation of history makes it possible for many in the oppressed corporate community to interpret their behavior as being Christlike. In fact, the posture adopted by Nanny is necessary for the maintenance of self-esteem, rather than as the realization of the Christian ideal. With each of her three marriages, Janie challenges this externally imposed stereotype, which served in slave days as the ideal self-image for the corporate community (Fullinwider 27–28).

Janie's application of the text, her reinterpretation of history, provides her with the impetus to break free of gendered silence and inferior status. In her movement from passive looker to active participant, Janie discovers that, to change one's way of thinking, the individual must change her perceptions of the world. Whereas Nanny and Janie share the same mythic belief system, each differs in her choice of an end to reach the goal, the dream.

In many respects, the tension to be resolved in the Nanny-Janie argument involves the route to freedom and respectability for the black woman. This tension is presented in the novel as two competing perspectives on reality: Janie's romantic vision, and her grandmother's pragmatic grounding in reality. They, however, have different interpretations and applications of the dream of " 'whut a woman oughta be and to do' " (15), which is to say, they have different interpretations of history. Whereas Nanny, whose brooding presence dominates the narrative, sees the dream as protection and security, Janie sees Nanny's dream as restrictive; it circumscribed existence. The grandmother's dream has no room for an idyllic view of nature. For Nanny the pressure of history is a pressure in favor of remembering and not forgetting, whereas for Janie the pressure of history is in favor of forgetting and against remembering (Fish 6).

The tension between Nanny and Janie as presented in the opening paragraphs centers on the highly charged word *truth,* meaning 'to be free from other people's fictions.' What is the truth as socially constructed: (1) security and respect (Logan Killicks); (2) excessive competition and overcompensation as a result of marginalization (Joe Starks); or (3) the sensualization of pain and pleasure (Tea Cake and life on the Everglades)? These versions of the truth, presented from the perspective of black males, confront the female Looker as she stands before the horizon: "Now women forget all those things they don't want to remember and remember everything they don't want to forget. The dream is the truth. Then they act and do things accordingly."

This enigmatic paragraph begins to make sense in the wake of Jody's death, when Janie allows her suppressed emotions to surface: "She had an inside and an outside now and suddenly she knew how not to mix them" (68). Janie had come to an awareness that her grandmother had pointed her in the wrong direction—the realization that her grandmother's best of intentions had contributed to her divided self:

> She had been getting ready for her great journey to the horizons in search of *people;* it was important to all the world that she should find them and they find her. But she had been whipped like a cur dog, and run off down a back road after *things.* It was all according to the way you see things. Some people could look at a mud-puddle and see an ocean with ships. But Nanny belonged to that other kind that loved to deal in scraps. Here Nanny had taken the biggest thing God ever made, the horizon—for no matter how far a person can go the horizon is still way beyond you—and pinched it in to such a little bit of a thing that she could tie it about her granddaughter's neck tight enough to choke her. (85)

In the wake of this realization, Janie begins earnestly the process of her search for self and form, the process of finding a voice and creating a woman. The process of healing her divided mind includes the rejection of protection and security, which Nanny, Logan, and Jody sought to provide, and entering into a relationship with a man regarded as her social inferior. Coming to see her grandmother's well-intended actions as a fiction, Janie, in her search for self and form, turns her world upside down in order to make it rightside up. The break from gendered silence—exemplified by the negative community of gossiping women who sit on the front porch—involves the reconnection of subject (Janie) and object (pear tree) on the same imaginative plane; that is, Janie, in her quest, unknowingly sets out to smash a fiction that has outlived its usefulness—black women as the mules of the world.

The polarities represented by Nanny and Janie in her movement toward the horizon stem from Janie's desire to seek an authentic place for an expression of the autonomy and independence of her consciousness:

The desire for an authentic place for the expression of this reality is the source of the revolutionary tendencies in [black religion]. But on the level of human consciousness, religions of the oppressed create in another manner. The hegemony of the oppressors is understood as a myth—a myth in the two major senses, as true and as fictive. It is true as a structure with which one must deal in a day-to-day manner if one is to persevere, but it is fictive as far as any ontological significance is concerned. (Long 169–70)

It is in their day-to-day existence as laborers that members of the oppressed community challenge the oppressors' definition of them. Their autonomy arises from their labor, but paradoxically their autonomy takes on a fictive character. The principal figures in Janie's life respond to the contradictory nature of myth as true in a variety of ways. Nanny's intimate knowledge of the violence perpetuated upon the corporate community dictates her determination to have Janie marry in order to protect her granddaughter from such a history. Joe Starks's response to history is to overcompensate by lording his accomplishments over those of his fellow citizens. Tea Cake's response is to seek freedom and release through his music and style of life; the perpetual mobility of this blues figure is indicative of his not becoming "institutionally" dependent on a system over which he exercises no control. Tea Cake remains outside the system. Though the blues as a "religious" counterstatement against the fictive character of the autonomy of the corporate community stands outside the sway of the institutional church, the community of faith (Nanny) understands its anarchic personality. In her movement toward the horizon, the sheltered Janie will come to understand the fugitive element that makes the music swing, jump, and cry.

CRAYON ENLARGEMENTS

In the Eatonville section of the novel, Hurston focuses on the style of life in a vibrant and dynamic community. From her perspective, best-foot forward presentations of the folk represent the triumph of the human spirit over oppression, meaning that black enjoyment of life "is not solely a product of defensive *re*actions" to the dominant white culture.[1] Hurston believes that the distinguishing feature, the corporate signature, of the African imagination to America is creativity—the ability to invest the Other's linguistic structure with new meanings. In "Characteristics of Negro Expression," she refers to this irrepressible quality as "the will to adorn" (50). That which permeates the soul of the black community is drama. Hurston comments:

Every phase of Negro life is highly dramatized. No matter how joyful or how sad the case there is sufficient poise for drama. Everything is acted out. Unconsciously for the most part of course. There is an impromptu ceremony always ready for every hour of life. No little moment passes unadorned. ("Characteristics" 49)

Hurston implicitly presents blacks as offering an image of vitality to a civilization dimly aware of its lack of both vitality and color (Bennett 149).

In terms of narrative tension, Hurston contrasts this vitality with the increasingly withdrawn Janie, who is excluded from participating in the storytelling sessions, the "crayon enlargements of life" (48) on the store front porch. She has become a prisoner of the pretty picture of " 'whut a woman oughta be and to do' " as outlined by Joe when he courted her: " 'A pretty doll-baby lak you is made to sit on de front porch and rock and fan yo'self and eat p'taters dat other folks plant just special for you' " (28).

The imaginative freedom that the big-picture talkers have on the front porch contrasts with Janie's despair inside the store, where she silently listens with the dumb obedience of a mule. Forced to become a passive observer, Janie longs to participate in these spirited storytelling sessions, the male community in unison enjoying release from the day's work. "Janie loved the conversation and sometimes she thought up good stories on the mule, but Joe had forbidden her to indulge" (50). The restricted space gnaws away at her soul. Squeezed out of the big picture, an appendage that derives her identity through her husband, Mrs. Mayor Starks finds herself ensnared in a choking kind of love; this is not what she envisioned under the pear tree.

Reserved for the big-picture talkers, the porch of Joe Starks's store is treated as a sacred space wherein secular performances take place. Within this space, the storytellers exhibit the creative capacities of black people defining themselves in the order of things. Like their preacher counterparts, the personae the storytellers employ in performance sanction these men as guardians of the word, of the text—of the aesthetic values of the community. The performance, with its dynamic give-and-take that one associates with the black church, runs through all segments of black life.

Matt Bonner's decrepit mule is the focal paint of the daily drama played out in the ritual space of Joe's storefront porch. Sam and Lige and Walter take the lead in creating the "pictures" the male members pass around, which an envious Janie rightly divines as "crayon enlargements of life" (48):

"Dat mule uh yourn, Matt. You better go see 'bout him. He's bad off."
"Where 'bouts? Did he wade in de lake and uh alligator ketch him?"
"Worser'n dat. De womenfolks got yo' mule. When Ah come round de lake 'bout noontime mah wife and some others had 'im flat on de ground usin' his sides fuh uh wash board."
The great clap of laughter that they have been holding in, bursts out. Sam never cracks a smile. "Yeah, Matt, dat mule so skinny till de women is usin' his rib bones fuh uh rub-board, and hangin' things out on his hock-bones tuh dry." (49)

As a mode of religious expression, these good-natured stories show that the creative capacities of blacks are not dependent on living in trembling and fear of the white man—nor do the tales use white oppression as a point of departure. Coexisting with the laughter, banter, and humor of the jokes about Matt Bonner's mule are references to poverty and marginality, as well as the life-and-death struggle for survival, especially when the buzzards swoop down to eat the dead mule. The humor, however, takes the edge off the tale tellers' poverty and marginality (the sides of the mule are so flat as to be used as wash boards).

The stories told on Joe Starks's porch appear to have significance beyond their immediate entertainment value. The people who make fun of Matt Bonner's tired mule can identify with this beast of burden, that works in dumb obedience and silence much as they have been trained—and more, *pronounced*—to do, and as Joe has trained Janie to do. But unlike the mule, Janie rebels rather than going silently to her grave.

Imagistically, the humor inherent in the mock funeral for the mule may be read on two levels. First, the parody of mule heaven crystallizes the people's desire for a better world—plenty of food and no work. Second, it echoes Nanny's desire not to have Janie work with little or no tangible reward for self. The frustrated Janie is isolated from the imaginative life of the community, where ". . . the people [specifically, the *men*] sat around on the porch and passed around the pictures of their thoughts for the others to look at and see . . ." (48).

Overall the stories in this section are not so much documents for understanding black life as they are representations of Hurston's attempt to capture the vibrancy and drama that are part of the creative soul of black America. As Hemenway notes, Hurston's efforts "are intended to show rather than tell, the assumption being that both behavior and art will become self-evident as the tale texts (performance events) accrued during the reading" (168).

To know how people view the world around them is to understand how they evaluate life; and people's temporal and nontemporal evaluations of life provide them with a "charter" of action, a guide to behavior. In this regard, Hurston makes it explicit that Christian explanations have never proved fully adequate for blacks, whose sensibilities are deeply rooted in folk traditions. In chapter 8, for example, the reader/spectator is more inclined to rejoice in Janie's confronting Joe on his deathbed about the woman she has become—declaring her independence—than to note the extent in which the extra-church (remnants of African traditional religion) informs this pivotal scene. Hurston, in a statement radical for its time, brings to the surface these submerged values, beliefs, and practices in the root doctor and Janie's description of Joe's death. Though Hurston does not give an exegetical explanation of the religious values which underlie Joe's calling on the root doctor, she makes it clear that his apparent act of desperation is interrelated with Janie's description of her husband's death. In making these extrachurch forms of expressions central to our understanding of Joe and Janie Starks, the town's most venerated citizens, Hurston perceptively reveals the epic complexity of black life.

As he nears death, the status-conscious Joe engages the assistance of a conjure man to ward off the spell he believes Janie, his wife of twenty years, has had put on him. Hurston suggests that, though African traditional religion and medicine, which the root doctor represents, have been forced underground, these once-viable traditional values and outlooks continue to exist and to exercise an influence among segments of the corporate community, as Pheoby indicates in her all-knowing, sympathetic response to the shocked Janie: " 'Janie, Ah thought maybe de thing would die down and you never would know nothin' 'bout it, but it's been singin' round here ever since de big fuss in de store dat Joe was 'fixed' and you wuz de one dat did it' " (78).

As a representative of a once-proud living tradition, the root doctor has been forced underground and divested of an essential dimension of his *raison d'être*. Known in Africa as medicine men, herbalists, traditional doctors, or *wagangas;* knowledgeable in religious matters, these influential African men and women are expected "to be trustworthy, upright morally, friendly, willing and ready to serve, able to discern people's needs and not be exorbitant in their charges" (Mbiti 218). But in the fare of an uncompromising and indifferent Christianity, Hurston's root doctor, as a remnant of African traditional religion and medicine on the North American continent, is forced to stand outside the dominant Christian culture as something foreign and alien (Shorter 1–2). The root doctor in America, as the public face of a submerged religion, is reduced to a caricature of his or her former self. Operating at the edge of American society, the root doctor is more likely to be a charlatan or hustler than "the friend of the community [who] comes into the picture at many points in individual and community life" (Mbiti 218).

Hurston demonstrates her understanding of the complexity of the black experience with its discontinuity-within-continuity in the stressful departure scene between Joe and Janie. That this scene is filled with subtle juxtaposition of thought and idea becomes apparent when Janie begins to think of Death,

> that strange being with the huge square toes who lived way in the West. The great one who lived in the straight house like a platform without sides to it, and without a roof. What need has Death for a cover, and what winds can blow against him? He stands in his high house that overlooks the world. Stands watchful and motionless all day with his sword drawn back, waiting for the messenger to bid him come. Been standing there before there was a where or a when or a then. (79–80)

Janie's conception of death reveals the manner in which language itself is alive with history and the historical to tell of the emergence of a black ethos in an Eurocentric world. Like her African American ancestors before her, Janie uses the language and imagery of the Christian Bible because it was readily available. Nevertheless, her aesthetic orientation differed from those in the dominant community, as is evident in her conceptualization of death. Hurston presents a well-developed religious consciousness that has penetrated the universe in ways the dominant culture has not. The attitude toward death and dying Janie expresses displays a certain intimacy. Her conceptualization is not predicated on fear and stands in sharp contrast to the conventional Western attitude toward death. Death is not final; God has not died in Africa. Physical death is a passage from one realm of existence to another. As long as there is God, man or woman will never be a *finite* being.

In conjoining the root doctor and death, Hurston is not attempting to depict one woman's knee-jerk rejection based on submerged religious belief. While one might argue that, as a matter of historical genesis, the association might have been awakened in Janie's mind during a moment of stress, the inward and lasting character of these interlocking passages is to make the connection that, in the United States, the root doctor has become separated from his divine calling. Hurston would have us understand that African traditional medicine is a part of African traditional religion (Mbiti 217–52; Shorter 1–19).[2]

What Hurston, in effect, is evoking is the historical genesis of the blues—the reconstitution of self out of a religion that has come to be viewed as foreign and alien. She is talking about black people's ability to squeeze out a song, story, or sermon from the near-lyric, near-tragic situation of their lives as a result of their inability to texturize the world. Ultimately, the text for Hurston is not a fixed object, but a dialectical process in which contradictory elements coexist, in which parts and wholes depend upon each other, and in which negation and affirmation are closely joined. It is in this sense that we can speak of Hurston as showing how an African continuum is maintained. In spite of the fragmentation that has occurred, the corporate community maintains continuity in the face of discontinuity, and discontinuity in the face of continuity.

THE BLUES IMPULSE

If Hurston's intent in the first two sections of *Their Eyes Were Watching God* is to screen out white antipathy, then the last section shows the response of the community to this oppression and to black society's assigned marginality. Hurston does not view the blues so much as the failure of religion as it is the intensification of religious expression in the absence of fundamental checks and balances of the strong against the weak. While the perpetrators of the oppression remain essentially in the background, the effects of their oppression manifest themselves in the hedonistic lifestyle of many in the black community. Not surprisingly, Janie discovers her voice among the socially downcast segment of society, who sensualize pain and pleasure. After twenty years of marriage, Jody dies and Janie falls in love with Vergible "Tea Cake" Woods, a man twelve years younger than she and, by most people's estimations, her social inferior. In a reversal of the romantic moment that we associate with fairy tales such as the Cinderella story, Janie and Tea Cake go to live in the Everglades, rejecting the finery and status of the mayor's house because of their desire to know and love each other.

Janie's life with Tea Cake, a cultural archetype, represents the third and final movement in her march toward the horizon, toward self-definition. Tea Cake, as the blues-made-flesh, is the objectification of Janie's desire. In spite of his sexism, Tea Cake, a rounder, drifter, and day laborer, is the embodiment of the freedom which Janie's divided mind has long sought. And unlike the traditional bluesman, Tea Cake does not love Janie and then leave her.

Tea Cake's life style expresses a practical, existential response to the world, and stands in direct opposition to the values Nanny had attempted to instill in Janie. A hedonistic howl replaces silent worship; a desire for security and stability yields to comfort with flux. Whereas Nanny's life is dedicated to the patient forbearance of Protestant Christian worship, Tea Cake's life—with its roots in the slave seculars—represents another dimension of the day-to-day secular expression of the community. Tea Cake's irrepressible laughter embodies the tough-minded spirit of the blues. It stands as a reminder that there is more to the everyday than the struggle for material subsistence.

The tradition which Tea Cake embodies recognizes no dichotomy between a spiritual and a blues mystique. The blues are the spirituals, good is bad, God is the devil, and every day is Saturday. The essence of the tradition is the extraordinary tension between the poles of pain and joy, agony and ecstasy, good and bad, Sunday and Saturday (Bennett 50). Unlike the spiritual vision, the blues vision "deals with a world where the inability to solve a problem does not necessarily mean that one can, or ought, to transcend it" (Williams 74–75). Tea Cake, who stands outside the influence of the institutional church, responds to his circumscribed existence by squeezing as much pleasure out of the moment as possible. Needless to say, his life style, in contrast to Nanny's patient forbearance, is tantamount to paganism.

Tea Cake, who appears to live only for the moment, comes from "an environment filled with heroic violence, flashing knives, Saturday night liquor fights, and the magnificent turbulence of a blues-filled weekend of pleasure and joy" (Barksdale 110–11). This child of the morning star makes Janie feel alive, vital, needed, loved, unlimited—and she gives of herself freely. Janie's blissful "marriage" with Tea Cake lasts for about two years; then a storm hits the Everglades, and God takes His glance away.

During the raging storm, God seems to be speaking. Janie and Tea Cake wait for God to make His move, and when destruction appears imminent,

Janie and Tea Cake strike out for the high ground. In a heroic struggle against the raw power of nature, they make it, but not before Tea Cake is bitten by a rabid dog in an effort to save Janie. Several weeks later, Janie is forced to kill the man she loves. As "a glance from God"(102), Tea Cake has been temporary. "The Lord giveth, and the Lord taketh away" (Howard 105–6).

Janie's response to the flood is not simply intellectual; it is experiential and total. It is a religious response born out of her having come to terms with the impenetrable majesty of the divine. For Janie, the experience of *mysterium tremendum* is brought to bear when she is suspended between life and death:

> "If you kin see de light at daybreak, you don't keer if you die at dusk. It's so many people never seen de light at all. Ah wuz fumblin' round and God opened de door." . . .
> The wind came back with triple fury, and put out the light for the last time. They sat in company with the others in other shanties, their eyes straining against crude walls and their souls asking if He meant to measure their puny might against His. They seemed to be staring at the dark, but their eyes were watching God. (151)

The storm in this, Janie's last movement toward the horizon, symbolizes the struggle the corporate black community has to come to terms with in the oppressor's negation of its image. Out of this negation, the mythic consciousness seeks a *new* beginning in the future by imagining an *original* beginning. The social implications of this religious experience enable the oppressed community to dehistoricize the oppressor's hegemonic dominance. Metaphorically, the phrase *their eyes were watching God* means the creation of a new form of humanity—one that is no longer based on the master-slave dialectic. The utopian and eschatological dimensions of the religions of the oppressed stem from this modality—which Hurston arrests by concluding her moving story of romantic love with a flourish of Christian iconography (Long 158–72).

With the spellbound Pheoby at her side, Janie struggles to find her voice and, equally important, an audience that will give assent to her testimony. Janie taps into the responsive mythology of the black sermon as she assigns meaning to her experience. She exercises autonomy in making her world through language. However, while the language of the black church provides her one means of translating her experience into a medium which can be comprehended easily by a member of her aesthetic community, Hurston keeps before us the inescapable fact that the community acts upon Janie, and Janie upon the community. She differs from her community in that her action represents a break from gendered silence.

The logical conclusion to Janie's female-centered discourse occurs when Pheoby, who aspires " 'to sit on de front porch' " (28), undergoes a transformation. With the exhilaration that only the newly converted can know, Pheoby enthusiastically becomes Janie's disciple:

"Lawd!" Pheoby breathed out heavily, "Ah done growed ten feet higher from jus' listenin' tuh you, Janie. Ah ain't satisfied wid mahself no mo'. Ah means tuh make Sam take me fishin' wid him after this. Nobody [i.e., the negative community of women and the signifying men] better not criticize yuh in mah hearin'." (182–83)

Pheoby responds excitedly to Janie's call to break with hierarchies of representation and to stop seeing herself as a silent subject. It is significant that Janie comes to Pheoby, religiously speaking, from a point of strength, not coping. She knows who her God is. She does not seek confirmation for her actions, but affirmation of her voice. The religious imagination of the community enters into Janie's verbal consciousness and shapes her response to historical pressures.

The language of the black church is a communal language invested with authority. Not only does this communal language give Janie voice and legitimacy, but it also sustains her. Through it, she can prevent the memory of Tea Cake from dying. The connection to romance—a vertical language— becomes apparent to the mesmerized Pheoby, as well as the reader/spectator. Janie's ritual retelling of her journey toward the horizon enables her to suspend the rules of time and space as she moves toward the climactic moment in her sermon—the tragic death of her beloved Tea Cake. Each time Janie tells of their short but intense life together, she relives the experience, much as Christians do when they participate in the Eucharist. In fact *Their Eyes Were Watching God* may be viewed as a series of revelations leading toward ultimate revelation—Janie's being reunited in the spirit with Tea Cake.

The novel ends where it began, with the perceptual field of the narrator, who releases it from the temporal world. In this way, Janie and Tea Cake achieve a greater freedom in the world tomorrow, and Janie triumphs over her critics, the negative community of gossiping women to whom the reader is introduced in the book's opening sequence. With her spiritual loyalties no longer divided, Janie, in a picture at least as arresting as the novel's opening scene, draws the various strands of her sermon together:

She pulled in her horizon like a great fish-net. Pulled it from around the waist of the world and draped it over her shoulder. So much of life in its meshes! She called in her soul to come and see. (184)

In pulling the fish net around her shoulders, Janie arrests the "eschatological despair" she has experienced (Kermode 9). An optimist and romantic, Janie seeks a larger space for herself and her life's story; her quest involves woman's timeless search for freedom and wholeness. Her charge to her new convert is " '. . . you got to *go* there tuh *know* there' " (183). Janie, in her movement toward the horizon (i.e., in the successful execution of her performance via the sermon), is transformed from blues figure to prophet. In so doing, she both achieves personal fulfillment and assumes a communal role traditionally reserved for males. She appropriates tropes of creation ("She had given away everything in their little house except a package of garden seed that Tea Cake had bought to plant" [182]) and reunion ("She pulled in her horizon like a great fish-net") in order to insert her voice into history.[3]

In the end, Janie's sermon becomes a poetry of affirmation—with self, community, and loved ones. Janie and Pheoby are uplifted through the preached word. Operating from a position of strength within the ethos of her community, Janie achieves an unspeakable intimacy that bonds her community of faith.

Notes

1. My comments in this section are informed by the observations of Hurston's biographer Robert Hemenway (221). Part of Hazel Carby's project is to demystify the idealization of the folk.

2. I have written at greater length about voodoo as a submerged religion in "Society and Self."

3. For a critique of the "prophetic moment" as a distinctly male enterprise, see Krasner 113.

Works Cited

Barksdale, Richard "Margaret Walker: Folk Orature and Historical Prophecy." *Black American Poets Between Worlds, 1940–1960.* ed. R. Baxter Miller. Knoxville: U of Tennessee P, 1986. 104–17.

Bennett, Lerone, Jr. *The Negro Mood.* Chicago: Johnson, 1964.

Carby, Hazel. "Ideologies of Black Folk: The Historical Novel of Slavery." *Slavery and the Literary Imagination.* ed. Deborah E. McDowell and Arnold Rampersad. Baltimore: John Hopkins UP, 1989. 125–43.

Dixon, Melvin. *Ride Out the Wilderness: Geography and Identity in Afro-American Literature.* Urbana: U of Illinois P, 1987.

Fish, Stanley E. *Self-Consuming Artifacts.* Berkeley: U of California P, 1972.

Fontenot, Chester. J., Jr., Rev. of *The Craft of Ralph Ellison*, by Robert G. O'Meally. *Black American Literature Forum* 15.2 (1981): 79–80.

Fullinwider, S. P. *The Mind and Mood of the Black America.* Homewood: Dorsey, 1969.

Hemenway, Robert. *Zora Neale Hurston: A Literary Biography.* Urbana: U of Illinois P, 1977.

Howard, Lillie P. *Zora Neale Hurston.* Boston: Twayne, 1980.

Hubbard, Dolan. "Society and Self in Alice Walker's *In Love and Trouble.*" *Obsidian II* 6.2 (1991): 50–75.

Hurston, Zora Neale. "Characteristics of Negro Expression." 1935. *The Sanctified Church.* Berkeley: Turtle Island, 1983. 49–68.

———. *Their Eyes Were Watching God.* 1937. New York: Harper, 1990.

Kermode, Frank. *The Sense of an Ending.* Oxford: Oxford UP, 1966.

Krasner, James. "Zora Neale Hurston and Female Autobiography." *Black American Literature Forum* 23 (1989): 113–26.

Long, Charles H. "The Oppressive Elements in Religion and the Religions of the Oppressed." *Significations: Signs, Symbols, and Images in the Interpretation of Religion.* Philadelphia: Fortress, 1986. 158–72.

Mbiti, John S. *African Religions and Philosophy.* London: Heinemann, 1969.

Otto, Rudolf. *The Idea of the Holy.* Trans. John W. Harvey. Rev. ed. London: Oxford UP, 1936.

Shorter, Alyward. *African Christian Theology.* Maryknoll: Orbis, 1977.

Vivas, Eliseo. "The Object of the Poem." *Critical Theory since Plato.* ed. Hazard Adams. New York: Harcourt, 1971. 1069–77.

Walker, Alice. "In Search of Our Mothers' Gardens." 1974. *In Search of Our Mothers' Gardens: Womanist Prose.* San Diego: Harcourt, 1983. 231–43.

Williams, Sherley Anne. "The Blues Roots of Contemporary Afro-American Poetry." *Afro-American Literature: The Reconstruction of Instruction.* ed. Dexter Fisher and Robert B. Stepto. New York: MLA, 1979. 73–87.

Naming and Power in Zora Neale Hurston's
Their Eyes Were Watching God

> The women say, unhappy one, men have expelled you from the world of symbols and yet they have given you names, they have called you slave, you unhappy slave. Masters, they have exercised their rights as masters.
> —Monique Wittig, *Les Guerilleres*

Naming has always been an important issue in the Afro-American tradition because of its link to the exercise of power. From their earliest experiences in America, Afro-Americans have been made aware that those who name also control, and those who are named are subjugated. Slaves were forced to abandon their African identities when they were captured, and were renamed with their masters' identities when they arrived in America. In *Orality and Literacy,* Walter Ong points out that for primarily oral cultures (such as the early slave communities) naming conveyed a power over things, for without learning a vast store of names, one was simply "powerless to understand" (33). This sense of powerlessness could extend beyond the individual to include an entire community of "unnamed" people. Naming is tied to racial as well as individual identity: "To have a name is to have a means of locating, extending, and preserving oneself in the human community, so as to be able to answer the question 'who?' with reference to ancestry, current status, and particular bearing, with reference to the full panoply of time" (Cooke 171). William Halsey in his essay "Signify(cant) Correspondences" further emphasizes the importance of naming for Afro-Americans, saying that names and naming are "a heavily ritualized rite (or is that right?) of passage and theme prevalent in African culture" (259).

This concern with naming in Afro-American culture is evident in black literature from the earliest slave narratives to more contemporary works. The titles of many of these works, such as *Black Boy, Invisible Man,* and *Nobody Knows My Name,* indicate their authors' awareness of the correspondence between namelessness and lack of power. Ralph Ellison, in "Hidden Name

Reprinted from *Black American Literature Forum* (currently the *African American Review*) 24 (Winter 1990): 683–96. © 1990 Indiana State University. Reprinted by permission of the publisher.

and Complex Fate" stressed that "our names, being the gift of others, must be made our own" (147). Taking possession of one's own name and thus claiming sovereignty over one's self is an act of power. In his article " 'I Yam What I Am': Naming and Unnaming in Afro-American Literature," Kimberly Benston defines language in a way which is particularly relevant to a discussion of naming and power:

> Language—that fundamental act of organizing the mind's encounter with an experienced world—is propelled by a rhythm of naming. It is the means by which the mind takes possession of the named, at once fixing the named as irreversibly Other and representing it in crystallized isolation from all conditions of externality. (3)

Benston's use of the phrase *take possession* shows clearly the underlying text in the naming of slaves by their masters. Fixing the named as "Other" also implies an interpretation of the named as an object, rather than a subject— something which cannot be part of the namer's self. The objectification of slaves is a well-documented method used by slave owners to distance themselves enough from their slaves to treat them as nonhuman. The namer has the power; the named is powerless. For the powerless, being named carries with it the threat of limitation, reduction, and destruction.

In order to break away from this sense of powerlessness, Afro-Americans have historically "unnamed" or renamed themselves. As Benston points out, renaming can be a means of self-creation and reformation of a fragmented familial past. Former slaves discarded their masters' names and created new names for themselves. Self-designation indicated social and economic freedom, the birth of a truly new self (3). Benston points out that unnaming has a particular significance for the questing hero or heroine in much of Western literature. Many questing literary characters come to the realization that names are fictions, that no particular name can satisfy the energy of the questing self. So long as the questing character seeks a name through a prescribed social role, he or she discovers only limitation, whereas, when a character is unnamed, he or she can have limitless designations which disrupt the function of social labeling and deny the applicability of words' topical function to his or her unfolding experience (7–9).

Benston's essay is an important introduction to the relationship between naming and power, but his examples only explore this issue in the literature of men. Naming has a double importance in the tradition of Afro-American women writers. One of the crucial issues for women writing within the Western tradition is the dichotomy between woman's command of language as opposed to language's command of woman (Gilbert and Gubar 236). Gilbert and Gubar point out that "the female need to achieve a command over language has, to begin with, been most practically expressed through strategies of unnaming and renaming, strategies that directly address the problem of woman's patronymically defined identity in western culture" (237). Black women have experienced a "double dispossession" (238). Lorraine Bethel discusses the two ways in which black women are oppressed: "The codification of Blackness and femaleness by whites and males is contained in the terms 'thinking like a woman' and 'acting like a nigger . . .' " (178). To counterbalance this, black women writers often focus on connection rather than separation, transforming silence into speech, and giving back power to the culturally disenfranchised (Pryse 5).

One of the most important and innovative Afro-American women writing in this tradition is Zora Neale Hurston. Hurston was a pioneer in the attempt to define the totality of Afro-American women in literature and anthropological studies, rather than their being defined by others (Bush 1035). Hurston's novel *Their Eyes Were Watching God* focuses on the character Janie, whose quest for the "horizons" of herself finally leads her to a place where she defines herself, despite a society which wants to deny her power because she is a black woman. The importance of naming and unnaming in Hurston's novel fixes it firmly within the tradition of Afro-American women writers. As Janie develops in the novel, she experiences the oppressive power of those who name her, the growing potential of being renamed, and finally the freeing experience of being unnamed.

Near the start of the novel, Janie has no name when she returns to Eatonville: "So the beginning of this was a woman" (9). The sentence places her within the larger context of the women mentioned in the book's second paragraph: "Now, women forget all those things they don't want to remember, and remember everything they don't want to forget" (9). As Janie walks into town she remains nameless; in fact, it is not until several pages into the novel that she is finally named by the townspeople on the porch. Ironically, when they say her name, they do so incorrectly; since she had married for a third time, her name is no longer " 'Janie Starks' " (12). Naming is clearly a source of power for the watchers on the porch, yet their power cannot affect Janie. Because the townspeople have been under the "bossman's" eye all day, they now need to exercise some power in the only way they can—within their oral tradition. "They became lords of sounds and lesser things. They passed nations through their mouths. They sat in Judgment" (10). The metaphors used to describe their words equate them with weapons. Janie recognizes the negative relationship between her neighbors' sense of power and naming. Speaking to Pheoby later, she calls them collectively " 'Mouth-Almighty' " (16), and Pheoby comments that "so long as they get a name to gnaw on they don't care whose it is, and what about, 'specially if they can make it sound like evil" (17).

According to Hortense Spillers, it is important that Hurston chose to name her character Janie because it differentiates her from a literary type (such as the women found in literature by Larsen and Fauset) whose life possibilities have been circumscribed and prescribed by preconditions (253).

Janie's name gives her an identifiable status, yet it does not limit her to one role or life experience.

As Janie and Pheoby talk, Janie begins to trace the experiences that have brought her back to Eatonville. Starting with her years as a little girl, Janie makes it clear that naming was used as a limiting or prescribing force by people around her and that, at a young age, she adopted their views of naming as her own. Janie relates how she was raised by her grandmother, Nanny, in the home of a wealthy white family, the Washburns. Because of her protected environment, Janie did not know she was black until she was six years old. As she explains the event in which she discovered her racial heritage, Janie mentions that the white family named her "Alphabet": " 'Dey all useter call me Alphabet cause so many people had done named me different names' " (21). As "Alphabet," Janie seems to be no more than a character (like a letter of the alphabet) who signifies nothing for herself while facilitating the "circulation of signs" that reinforces communication among those who exercise power (Gilbert and Gubar 238).

Elizabeth Meese feels that Janie, at the beginning of her life, "receives her sense of definition from others. She is woman as object in a racist, patriarchal culture. Failing to recognize herself as the one black child in a photograph, she begins her story without name or color"(61–62). It is interesting that Hurston begins both the narrative frame and Janie's narrative with Janie as a nameless character. The effect is one more of contrast than of resonance, though, since Janie as an adult is well-defined and does not need to be named to identify herself, as she did as a girl.

Janie's first lessons about naming come from a woman whose name, Nanny, exemplifies her place within the white patriarchal structure. One of Nanny's responsibilities was to look after the four white grandchildren who lived in the Washburn house. Janie says, " 'Dat's how come Ah never called mah Grandma nothin' but Nanny, 'cause dat's what everybody on de place called her' " (20). Nanny lived under the naming system of the white slave owners who used force to teach her the connection between names and power. Nanny relates an incident to Janie in which the mistress of the plantation where she was enslaved confronted her in the slave cabins. The mistress, angry over Nanny's illegitimate child, tells her, " ' "Look lak you don't know who is Mistis on dis plantation, Madam. But Ah aims to show you" ' " (33). The white woman invokes her own name, Mistress, and ties it to the brutal power of the whip which she will use to "show" Nanny.

Nanny teaches Janie the same lessons she learned about naming: Names are bound within the white male power structure, and the most a black woman can hope for is to endure within them; Nanny's explanation of the power hierarchy places black women on the bottom as " 'de mule[s] uh de world' " (29). Nanny's naming of all black women, including Janie, as "mules" will haunt Janie for the next twenty years. She will be identified with the work animal first by Logan Killicks and then by Joe Starks when he buys a mule many years later in Eatonville. Janie will not be free of the mule name until Joe's mule finally dies.

In her adolescence, Janie tries her own hand at naming. As she is stretched on her back beneath the pear tree in Nanny's back yard one afternoon, she has an intense sensory experience of delight and responds by naming it "marriage" (24). By misinterpreting her own deepening sense of her self as a sign of possible joy with another, Janie limits the thing she names. Missy Dehn Kubitschek states that this identification of marriage with total fulfillment reflects Janie's immature consciousness, and that her interpretation of the tree is essentially static, focused on a prescribed social institution (22).

Because Janie associates marriage with her experience under the pear tree, she allows Nanny to arrange for her first legal name change to Mrs. Logan Killicks. Killicks's name is ironic, for his relationship to Janie quickly "kills" her definition of marriage: "She knew now that marriage did not make love. Janie's first dream was dead, so she became a woman" (144). With Killicks, Janie also learns more about the power associated with names. When they argue about her doing outside work in their yard, she calls him " 'Mist' Killicks,' " a name which ironically reflects his attempt to be her master. He, on the other hand calls her " 'LilBit,' " a name which reveals her position of powerlessness in his mind. Logan Killicks finally goes too far when he associates Janie with a second mule for working in the fields. Janie knows from Nanny's narrative that the mule has the least powerful position, and she knows that is not what she wants.

Janie finds her way out when Joe Starks appears. The first thing Joe does after asking for a drink of water is to name himself: "Joe Starks was the name, yeah Joe Starks from in and through Georgy" (47). Hurston's naming of Starks is ironic for several reasons. The word *stark* is often used as a synonym for barren, and Joe Starks and Janie never have any children. Hurston hints at sexual problems that develop between the pair because of their separate beds and Janie's eventual verbal "castration" of Joe in the store. Starks's name is also ironic because of his focus on capitalistic pursuits. Starks's wealth gives him a false sense of power because the townspeople resent him and the things he does to gain his wealth. Starks's name could also be seen as a comment on his desire to be a "big voice." As Janie eventually finds out, there is not much behind the big voice: it is a facade for the starkness inside Joe.

Hurston provides some hints about Joe's true nature through the limiting and subjugating names he calls Janie when they first meet. He calls her " 'lil girl-chile' " and " 'pretty doll-baby' " (48–49), indications of the role that he will want her to play once he becomes mayor of Eatonville. When Jody names her in the socially prescribed role of "wife," he says, " 'Ah wants to make a wife outa you' " (50). He clearly places himself in the position of power by his naming Janie. When Janie tries to name him, substituting the more affectionate "Jody" for "Joe," he is pleased but still controls the naming. He asks her to " 'Call me Jody lak you do sometime,' " and after she starts a sentence with his new name, he cuts her off with " 'Leave de s'posin and everything else to me' " (50). Janie is satisfied to stop " 's'posin' " for the time being. As she rides away with Joe Starks, she realizes that "her old thoughts were going to come in handy now, but new words would have to be made and said to fit them" (54).

Although Joe seems better than Logan at first, once he and Janie are together, he quickly assumes the "master" role. Janie unconsciously associates him with the white patriarchal system from the beginning. When she first sees him coming down the road, she notes that "he was a seal-brown color but he acted like Mr. Washburn or somebody like that to Janie" (47). When Joe and Janie are on the train the day after their marriage, she proudly describes him as "kind of portly like rich white folks" (56). When they arrive in Eatonville, Joe begins to use a habitual expression "I god," which ironically sounds as though he is naming himself God. Joe's association of naming with power is apparent when he finds out that Eatonville has no mayor: " 'Ain't got no Mayor! Well, who tells y'all what to do?' " (57). The name *mayor* connotes control over others to Joe. Hurston's synthesis of the name *mayor* with the phrase *I god* may have come from her own life, since her father was a minister and mayor of the all-black Eatonville when she was born (Bloom, "Chronology" 115).

Once Joe finds out there is no named authority, he sets himself up in the town's highest position of power. He gathers the men around him and asks, " 'Whut is de real name of de place?' " (59). Ironically, Eatonville is named for Captain Eaton, a white landowner who has exercised power over the small, black community. Joe replaces Captain Eaton as the power broker when he uses his capital literally to "buy" Eatonville for his own. Once he has bought the town, Joe sets himself up as God; he creates new buildings and names them and brings light to Eatonville in the form of the lamp post.

Once Joe is officially named mayor, Janie becomes "Mrs. Mayor Starks." Unfortunately, the power that Joe readily adopts with his new name is not meant to be shared with Janie. Her name simply becomes a reflection of the new power of Joe. When the townspeople ask "Mrs. Mayor Starks" to make a speech, Joe cuts in: " 'Thank yuh fuh yo compliments, but mah wife don't know nothin' 'bout no speech-makin'. Ah never married her for nothin' lak dat. She's uh woman and her place is in de home' " (69). John Callahan points out that Joe views Janie as his "appendage" (102). Joe says, " 'Ah told you in de very first beginnin' dat Ah aimed tuh be uh big voice. You oughta be glad, 'cause dat makes uh big woman outa you' " (74). Joe reasons that because he loves being Mr. Mayor, Janie should gratefully accept the name and identity of Mrs. Mayor (Callahan 102). Joe does not understand that Janie can make a " 'big woman outa' " herself. This relationship of power with Joe "t[a]k[es] the bloom off of things" (70) for Janie, and "a feeling of coldness and fear" takes hold of her (74).

Janie's fears are well-founded, for the role of the mule returns to haunt her in her second marriage. When Joe first met Janie he protested against Logan Killicks's treatment of her as a beast of burden: " 'You behind a plow! You ain't got no mo' business wid uh plow than uh hog is got wid uh holiday!' " (49). After Joe's store and house are completed, though, he comes increasingly to treat her like an animal obliged to work his property. One day as she is working in the store, she sees some of the men tormenting Matt Bonner's mule outside. Her thoughts reveal an unconscious identification of her situation with that of the mule:

> She snatched her head away from the spectacle and began muttering to herself. "They oughta be shamed uh theyselves! Teasin' dat poor brute lak they is! Done been worked tuh death: done had his disposition ruint wid mistreatment, and now they got tuh finish devilin' 'im tuh death. Wisht Ah had mah way wid em all." (89)

Janie feels as powerless as Matt's mule; she's being mistreated and "worked to death" by Joe. As she turns away from the window, "a little war of defense for helpless things" goes on inside her, and she thinks, "People ought to have some regard for helpless things" (90). When Joe overhears what Janie has muttered, he buys the mule from Matt, pretending that "freeing" the mule is his idea. In front of the others, Janie delivers an ironic speech in which she compares Joe to George Washington and Abraham Lincoln:

> "Abraham Lincoln, he had de whole United States tuh rule so he freed de Negroes. You got uh town so you freed uh mule. You have tuh have power tuh free things and dat makes you lak uh king uh something." (92)

Janie's juxtaposition of the freeing of slaves with the freeing of the mule shows the ironic contrast between the importance of what Joe has done and what Lincoln did. It also links servitude to the state of the mule; thus, Janie's servitude to Joe is clearly less important to him than the "servitude" of the mule.

After this incident, Janie begins to feel a stronger desire for freedom and a greater dissatisfaction with her relationship with Joe. One night, Joe hits her because her dinner does not please him. After that, Janie's image of Joe "tumble[s] down and [is] shattered," and her association of him with the pear tree ideals is ruined (112). He becomes " 'nothin' . . . in [her] mouth' " (118), and she starts to use words to fight back at him. Janie finally defeats Joe with her words, during their fight in the store, and the "big voice" of Joe is silenced. When Joe hears Janie expose the truth about his sexuality, he feels humiliation and rage: "Joe Starks didn't know the words for all this, but he knew the feeling. So he struck Janie with all his might" (124). When this happens, Janie's power relationship with Joe is reversed. For Janie, "new thoughts had to be thought and new words said" (125). Joe becomes ill and retreats from contact with Janie. His last attempt to control her is to name her as his murderer. When Janie finds out he is spreading this rumor, she tearfully tells Pheoby, " 'Tuh think Ah been wid Jody twenty years and Ah just now got tuh bear de name uh poisonin' him' " (127). Joe's final actions toward her make Janie sad, but she refuses to be controlled by him.

When she realizes that Joe is about to die, she ignores his order for her to stay out of the sick room and confronts him one last time. When she faces her oppressor, she reverses the seat of power; Janie becomes the one who names. Janie sees that "Jody, no Joe, gave her a ferocious look. A look with all the unthinkable coldness of outer space. She must talk to a man who was ten immensities away" (130). Janie recognizes the difference between the man she affectionately named "Jody" twenty years ago and the man named "Joe Starks," the "big voice." Janie tells him, " 'Listen, Jody, you ain't de Jody ah run off down de road wid. You'se whut's left after he died' " (133). Starks protests against the truth, but then Death, "the square-toed one," takes him. Janie muses for a while on the transformation of her Jody into Joe Starks, "the making of a voice out of a man" (134), and then she calls in the community to mourn.

Janie takes on a new name at this stage in her life; she becomes the "widow of Joe Starks," a woman of property. It is readily apparent that the attraction associated with her new name is still linked to Joe Starks. She sees the difference between her state as a "widow" and the status of the other widows in town; men will woo her because she has Joe Starks's money and property. John Callahan feels that with his "big voice" Joe Starks, in effect, became Nanny's successor, and so it is appropriate that after his death and burial Janie discovers her true feelings about Nanny (105). Nanny's dream for Janie has been realized in the security offered by Joe's wealth, but for Janie, Nanny's definition of happiness is not enough:

> . . . Nanny had taken the biggest thing God ever made, the horizon—for no matter how far a person can go the horizon is still way beyond you—and pinched it in to such a little bit of a thing that she could tie it about her grand-daughter's neck tight enough to choke her. She hated the old woman who had twisted her so in the name of love. (138)

What Nanny had named "love" Janie renames as "mis-love" (138). Janie recognizes that she must define her own horizons now. Maria Tai Wolff states that Janie knows that another's ideas are never adequate; the only truths she will now accept are those derived from her own experience (31).

As soon as Janie has this realization, she imagines her own creation. Missy Dehn Kubitschek says that Hurston underscores Janie's rebirth by associating her reflections on her marriages with a creation myth (24). Janie finds a "jewel" within herself and opposes that image to "tumbling mudballs" (139). Janie has a new sense of strength and identity which comes from within herself rather than from her association with someone else.

Tea Cake's entrance into Janie's life and his relationship to naming foreshadow the kind of relationship they will share. Whereas Joe Starks's first words were to name himself ("Joe Starks was the name"), Tea Cake's first words call Janie by name, " 'Good evenin', Mis' Starks,' " (144). Janie tells him that he has " 'all de advantage 'cause Ah don't know yo' name' " (144), but Tea Cake does not view his name as important. " 'People wouldn't know me lak dey would *you*,' " he tells her (145). Janie finds herself relaxed and laughing as she talks to Tea Cake because he uses his words to entertain her. John Callahan says that Tea Cake "revivifies" names (106): instead of asking Janie for a match, he says, " 'You got a lil piece uh fire over dere, lady?' " (145). When Janie finally learns his name, she finds that he has been renamed from Vergible Woods to Tea Cake. Janie likes the renaming and asks Tea Cake if it suits his nature: " 'Tea Cake! So you sweet as all dat?' " (149). Tea Cake does not name to gain power; he names to explore the true nature of a thing.

As their relationship develops, Janie finds that naming no longer holds the limiting power that it manifested in her relationships with Logan and Joe. She explains to Pheoby that the age difference between her and Tea Cake does not affect them because they " 'thinks de same' " (173). Janie forms a new relationship to language, but this time she has power over it rather than its having power over her: " 'So in the beginnin' new thoughts had tuh be thought and new words said. After Ah got used tuh dat, we gits 'long jus' fine. He done taught me de maiden language all over' " (173). Tea Cake's use of language is positive and creative, rather than limiting and destructive.

Soon after this, Janie and Tea Cake are married. This time, her name change does not bring about a relationship of unequal power. Instead, she and Tea Cake move away from Eatonville and form a new life in the " 'Glades." Their trust and love for each other develop so far that Janie can finally feel free to say to Tea Cake, " 'All right then, you name somethin' and we'll do it' " (250). She knows that, because she and Tea Cake think "the same," he will never use his naming as a source of power over her.

Although their move away from Eatonville provides them with a place where they can create their own relationship to language, it also places them in a larger world, a world which is not racially segregated and which brings them face to face with the forces they name "God" and "Death." The issues of race and name are, however, inextricably combined by Mrs. Turner, Janie and Tea Cake's neighbor in the " 'Glades." Mrs. Turner's use of naming falls into the Western literary tradition described by Benston. The privileging of "white" over "black" and the reduction of a human being to the word *nigger* are methods used by Mrs. Turner to give her a sense of power. She tells Janie:

"Ah can't stand black niggers. Ah don't blame de white folks from hatin' 'em cause Ah can't stand 'em mahself. 'Nother thing, Ah hates tuh see folks lak me and you mixed up wid 'em. . . . If it wuzn't for so many black folks it wouldn't be no race problem. De white folks would take us in wid dem. De black ones is holdin' us back." (210)

Mrs. Turner names people by their skin color rather than their individual names. Her rejection of "black niggers" is a complete denial of her Afro-American heritage.

Mrs. Turner is not Janie's only exposure to the destructive naming based on skin color. After the hurricane, when Tea Cake and Janie are recovering in Palm Beach, Tea Cake is approached by two white men with guns. He is concerned because they do not know him, but he soon discovers that they are not interested in his real name:

> "Hello, there, Jim," the tallest one called out. "We been lookin' fuh you."
> "Mah name ain't no Jim," Tea Cake said watchfully. "Whut you been lookin' fuh *me* fuh? Ah ain't done nothin.' " (251)

The men's generic misnaming demeans Tea Cake by grouping him with all black men, denying him a separate identity. Tea Cake is forced to go with the men to bury the dead, and again he sees the denial of identity based on skin color. The white men have the workers separate the bodies according to color and save the white bodies for burial in a box, whereas the black bodies will be covered in a mass grave. Tea Cake remarks ironically on the fact that, with the shape these bodies are in, he " 'can't tell whether dey's white or black' " (253).

When he escapes back to Janie, he tells her, " 'It's bad bein' strange niggers wid white folks. Everybody is aginst yuh' " (255). Because the white people of Palm Beach do not know Tea Cake and Janie by name, he feels, they are not safe there. Janie comments further on the naming according to race: " 'Dat sho is de truth. De ones de white man know is nice colored folks. De ones he don't know is bad niggers' " (255). Janie and Tea Cake decide to return to their former home in the "Muck" where they control the naming, and through their naming maintain a sense of control.

It is on the "Muck" that Janie comes up against two powerful forces which she cannot control: the force which causes the hurricane and the force which she describes as the "being with . . . square toes" (129). Janie names these abstractions to try to understand them. The first force, the one she and Tea Cake encounter in the hurricane, she names "God." Janie has already used the name *God* in association with Tea Cake. She describes him earlier in the novel as "a glance from God," bringing him together with her vision of the pear tree blossoming in the spring (161). During the storm, she reiterates Tea Cake's connection to the force she names "God" when she explains her love for him:

> "We been tuhgether round two years. If you kin see de light at daybreak, you don't keer if you die at dusk. It's so many people never seen de light at all. Ah wuz fumblin' round and God opened de door." (236)

For Janie, then, *God* is a name for what she has learned through her own growth and through her relationship with Tea Cake. *God* is the unexplainable force which is located somewhere beyond the horizon, the goal which Janie is constantly seeking. As Janie and Tea Cake sit together in the darkened shanty, they become aware of their connection with this unknown force:

> They sat in company with others in other shanties, their eyes straining against crude walls and their souls asking if He meant to measure their puny might against His. They seemed to be staring at the dark, but their eyes were watching God.(236).

Hurston's use of the final clause as the title of her novel emphasizes its importance. The name *God* is not defined by Hurston in the way that it is used in the Western literary tradition. Hurston's renaming of this force (or potential) places her novel outside the white male literary canon, and creates a powerful new place for black women writers to rename their experience.

Along with her re-signification of the name *God,* Hurston also re-signifies the name *Death.* When Joe Starks is dying, Janie personifies Death as the "strange being with the huge square toes" who has been standing in his high house since "before there was a where or a when or a then" (129). Janie's renaming of death as a being identified by the shape of his toes (tombstones) helps her understand the phenomenon of death and helps her control her fear of it. She describes the time after the hurricane like a reprieve after the visitation of a dreaded neighbor or relative:

> And then again Him-with-the-square-toes had gone back to his house. He stood once more and again in his high flat house without sides to it and without a roof with his soulless sword standing upright in his hand. . . . The time of dying was over. It was time to bury the dead. (249)

By naming death, Janie gains an understanding of it. It is this understanding of death that enables Janie to shoot Tea Cake when she is forced by his illness to become an instrument of death. Although she is filled with sorrow at the thought of killing him, she recognizes that she must do it for her own life to continue.

When Janie kills Tea Cake, she becomes once again unnamed. She has actively ended her role as his wife, which leaves her an option to name her own roles. She easily overcomes the last attempt by someone in the novel to name her when she is tried for Tea Cake's murder. The white lawyers designate her " 'the defendant,' " rather than Janie (279). In their arguments, the lawyers offer the jury a variety of other names: " 'poor broken creature,' " " 'devoted wife,' " or " 'wanton killer.' " Janie knows that the assignment of any of these names to her would be untrue and would limit the "horizon" she has come to know. The assignment of one of these names to Janie would result in a misunderstanding of her relationship with Tea Cake, and Janie fears such a misunderstanding more than death (279). To counter this last attempt at naming, Janie tells her own story to the jury. Her words hold more power than the names: "She just sat there and told and when she was through she hushed. She had been through for some time before the Judge and the lawyer and the rest seemed to know it" (278). The Jury comes to an understanding of Janie through her own words, and so she is freed.

Janie has been to the horizon and back (284), as she tells Pheoby. Her return to Eatonville is not a defeat, as the watchers on the porch interpret it to be. Instead, Janie returns full of new knowledge and power, able to rename her surroundings because she has unnamed herself. She tells Pheoby, " 'Dis house ain't so absent of things lak it used tuh be befo' Tea Cake come along. It's full uh thoughts, 'specially dat bedroom' " (284). Janie transforms her experiences with renaming: Tea Cake becomes the "son of Evening Sun" (281), and the lamp in Janie's hand is a "spark of sun-stuff washing her face in fire" (285). Janie Crawford Killicks Starks Woods has survived a succession of marital and other identities, and at the end of the novel, empowered to tell her own story, she has become a sort of goddess who pulls "in her horizon like a great fish-net" (Gilbert and Gubar 238–39).

Janie's last act is an invocation of her self: "She called in her soul to come and see" (286). Janie is the final one who names in Hurston's novel, and with her call to herself, Janie becomes a model of powerful self-identification for later Afro-American women writers.

Works Cited

Benston, Kimberly W. " ' I Yam What I Am': Naming and Unnaming in Afro-American Literature." *Black American Literature Forum* 16 (1982): 3–11.

Bethel, Lorraine. " 'This Infinity of Conscious Pain': Zora Neale Hurston and the Black Female Literary Tradition." *But Some of Us Are Brave.* ed. Gloria Hull, Patricia Bell Scott, and Barbara Smith. New York: Feminist. 1982. 176–88.

Bloom, Harold. "Chronology." Bloom, *Zora* 115–18.

———, ed. *Zora Neale Hurston's* Their Eyes Were Watching God. New York: Chelsea, 1987.

Bush, Trudy. "Transforming Vision: Alice Walker and Zora Neale Hurston." *Christian Century* 105(1988): 1035–38.

Callahan, John F. " 'Mah Tongue Is In Mah Friend's Mouf': The Rhetoric of Intimacy and Immensity in *Their Eyes Were Watching God.*" Bloom, *Zora,* 87–113.

Cooke, Michael G. "Naming, Being, and Black Experience." *Yale Review* 67.2 (1977): 167–86.

Ellison, Ralph. "Hidden Name and Complex Fate." *Shadow and Act* New York: Random, 1964. 144–66.

Gilbert, Sandra, and Susan Gubar. *No Man's Land.* 2 vols. New Haven: Yale UP, 1988. Vol. 1.

Halsey, William. "Signify(cant) Correspondences." *Black American Literature Forum* 22 (1988): 257–61.

Hurston, Zora Neale. *Their Eyes Were Watching God.* 1937. Urbana: U of Illinois P, 1978.

Kubitschek, Missy Dehn. " 'Tuh de Horizon and Back': The Female Quest in *Their Eyes Were Watching God.*" Bloom, *Zora* 19–34.

Meese, Elizabeth. "Orality and Textuality in *Their Eyes Were Watching God.*" Bloom, *Zora* 59–72.

Ong, Walter J. *Orality and Literacy: The Technologizing of the Word.* London: Methuen, 1982.

Pryse. Marjorie. "Zora Neale Hurston, Alice Walker, and the 'Ancient Power' of Black Women." Pryse and Spillers 1–24.

Pryse, Marjorie, and Hortense Spillers, ed. *Conjuring: Black Women, Fiction and Literary Tradition.* Bloomington: Indiana UP. 1985.

Spillers, Hortense. "Cross-Currents, Discontinuities: Black Women's Fiction." Pryse and Spillers 249–61.

Wittig, Monique. *Les Guerilleres.* Trans. David Le Vay. Boston: Beacon, 1985.

Wolff, Maria Tai. "Listening and Living: Reading and Experience in *Their Eyes Were Watching God.*" *Black American Literature Forum* 16 (1982): 29–33.

Gender and Ambition:
Zora Neale Hurston in the
Harlem Renaissance

Ralph D. Story

In the literary world the "battle" between the sexes for publicity, publications and position is a conflict rooted historically in the dynamics of race, class and gender as they have existed and continue to exist in the United States.

It is thus enlightening and intriguing to illustrate and examine the antecedents of the contemporary situation by way of the literary skirmishes and aesthetic debates between Zora Neale Hurston (1901–1960) and two of her well-known contemporaries, Langston Hughes (1902–1967) and Richard Wright (1908–1960) beginning in the Harlem Renaissance (hereafter referred to as HR).

Although many of the more recent in-depth analyses of the Harlem Renaissance contain contrasting points of view on quite a few issues, most of the accounts and descriptions of Hurston as a person during the era are relatively consistent.[1] Yet relative judgement in the case of Hurston seems to be determined by the gender of the scholar or writer; black male scholars hold one view of her and black female writers hold another.

The typical, and male, rendering of Hurston during the HR can be seen in Langston Hughes' autobiography, *The Big Sea* (1940). In this work she is depicted as a joke-telling, uproariously funny woman who went out of her way to ingratiate herself with influential, rich whites—her purpose being to receive material rewards and financial sponsorship to further her literary career.

Yet very few of the scholars who hold such views of her are willing to concede that such a characterization tells us little about her abilities as a writer. Implicitly, the HR Hurston "character" (some would say caricature) seems to be more important than the characters which people her fiction and folklore, most of which was not published during the HR but instead in the 1930's.[2]

Reprinted from *The Black Scholar* 20.2 (1989): 25–31. © 1989 The Black Scholar. Reprinted by permission of the journal.

In sharp contrast to the views of most HR scholars and the various depictions of the era, the views of contemporary black women writers, and Alice Walker's specifically, are almost exclusively devoted to the lasting importance of Hurston's work. Walker sees Hurston's work as a rare body of literature, "an indication of the quality I feel is most characteristic of Zora's work—a sense of black people as complete, complex, and undiminished human beings. . ."[3]

June Jordan, herself a very great African-American poet, provides a positive analysis of Zora Neale Hurston's Eatonville (Fla.) environment, seeing it as an inspiration for Hurston's fiction in which black folk play, "their own particular selves in a family and community setting that permits relaxation from hunted/warrior postures and that fosters the natural person-postures of courting, jealousy, ambition, dream, sex, work, partying, sorrow, bitterness, celebration and fellowship."[4]

Such complimentary analyses make one wonder just how the work of Hurston the writer fits the HR persona of Hurston, a person who has been disparagingly characterized by an African scholar as a woman "predisposed to identify more with whites (and whose) parents had large quantities of white blood in their veins,"[5] and by scholar David L. Lewis as a "minion" to the white patron Charlotte Osgood Mason.[6]

It is compelling to consider, moreover, that Hurston, who her astute biographer Hemenway acknowledges as "one of the most memorable personages of the period," has been singled out for biting criticism as if she was the only player in the artist-gatekeeper-patron literary game that was, in fact, so much a part of the entire HR. Perhaps condemnation of Hurston's behavior is in part attributable to the scarcity of information on those hard-to-describe but fairly well-known relationships between other black writers, "race" leaders, and their white patrons whom Hurston jokingly labeled "Negrotarians."

As it is, however, the publication of David Lewis' *When Harlem Was In Vogue* (1982), an innovative and primary source of information on the HR, makes it obvious that Hurston was not the only writer "on the take." Indeed, many of the major black HR writers had a benefactor or benefactors: a patronage system which makes the HR seem just as much a matter of interracial connections and networking as it was a matter of black talent in abundance so obvious that the dominant culture's literary world had to acknowledge it through social liaisons and publication opportunities.

It is very surprising that this well-known nexus of interracial relationships had not been adequately addressed prior to Lewis' incisive analysis and commentary. In his close examination, the linkages between major HR black artists, influential black intermediaries, and white philanthropy and/or patronage, are clearly discernible.[6]

Hurston, contrary to popular belief, was not the only HR writer who had clear-cut financial ties to a white patron—Charlotte Osgood Mason. Langston Hughes, Claude McKay, Aaron Douglas and Alain Locke were all recipients of Mason's financial and moral support. Hughes, in particular, was emotionally traumatized by his break with Mason after three years of relatively heavy-handed if not generous guidance (since Mason preferred to have "her artists" address her as "Godmother.")

It shouldn't be surprising to contemporary readers that the second phase of the HR, as part and parcel of the more visible forays of rich whites who flocked to Harlem to have a good time, was distinguishable as the era of widespread white support of black creative intellectuals. Joel Spingarn, one of the founders and supporters of the NAACP, had discernible linkages to Harcourt Brace Publishing Company which published the works of Claude McKay and James Weldon Johnson; Alfred Knopf, a personal friend of Carl Van Vechten and an associate of Walter White, a writer and longtime secretary of the NAACP, was the publisher for both Hughes and White.

Horace Liveright (of Boni and Liveright publishers) was one of the notable publishers in attendance at the Opportunity Awards banquets. His company published Jean Toomer, Jessie Fauset and Alain Locke. Charles S. Johnson and Locke were the managers of the Rosewald and Harmon Funds respectively—funds which were responsible (beyond literary support for artists) for building YMCAs in the black community and the funding of Tuskeegee Institute and other traditional black colleges' endowments.[7]

In a scenario such as that indicated by the associations described above, Zora Neale Hurston's "behavior" seems to be more of a variation on the same theme rather than the conspicuous activities of an individual artist desperately coveting the kind of support which had been extended to black male writers. Lewis' delineation of this broader issue makes her actions all the more understandable and thereby exposes certain characterizations of her as sexist at worst and suspect at best. As Lewis perceives the HR,

> . . .white capital and influence were crucial and the white presence. . .hovered over the New Negro world art and literature like a benevolent censor, politely but pervasively setting the outer limits of its creative boundaries.[8]

Another aspect of the game in which Hurston was a participant was that of the much talked about—but rarely documented—literary infighting for recognition and publication engaged in by struggling artists. In the fishbowl world of that infighting, publicity was precious and each artist was in competition with all others to be seen and heard at book parties and social events where work and play were merged.

It was also at such gatherings that influential patrons would hear the creative work of the writers and choose a rising star (or stars) to sponsor. Hurston, like her male counterparts, was merely acting as any other artist would in a competitive situation. Claude McKay, an HR participant, made it clear in his autobiography, *A Long Way From Home* (1937), that Hurston was merely one of many who found it necessary to court and covet connections with rich white patrons:

Also, among the Negro artists there was much of that Uncle Tom attitude which works like Satan against the idea of a coherent and purposeful Negro group. Each one wanted to be the first Negro, the one Negro, and the only Negro, *for the whites* instead of for their group. Because an unusual number of them were receiving grants to do creative work, they actually and naively believed that Negro artists as a group would always be treated differently from white artists and be protected by powerful white patrons.[9]

Hurston was a player in a game which had many unwritten rules of convention for women—a game any woman at the time would have found impossible to win and especially a black woman writer-intellectual unwilling to discard her rural-southern black folk background.

One rule which she violated was the rule stipulating conventional and conservative public behavior; she smoked in public and consistently and candidly spoke her mind. And despite much retrospective glamor attached to this era, the "Roaring Twenties," despite its rich flapper veneer, was still a decade dominated behaviorally by straightlaced conventions and ideals and particularly so for black women.

One only has to read the works produced during the era by the other well-known black woman editor-novelist-writer, Jessie Fauset, to understand how far afield Hurston truly was from her mostly middle-class (or, if not from that background, certainly aspiring to it) black male contemporaries.[10]

Additionally, within the smaller, private black literary city of the Harlem Renaissance, there was still the need for the artist to prove her/himself deserving of a major publisher to financially support and distribute her/his work. Thus, the task for Hurston as a black woman player in the interracial literary game was to make it: to win in a game dominated at the time by white men who controlled the game, by white spectator-readers who comprised the primary audience, and by black men who functioned as gatekeepers and occasionally as players themselves.

For Hurston was in fierce competition with her own peers when it came to seeking entry at the dominant culture's gates of fame and fortune. *She recognized it for what it was and made no attempt to disguise it;* as a result, those who were unwilling or afraid to expose such widespread accommodation and courting of favors criticized her repeatedly as if her behavior was unusual and revealed a secret ritual most others agreed upon privately to keep off the record.[11]

It is much easier to understand Hurston's energetic presence as well as the contrasting behavior and work of Jessie Faucet, who focused her imaginative attention on the black middle class and its "cultured" and Victorian behavior in this context.[12] The eventual conflict between Hurston and one of her best HR friends, Langston Hughes, over the play *Mule Bone* can be perceived as an inevitable clash which began during the HR but was lurking just underneath the surface, obscured by the retrospective glitter of an era which seemed so promising but ended so abruptly.

An even more interesting context in which to place Hurston is as a southern black woman challenging the traditional position of women and exceeding the aesthetic space they had been traditionally provided: She dared to see herself as a writer with talent equal to if not greater than her peers at representing the "folk" orally and in writing. She was, essentially, more "downhome" than all the other Negro artists who "were" the HR and was not afraid to flaunt it.

The controversy and bitter dispute between Hurston and Hughes over *Mule Bone* and especially Hurston's role in the affair contain all the aforementioned elements and tensions. *Mule Bone*, understood in this manner, becomes a compelling drama, a play underwritten by larger societal forces and staged with the traditional conflicts between men and women which are and have been all too universal. In this case, Hurston was an emergent, adlibbing and provocative leading lady.[13]

> "But Tea Cake, it's too awful out dere. Maybe it's better tuh stay heah in de wet than it is tuh try tuh—" He stunned the argument with half a word. "Fix," he said and fought his way outside. He had seen more than Janie had.

This brief dialogue, an exchange between Janie Crawford and Tea Cake, two lovers whose relationship takes on epic proportions in Hurston's *Their Eyes Were Watching God* (1937), symbolically etches out and foreshadows the aesthetic debate between black female and black male writers. In short, the debate (which is still ongoing but discussed only occasionally) can be reduced to some basic questions. *To what extent are the experiences of black folk—and especially their interaction with whites, typically symbolizing the dominant (and oppressive) culture— important or significant enough to warrant their heavy-handed inclusion and/or subsequently dominant role in most twentieth century fictional depictions of black life? Or, are the day-to-day lives of black folk interior lives in which whites only occasionally appear and then as mere bit players, more representative of the "core" black experience and hence, more appropriate subject matter for artistic renderings by black writers?*[14] The most fitting response to these queries is that both situational realities deserve literary attention and that black men and black women writers have fictionalized those experiences in their lives which have appeared to be the most compelling, enduring and collectively encompassing. But what happens if those experiences are divergent, and uniquely so, because of gender, i.e., if the perspectives of black women writers were in sharp contrast to those of black male writers as a result of their respective sexes and the realities so intimately linked to their sex-specific experiences? The actual dialogue on this matter would seem to indicate as much. Alice Walker, for instance, has written rather bluntly on the issue:

> It seems to me that black writing has suffered because even black critics have assumed that a book that deals with the relationship between members of a

black family—or between a man and a woman—is less important than one that has white people as a primary antagonist. The consequence of this is that many of our books by "major" writers (always male) tell us little about the culture, history, or future, imagination, fantasies, etc., of black people, and a lot about isolated (often improbable) or limited encounters with a nonspecific white world.[15]

Mary Helen Washington, in the course of an essay on Hurston's *Their Eyes Were Watching God,* has also commented on what might be considered a skewed version of black life rendered by black male writers:

> The black writer sometimes gets his eyes so fixed on the white world and its ways of acting toward us that his vision becomes constricted. He reflects, if he is not careful, but one aspect of his people's experiences: suffering, humiliation, degradation. And he may fail to show that black people are more than simply reactors, that among ourselves, we have laughter, tears, and loving that are far removed from the white horror out there.[16]

The gist of this debate, even considering Walker's and Washington's comments to be accurate, however, has more to do with the specific focus of the writer at a given point in historical time and space. Black male writers, throughout most of the twentieth century, have seen the macrocosmic issues affecting black folk—justice, equality and respect for the "race"—as being more suitable for fictional recreations of black life because these issues were more important for the vast majority of black folk. This was especially true during the pre-WWII era. Black women writers, however, have generally taken the opposite stance which, loosely translated, says the black community—its women and men in that order—should have always been the central focus for black writers. Thus, the moment Hurston's novel appeared in print black male writers critiqued it negatively.

Their Eyes Were Watching God was reviewed by Richard Wright for *New Masses* shortly after its release. In his critique he accused Hurston of perpetuating stereotypes.[17] Moreover, Sterling Brown and Ralph Ellison shortly thereafter voiced similar misgivings about Hurston's work which they felt consciously or unconsciously avoided the more serious and consequential tensions and issues in black life, i.e., the struggle of blacks against whites to achieve justice, which both deemed as the major task for serious black fiction writers.[18]

Despite such disparaging criticism from such African-American literary giants, the work is a significant, very well-written novel with obvious philosophical and social significance that Wright, Brown and Ellison either dismissed as irrelevant or overlooked when writing their reviews. Indeed, *Their Eyes Were Watching God* is a novel that exposed philosophical differences between black men and women; equally significant, the reviews of the novel revealed a literary division of labor and hierarchy before there was a concerted and consistently visible women's movement, which has provided the ideological and literary foreground for the views of black women writers.

To put it in simple terms, black male writers during the 1930's were unwilling to concede their own territorial literary dominance over the most "serious" subject matters—interracial conflicts, the "state's" inadequacies, the fight of black folk against racism and poverty and the recreation of black historical figures in fictional form. Thus, even if a talented black female writer had emerged who wanted to deal with such issues, it would have been extremely difficult for her to convince publishers and/or readers that she was up to the task given the chauvinism and sexism (and not to mention racism) so characteristic of American life in the pre-WWII era. Black male writers, perhaps unconsciously, were also unwilling to perceive the struggle of black women for sexual equality and the perspective brought to bear on that struggle by a great black woman writer as literary territory and as an orientation worthy of detailed delineation in Hurston's novel.

Wright, Brown and Ellison wanted to insist that man's inhumanity to man, in this instance the oppression of black people as a group by those with money and power, makes the possibility of genuine, reciprocal and enduring love remote at best and willful self-delusion at worst. They would have contended that the more serious problems affecting black people are those problems which stemmed from powerlessness and minority status.

It follows in their view then that any writer attempting serious fiction has to address the more encompassing global, political, psychological and material conflicts of a people in the symbolically collective sense. *Their Eyes Were Watching God* was for them a work which they very easily dismissed as minor and of secondary importance given "the struggle of the people" at the time. A black love story which took place in an all-black setting was not sufficiently realistic nor artistically sound for all the aforementioned reasons.

Hurston's view, had she articulated it, might have been just the opposite. Black women, more than anything else, have wanted love whereas black men have wanted justice and power; yet neither is guaranteed. She might have also asserted that if one were given the choice, the quest for love and its subsequent attainment by black men and women are ultimately more realizable and necessary for black folk as a *precondition* to their engagement in any protracted, life-threatening struggle.

Hurston, in this imaginary dialogue, symbolizes the woman's perspective and demonstrates that women have had a different set of values than black male writers and this is made clear in their fictional recreations of black life. *Their Eyes Were Watching God* embodies a different value system in that it is clearly a delineation of the quest for love and self-fulfillment by Janie Crawford (the protagonist of the novel).

Black women writers, in addition to their different values, have also had a different set of experiences than black male writers and this is made patently obvious in their fictional recreations of black life, with Hurston's novel being an exceptional case in point. This work begins with this understanding and from the very first page presents the perspectives of men and women which are then substantiated by the work:

> Ships at a distance have every man's wish on board. For some they come with the tide. For others they sail forever on the horizon, never out of sight, never landing until the Watcher turns his eyes away in resignation, his dreams mocked to death by TIME. That is the life of men. Now, women forget all those things they don't want to remember, and remember everything they don't want to forget. The dream is the truth. Then they act and do things accordingly.[19]

By the tale's end Janie Crawford is a fully developed, complex black female character. Indeed, Hurston revised, as Barbara Christian contends, "the previously drawn images of the mulatta, (and) the author's rendition of her major characters beautifully revealed the many dimensions of the black woman's soul as well as the restrictions imposed upon her by her own community—that she, like all others, seeks not only security but fulfilment."[20] It is rather refreshing and poignant that Janie's reaction to the death of Tea Cake (her last lover in the novel) is not one of morbid resignation but instead an elevated, heightened consciousness:

> She pulled in her horizon like a great fishnet. Pulled it from around the waist of the world and draped it over her shoulder. So much of life in its meshes. She called in her soul to come and see.[21]

In effect, *Their Eyes Were Watching God,* Hurston's greatest literary accomplishment, established her as one of the great imaginative writer-folklorists in the twentieth century. Her characterization of Janie Crawford, the breath of strongly feminine perspective she gave Janie and her authentic rendering of black folk speech and legend should make it impossible for any African-American scholar to disparage her importance to the African-American and American literary traditions respectively.

Yet, Hurston's non-fiction, excluding the folklore, and particularly her later statements in articles on race are another issue.[22] She reacted bitterly to disparagement and what she considered to be generalizations about race which she resisted. Nevertheless, even on this count contemporary black women writers are more sympathetic and have a more specific understanding of Hurston's tragic life and unappreciated work than do black male writers (with the exception of the late Larry Neal). Barbara Christian, an astute contemporary black female literary critic, sees Hurston's life and work as example and creative precedent:

> One of the first writers to use folk images and speech as well as the insular folk culture, Hurston anticipated future black women writers who would attempt

to define themselves as persons within a specific culture rather than primarily through their relationships with whites. Faucet's characters, particularly in *The Chinaberry Tree,* also insulated themselves with a particular class, but Hurston's *Their Eyes Were Watching God* invokes not one class but the total community— its language, images, mores, and prejudices—as its context. In so doing it articulates the Afro-American experience not only as a condition but as a culture.[23]

Christian's view of Hurston as a writer who "anticipated future black women writers" and one who had achieved a consciousness of a distinct black culture is an accurate assessment. For Hurston's work was in many ways culturally nationalistic (as in the late 1960's) and anticipated and surely inspired the literary works of black women writers of the 1970's and 1980's.

Indeed, her work foreshadowed the issues of black women which came to prominence in the early 1970's, specifically the plight of black women as a subject matter in and of itself deserving of literary and scholarly attention. The work of Ntozake Shange, and especially the brilliantly poetic *for colored girls who have considered suicide when the rainbow is enuf* (1975) and the reactions to that work are most comparable to that of Hurston's experiences as a writer for both political and aesthetic reasons. For Shange, like Hurston, has had to withstand some rather acerbic and pointed criticism from black male writers for her choreopoem. Hopefully, history will not repeat itself and Shange's talent and creative power will be appreciated in her lifetime. Zora Neale Hurston was not that fortunate.

Notes

1. See Nathan Huggins' *Harlem Renaissance;* Langston Hughes' *The Big Sea;* Arna Bontemps' (Ed.) *The Harlem Renaissance Remembered;* David Lewis' *When Harlem Was In Vogue.*

2. Zora Neale Hurston was the author of *Jonah's Gourd Vine* (1934), *Mules and Men* (1935), *Their Eyes Were Watching God* (1937), *Tell My Horse* (1938), *Moses, Man of the Mountain* (1939), *Dust Tracks on a Road* (1942) and *Seraph on the Suwanee* (1948) and numerous other anthropological, folklore and "race" articles.

3. Alice Walker's "Introduction" to *Zora Neale Hurston: A Literary Biography,* by Robert Hemenway (Chicago: University of Illinois Press, 1978), p. xii.

4. Hemenway, *Zora Neale Hurston,* p. 12.

5. Chidi Ikonne, *From DuBois to Van Vechten: The Early New Negro Literature, 1903–1926* (Westport, CT: Greenwood Press, 1981), p 183.

6. David Levering Lewis, *When Harlem Was In Vogue* (New York: Alfred A. Knopf, 1981), p. 151.

7. Ibid., pp. 75–78,152–153,50–58, 58–74, 125, 229–230, 277–281, 233–234, 127, 196–197, 143–149, 121–125, 152–155, 89–98, 66–67, 59, 99, 151, 262–263, 144- 46, 70–71, 78–88. Also see George Kent's "Patterns of the Harlem Renaissance," *The Harlem Renaissance Remembered,* Ed. Arna Bontemps (Dodd Mead & Co.: New York, 1972).

8. Ibid., p. 98.

9. Claude McKay, *A Long Way From Home* (New York: Harcourt, Brace & World, 1970), p. 322.

10. Jessie Faucet's fiction has been negatively criticized (for the most part justifiably) because of her almost exclusive focus on the black "upper class." Yet, her work in the real world as an editor for *Crisis* and as a literary raconteur has not received the positive attention it deserves.

11. Numerous writers who either lived through the Harlem Renaissance as participants or are considered expert on the era have barely skimmed the surface on the subjects of patrons and patronage during this era. Lewis' work is clearly a threshold investigation of this subject and exposes it in ways never before uncovered.

12. See Barbara Christian's *Black Women Novelists* (Westport, CT: Greenwood Press, 1980) for an excellent discussion of Faucet's work.

13. Hurston and Hughes were friends before and during the play's draft but "lifelong enemies" after its solo completion by Hurston. Subsequent to this conflict, Hurston and Hughes "avoided each other for the rest of their lives," or approximately forty years. It is also significant that Hurston's claim to sole authorship was grounded not only in her belief that the characters and story of *Mule Bone* were essentially hers; she probably believed, and rightfully so, that she was more representative of "the folk" (blacks residing in the rural south) and hence had a more legitimate claim to recreating their lives than Hughes who was essentially a writer who focused his attention on the urban black experience. This "hidden" posture is just underneath the surface in the following excerpt from her correspondence: "Now about the play itself. It was my story from beginning to end. It is my dialogue; my situations. But I am not concerned about that."

14. I am using John Langston Gwaltney's term "core" which he uses to characterize the most representative, germane experiences of "everyday" black people. See John Langston Gwaltney, *Drylongso* (New York: Random House, 1980), p. xxii.

15. John O'Brien, ed., *Interviews with Black Writers* (New York: Liveright, 1973), p. 202.

16. Mary Helen Washington, "Zora Neale Hurston's Work," *Black World*, August 1972, pp. 68–75.

17. Richard Wright, "Between Laughter and Tears," *New Masses*, October 6, 1937, pp. 24–25.

18. Ralph Ellison, "Recent Negro Fiction," *New Masses*, August 5, 1941, pp. 22-26.

19. Zora Neale Hurston, *Their Eyes Were Watching God* (Philadelphia: J. E. Lippincott, 1937), p. 1.

20. Christian, p. 47.

21. Hurston, p. 286.

22. One of the more controversial articles by Hurston detailing her positions on blacks and voting is "I Saw Negro Votes Peddled," *American Legion Magazine*, 49 (November 1950), pp. 12–13, 54–57, 59–60.

23. Christian, p. 46.

Works Cited

Berry, Faith. *Langston Hughes: Before and Beyond Harlem*. Westport, CT: Lawrence Hill & Co., 1983.

Bontemps, Arna. *The Harlem Renaissance Remembered*. New York: Dodd Mead & Co., 1972.

Brown, Sterling. "The New Negro In Literature." *The New Negro Thirty Years Afterwards*. ed. Rayford Logan. Washington D.C.: Howard University Press, 1955.

Christian, Barbara. *Black Women Novelists*. Westport, CT: Greenwood Press, 1980.

Ellison, Ralph. "Recent Negro Fiction." *New Masses*. August 5, 1941.

Fauset, Jessie. *The Chinaberry Tree*. New York: Stokes, 1933.

Gwaltney, John Langston. *Drylongso*. New York: Random House, 1980.

Hansberry, Lorraine. *A Raisin In the Sun*. New York: Random House, 1959.

Hemenway, Robert. *Zora Neale Hurston: A Literary Biography*. Chicago, IL: University of Illinois Press, 1978.

Huggins, Nathan. *Harlem Renaissance*. New York: Oxford University Press, 1971.

Hughes, Langston. *The Big Sea*. New York: Alfred A. Knopf, 1940.

———. *The Weary Blues*. New York: Alfred A. Knopf, 1926.

Hurston, Zora Neale. *Moses, Man of the Mountain*. Philadelphia: J. E. Lippincott, 1939.

———. *Their Eyes Were Watching God*. Philadelphia: J. E. Lippincott, 1937.

———. "I Saw Negro Votes Peddled." *American Legion Magazine*, Vol. 49, November 1950.

Ikonne, Chidi. *From DuBois to Van Vechten: The Early New Negro Literature, 1903–1926*. Westport, CT: Greenwood Press, 1981.

Lewis, David Levering. *When Harlem Was In Vogue*. New York: Alfred A. Knopf, 1981.

McKay, Claude. *A Long Way From Home*. New York: Harcourt, Brace & World, 1970.

O'Brien, John. ed. *Interviews with Black Writers*. New York: Liveright, 1971.

Shange, Ntozake. *for colored girls who have considered suicide when the rainbow is enuf.* New York: Bantam Books, 1977.

Walker, Alice. "In Search of Zora Neale Hurston." *Ms.* Vol. III, No. 9, March 1975.

Washington, Mary Helen. "Zora Neale Hurston's Work." *Black World*. August 1972.

Wright, Richard. "Between Laughter and Tears." *New Masses*. October 6, 1937.

TELL MY HORSE:
VOODOO AND LIFE
IN HAITI AND JAMAICA
(1938)

♦

Witchcraft in the Caribbean Island
[Review of *Tell My Horse*]

Harold Courlander

Miss Zora Neale Hurston has gone afield from the scene of her previous work (*Mules and Men* and *Their Eyes Were Watching God*) and turned to the inexhaustible mines of Voodoo and witchcraft in Haiti and Jamaica. *Tell My Horse* is a curious mixture of remembrances, travelogue, sensationalism, and anthropology. The remembrances are vivid, the travelogue tedious, the sensationalism reminiscent of Seabrook, and the anthropology a melange of misinterpretation and exceedingly good folk-lore.

Jamaica seems to be by way of introduction. Turning at the earliest opportunity to Haiti, Miss Hurston recounts once more, in her own terms, the story of the bloody assassination of President Sam and the entry of the U.S. Naval forces into the private life of Haitian politics; she tells this rather well, having a fine gift for tales. Then she remarks upon the good fortune of the Haitian population in having been, at last, freed from the terror of banditry and tropical politics. Yet this must be more a feeling with her than an idea; she could not have read the late Dr. James Weldon Johnson's articles which appeared in the *Nation* during the summer of 1920. The hardships inflicted by the occupation upon all but the merchants of Haiti have not been forgotten to this day.

Her protest comes in another connection, against the position of women in the Caribbean. That position, she says in effect, is the double standard carried to its furthest possible excess. She discusses the "Black Joan of Arc," Celestina Simon, daughter of President Simon. It is not quite clear why the girl merits the title, but there are stirring tales about her, how she, her father, and her father's pet goat held secret Voodoo rituals in the palace, under the noses of frightened and disapproving guests.

Mostly she writes of Voodoo as she saw it in Haiti, and of witchcraft. The Voodoo resolves out of her anthropological training. But it is in her blood, and would be inevitable under any circumstances. As one observer said, "She'd find Voodoo in anybody's kitchen." But Haiti is full of the real thing. Seabrook exposed it in sensational, wishful terms. Dr. Herskovitz exposed it

Reprinted from *Saturday Review of Literature* 18 (15 October 1938): 6.

in its coldest mathematical terms. Miss Hurston tries both. To an extent she is successful, for Voodoo in Haiti is both warmer, possessed of more poetry, than Dr. Herskovitz realized, and less wild and orgiastic than Seabrook intimated. *Tell My Horse* is full of fine things. Miss Hurston has an immense ability for catching the idiom of dialogue, of seeing the funniest of exaggeration, of recognizing the essence of a story. And yet, though these qualities do carry through at all times, there is a constant conflict between anthropological truth and tale-telling, between the obligation she feels to give the facts honestly and the attraction of (as one of her characters says in *Mules and Men*) the "big old lies we tell when we're jus' sittin' around here on the store porch doin' nothin'."

In dealing with Voodoo rites Miss Hurston is painstaking. There is a good deal of useful material crammed into her eye-witness account. But she seems to be at her best with witchcraft. It fires her imagination, gives impetus to the urge to create a story or a scene. The chapter on Zombies is good. She has gone into the subject extensively, and, in addition to collecting all the Zombie tales going the rounds in Port-au-Prince, has even seen one and photographed her. "But I saw the case of Felicia Felix-Mentor which was vouched for by the highest authority. So I know there are Zombies in Haiti." The reasoning sounds just a little like that of the lumberjack's explanation that Paul Bunyan's plow made the Grand Canyon: "If you don't believe it, go and look for yourself."

The photographs are exceptionally good. It is unfortunate that it is so generally known that many of the "rituals" portrayed in them were enacted in Port-au-Prince and accessible to the average run of tourists. This does not disqualify them as probably the best available pictorial record of Voodoo, but the pictures Miss Hurston took herself are more honest. It is also a matter of regret that the abundance of Creole was not properly edited before publication. A glossary would have been valuable.

That Miss Hurston loves Haiti is obvious, but there is a general feeling that the material was not completely digested.

In Haiti and Jamaica
[Review of *Tell My Horse*]

CARL CARMER

Folklore is a spontaneous product of vitality and imagination. It needs a careful interpreter whose reports have these same two qualities. Seldom has there been a happier combination than that of the vivid, fantastic folklore of the West Indies and interpreter Zora Neale Hurston. Miss Hurston is a trained scholar. She is also one of the most delightfully alive personalities of our day. She knows what she is talking about and she talks with a zest and a humor and a genuineness that make her work the best that I know in the field of contemporary folklore.

The first part of *Tell My Horse* is a sort of practice walk-around in Jamaica. There is, as Miss Hurston would be the first to admit, a lot more to be written about Jamaican folklore. Stopping off at that British island to hunt the wild hog, collect proverbs, observe marriage customs, hear the "Night Song after Death" served to let her get her hand in for the big job ahead.

It is when Zora Hurston begins writing about her life and observations among the denizens of the misty mountains of Haiti that she becomes incomparable. A few works on Haitian lore have been too dully sensational, a few have been dully academic. Miss Hurston's book is so filled with the spirit of her subject that the whole feeling of its spine-chilling supernatural grotesquerie encompasses the reader and he has a hard time convincing himself that he is reading the authentic work of an honest, painstaking scholar.

Perhaps because she is herself a Negro, Miss Hurston makes her readers conscious of the deep current of racial poetry that runs beneath the rituals of Haitian life. Her sympathies are so strong that she seems to identify herself with her subject. She is but another folk teller of the tales she has uncovered, even a better teller than those who have preceded her.

As for the strange practices she reports, the ceremonies of voodoo, the rites of the horrifying Sect Rouge, the inexplicable mystery of the Zombie, she has better opportunity through identity of race and of natural reactions to

Reprinted from *New York Herald Tribune Books* (23 October 1938): 2.

report the Haitian Negro's observance of folk customs than any other person capable of describing them.

Zora Hurston has come back from her visit to the two near islands with a harvest unbelievably rich. Her book is full of keen social comment relieved with constant humor, it is packed with good stories, accounts of folk religions, songs with both music and words as all songs should be reported. There are few more beautiful tellings of a folk tale than "God and the Pintards," the last story in the volume.

The judges who select the recipients of Guggenheim fellowships honored themselves and the purpose of the foundation they serve when they subsidized Zora Hurston's visit to Haiti. I hope the American reading public will encourage her further wanderings. She ought not to be allowed to rest. I am for putting her to work at once on the Virgin Islands, Cuba, Puerto Rico, the coastal islands off the Carolinas and each of our Southern states. I know she does not need vacations for every sentence she writes proves her work gives her a grand time.

[Review of *Tell My Horse*]

C. G. WOODSON

Zora Neale Hurston as a writer is almost *sui generis*. She is regarded as a novelist, but at the same time she is more of an anthropologist than a novelist. Most of us can appreciate a novel but few have any conception of the functions of an anthropologist. After being trained at Barnard College of Columbia University, where she came under the influence of Dr. Franz Boas, she did some field work in Alabama and Florida for the Association for the Study of Negro Life and History in cooperation with Dr. Elsie Clews Parson, representing the American Folklore Society. Her first production was an article entitled "Cudjo's Own Story of the Last African Slaver," published in the *Journal of Negro History* in 1927.

This was the story of the only survivor of the last cargo of slaves brought from Africa to the United States in 1859. These slaves were landed not far from Mobile, and there they developed as a community consisting of Africans, or of the children and grandchildren of these captives. In this service Miss Hurston gained an insight into the background of the Negro which few of her race have had the penetration to appreciate. She learned not only to appreciate the culture of these people but how to live and move among them in order to portray to the world their thought and feeling and action. The books which she has written since that time give evidence of her unusual ability thus to function as an investigator and an author.

In the recognition of her ability she has been fortunate in having had for two years a Guggenheim Fellowship to enable her to extend her efforts into the West Indies, especially Haiti and Jamaica. This work, *Tell My Horse,* is based upon the practices of the undeveloped element of the people in those parts. She did not collect stories from books. They are known to be inadequate. She went among the people in their daily walks, won their confidence and moved them to speak to her out of the depths of their hearts. She can give, then, the inside story of voodoo on these islands, for she saw these scenes enacted and participated in them herself. These interesting situations and manifestations she has described in highly literary, even poetic, language of which she is capable. Here we learn of superstition, primitive rites—strange

Reprinted from *Journal of Negro History* 24.1 (January 1939): 116–18. © 1939 Journal of Negro History. Reprinted by permission of the journal.

customs which few have taken time to study scientifically. These, moreover, are presented as mystery, weirdness, comedy and tragedy which give convincing evidence of the transplantation of African culture to America. The book, then, is an important chapter in the conflict and fusion of cultures.

The make-up of the book deserves consideration. It is not merely a reproduction of these stories in printed form. The book is neatly made and well illustrated to assist in grasping the meaning of these stories. From Jamaica we have such stories as the "Rooster's Nest," "Curry Goat," "Hunting the Wild Hog" and "Night Song after Death." From Haiti we learn of the "Voodoo and Voodoo Gods," the "Isles of La Gonave," "Archahaie," "Zombies," "Sect Rouge" and "Parlay Cheval," which means *Tell My Horse*. Interwoven are observations on the people of the present day and some account of their past. A number of selections of the music of Haiti appear in the appendix. The work is entertaining and at the same time one of value which scholars must take into consideration in the study of the Negro in the Western Hemisphere.

MOSES, MAN OF THE MOUNTAIN
(1942)

◆

Led His People Free
[Review of *Moses, Man of the Mountain*]

PERCY HUTCHISON

This is the story of Moses as the Negro interprets the "Man of the Mountain." None the less reverent in conception than that of the white man, there is one aspect of the work of the great leader of the Israelites which holds particular fascination for the Negro, so that his view becomes especially interesting, and again always in a reverent way, entertaining, now and again even amusing. All primitive peoples have an inordinate love of magic, or what appears to be magic, and the African most of all. His descendants in this country may hold that the magic of the radio is more awesome than such relics of voodoo prestidigitation as they may have witnessed or heard about. But even they have traditions that will not die, and one of them, according to Zora Neale Hurston, is that Moses was just about the greatest magician ever in the world. He led his followers out of bondage, because his was better "medicine" than that of Pharaoh's magicians. He talked to God face to face, but he had been singled out by God for this honor because Jehovah recognized the superlative magical power of Moses. Consequently there comes about almost a transposition of Moses and God in the Negro's point of view of their relationship, or so it would seem from Miss Hurston's pages. Moses seems almost to be greater than God. But this is not irreverence, for it is undoubtedly due to the fact that it was easier for a primitive mind to endow a human being with mystical powers than to grasp a purely rational concept of deity. The author's Man of the Mountain is a very living and very human person.

The narrative begins with a pathetically moving picture of the enslaved Israelites striving to comprehend the cruelty of the decrees suddenly issued against them by the new Pharaoh. They talk in the dialect made familiar by Roark Bradford's books, which formed the basis of "The Green Pastures." When Jochebed, mother of the three-months-old Moses, takes the child in a wicker basket to hide him in the bulrushes, she addresses the river as if it had personality.

Reprinted from *New York Times Book Review* (19 November 1939): 21. © 1939 by the New York Times Company. Reprinted by permission.

Nile, youse such a big river and he such a little bitty thing. Show him some mercy, please.

For some reason not apparent the author reduces the dialect as she proceeds, and although a more closely knit narrative is the result, the book loses something in flavor. Moses, rescued by Pharaoh's daughter, is brought up as an Egyptian prince, as the leader of an army; not for a long time is he to be the Mountain Man. According to the Book of Exodus Moses was threescore years of age when he delivered the children of Israel out of their bondage, but little is told of Moses during the intervening years. It is the legendary Moses whom the Negroes have built that Miss Hurston gives us in the first part of the book, a Moses painted in rich imagination.

It is after the plagues get under way that the subtle change from the Biblical relationship between Moses and the Lord becomes noticeable. However, it must not be concluded that Moses actually supplants the Lord. No matter how greatly Negro tradition exalts the Israelite leader it still stands in too much awe of Jehovah to belittle Him.

Moses, a fugitive out of Egypt, has gone up into the hills, where the Lord appears to him for the first time and commands him to go down and liberate his people. Moses retorts that Pharaoh won't listen to him. Answers the Lord,

Go ahead like I told you, Moses. I am tired of hearing the groaning in my ear. I mean to overcome Pharaoh this time.

Moses objects that he could never make a speech. Then the Lord,

You. Go. I'll go with you. Open your mouth and I'll speak for you.

But if the Lord, as "boss-man," as Moses calls Him, is in control of operations, we presently find Moses acting as Jehovah's adviser, pleading for one more plague after another. Pharaoh remains obdurate, and when the high priest of the Egyptians counsels him to let the Hebrews go because the people are tired of the plagues, Pharaoh replies that they are nothing but tricks, and that Moses is bound to run out of tricks after a while. Thus we see the personal contest waged between Moses and the Egyptian King as represented by his magicians. Then, of course, comes the end of the bondage and Moses leads his people across the Red Sea.

The close of the book is poetic and beautiful with its picture of Moses high up on the slopes of Nebo looking down on the Children of Israel fording the River Jordan into the Promised Land.

It is impossible to say to what extent Miss Hurston has woven many legends and interpretations into one and how often she is making verbatim use of given, but, presumably, only orally extant, tradition. But the narrative becomes one of great power. It is warm with friendly personality and pulsating with homely and profound eloquence and religious fervor. The author has done an exceptionally fine piece of work far off the beaten tracks of literature. Her homespun book is literature in every best sense of the word.

The Negro's Moses
[Review of *Moses, Man of the Mountain*]

PHILIP SLOMOVITZ

Moses, greatest prophet in Israel, remains one of the most widely studied and discussed personalities in history. In recent years especially there has been an avalanche of biographical material dealing with the life and the ethical teachings of this great prophet. Sigmund Freud's recent work, *Moses and Monotheism,* attracted considerable notice. Biographies of Moses have been written by Louis Untermeyer and Edmond Fleg. A number of years ago a German, Werner Jansen, devoted a book under the title *The Light of Egypt* to a study of Moses. Last year Louis Golding, the brilliant novelist, wrote two travel books, *In the Steps of Moses the Conqueror* and *In the Steps of Moses the Law-giver.*

From the Jewish point of view, the most significant of all studies of Moses continues to be the brilliant essay by Ahad Ha'am (Asher Ginzberg). The following words of his indicate the Jewish attitude toward attempts to dissect the personality and character of Moses and to treat him as an archeological dilemma: "It is not only the existence of this Moses that is clear and indisputable to me. His character is equally plain, and is not liable to be altered by any archeological discovery. This ideal—I reason—has been created in the spirit of the Jewish people; and the creator creates in his own image."

In the light of these modern studies of the life of Moses, it is exceedingly interesting to read a new biography of the Hebrew prophet written by an American Negro. Zora Neale Hurston has already acquired fame as a writer, and in *Moses: Man of the Mountain* she reveals marked ability as a student and interpreter of Negro folkways. It is a magnificent story, but it is weak in its interpretation of the ethical contributions of the prophet and in its treatment of the code of laws handed down by him. For to Jews, Moses is primarily the lawgiver, the great creator of the great code known as the Decalogue. But Miss Hurston presents Moses as a great "voodoo man," which is the position

Reprinted from *Christian Century* (6 December 1939): 1504. © 1939 Christian Century Foundation. Reprinted by permission of the publisher.

given him by the Negro. Her distinctive contribution is her brilliant study of the problem of emancipation, done as perhaps only a Negro could do it.

In the introduction, Miss Hurston explains that the reason Moses is revered as he is by her people is because he had the power to go up the mountain to bring down the laws and because he talked with God face to face. She describes the early life of the Hebrews in Egypt, and in the course of conversations she interprets their attitudes, fears, reactions and hopes. There is a discussion, for instance, between Amram and a comrade before the birth of Moses. They speak of Pharaoh and the lack of nerve on the part of the people to deal with him. Amram's comrade says that he hates himself for not trying violence against Pharaoh even if they kill him for it. Amram replies: "That's what I hate 'em for too, making me scared to die. It's a funny thing, the less people have to live for, the less nerve they have to risk losing—nothing." Throughout this study there is alternate defiance and determination. When bolstered up by a leader like Moses, the people gain courage. When their stomachs happen to be empty, they cry for slavery.

Miss Hurston portrays Moses as an Egyptian who had met with displeasure at Pharaoh's court. But aside from this deviation from accepted biblical fact, she adheres to the biblical story. She is especially effective when she deals with Moses' miracle-producing powers and she ascribes to him extreme strength in his right arm as the producer of miraculous results.

Her Moses knows his people and understands what it means to deal with slaves. When Aaron suggests to him a shorter road than the wilderness of the Red Sea, Moses replies, "I know it, Aaron, but our people are leaving slavery. It takes free men for fighting. The Philistines might let us through without fighting, but it is too much of a risk. If these people saw an army right now they would turn right and run right back into Goshen."

Equally significant is Miss Hurston's interpretation of Moses' reaction to the report of the spies sent to the Promised Land. When he finds that they are still dominated by a slave psychology, he decides that the only way out of the difficulty is to keep the Hebrews in the wilderness for forty years until the generation of slaves has disappeared and Israel has become a people of free men.

Miss Hurston has written a splendid study of slave emancipation. From this point of view her biography of Moses is invaluable.

Zora Neale Hurston's
Moses, Man of the Mountain:
A Fictionalized Manifesto on the
Imperatives of Black Leadership

RUTHE T. SHEFFEY

Anyone who has discovered even a small measure of Zora Neale Hurston's luminosity keeps also indelibly engraved in the memory the picture of Alice Walker, Zora's spiritual sister, walking waist-high in weeds in the segregated cemetery in Fort Pierce, Florida, and looking for Zora's unmarked burial plot. If Alice Walker had achieved nothing else since that time, had published no flow of words, had won no Pulitzer Prize, the placement of that granite marker in 1973 (reading "Zora Neale Hurston, 'A Genius of the South,' 1901–1960—Novelist, Folklorist, Anthropologist") would have secured her a place in American annals. In 1976 when she wrote the introduction to Robert Hemenway's definitive biography of Zora Neale Hurston, Alice Walker concluded, "We are a people. A people do not throw their geniuses away. If they do, it is our duty as witnesses for the future to collect them again for the sake of our children. If necessary, bone by bone."

In *Moses, Man of the Mountain* (1939), mentioned briefly by a handful of critics, Hurston rescues from the Judeo-Christian tradition, and from other African traditions in the diaspora, a true national leader, a folk hero, Moses. In this novel, Zora clearly espoused that conclusion, also promoted by Freud in *Moses and Monotheism* (1939), that Moses was probably Egyptian rather than Hebrew and that the monotheistic religion he brought to the Hebrews originated with a ruler of Egyptian antiquity. Although Zora was writing this novel in 1935, Freud's conclusions did not appear until 1937 in German in *Imago* and in English in 1939, the year in which Zora's *Moses* also appeared. In any event, just as Walker and Hemenway had given Zora back to us, Zora herself has reassembled this mystical leader—for the edification of an oppressed people—bone by bone, his oppressed followers now clearly Afro-

Reprinted from *CLA Journal* 29.2 (December 1985): 206–20. © 1985 College Literature Association Journal. Reprinted by permission of the journal.

American, his true birth now clearly African. In 1953, Blyden Jackson astutely observed that "[t]he method taken, then, by Miss Hurston to achieve her cross-pollination, of the Mosaic legend with the atmosphere of a Negro documentary, and of a Negro documentary with the impersonality of an ancient story possesses the beauty of simplicity."[1]

Of the Hebrew leader Moses, Freud, like Hurston, had attempted to inquire whether he was a historical personage or a creature of legend. They both concluded with the overwhelming majority of historians that Moses was a real person and that the Exodus from Egypt associated with him did, in fact, take place. After establishing the name as simply the Egyptian name for "child," "mose" being not uncommon on Egyptian monuments, Freud wondered that no historian had dared to draw the conclusion that Moses' nationality might be like his name—Egyptian.

Even as Freud mused over this troublesome question, Zora had dared already to posit the Hebrew Moses as a black leader. Freud concluded that perhaps reverence for Biblical tradition had been invincible and that the idea that Moses might have been anything but a Hebrew was too monstrous to consider.[2]

Clearly the personal life of Moses represents him as a typical hero of national legend—as Sir James Frazer pointed out in *Folklore in the Old Testament*—who comes into the world and departs from it in an aura of mystery:

> He was exposed in infancy beside a river and rescued by a princess. At the close of his career he disappears in a hilltop. His "call" is authenticated by three miraculous signs, and he is equipped with a wonder-working rod which divides a sea or a lake, makes the bitter waters sweet, and produces a stream from a rock. These traits are abundantly paralleled elsewhere in folk literature.[3]

Among the heroes of national legend are Semiramiss, queen of Assyria; Gilgamesh, the Mesopotamian hero; in Japanese mythology, Hiruko; and Cyrus, the first king of Persia. Legendary stories are often told about founders of dynasties and kingdoms. Freud remarked that the legend of Moses deviated from others in its kind because "whereas normally a hero, in the course of his life, rises above humble beginnings, the heroic life of the man Moses began with his stepping down from his exalted position and descending to the level of the children of Israel."[4] There are at other points parallels in many other traditions to the events with which Moses is associated. For example, in annals of Christian saints on March 24, 1400, according to a legend, the Virgin Mary was revealed at Chalons, France, in a burning bush, the blaze of which could be seen for miles, but which afterward remained green. It would be excessive here to follow Sir James Frazer's accounts of the many national folklores in which the national hero is buried on a mountain or whose spirit ascends a mountain.

In the introduction to *Moses, Man of the Mountain*, Miss Hurston reported that in Haiti, the highest god is identified as Moses, the serpent god. His home, she continued, is in Dahomey, where he is worshiped extensively:

> Wherever the children of Africa have been scattered by slavery, there is the acceptance of Moses as the fountain of mystic powers. . . . So all across Africa, America, the West Indies, there are tales of the powers of Moses and great worship of him and his powers.[5]

Zora and Freud both concluded that Moses was a leader who was needed by—nay, more willed by—an oppressed people into being one of their own nationality.

Another account, in addition to the Biblical account, which Zora clearly knew was the one by Flavius Josephus, *Antiquities of the Jews*. In that account, the exposure legend is accepted, although Josephus describes Moses as an Egyptian general who fought a victorious campaign against the Ethiopians and who captivated the heart of Tharbis, the Ethiopian princess, so much that she offered her hand in marriage in exchange for her city. Zora included the materials on Moses as the Egyptian general, which were available *only* in Flavius, although her novel simply had Tharbis given to Moses as a war-prize.[6]

The possibility of taking an Old Testament saga and applying it, in the manner of the slave preachers, to Afro-American everyday life had been explored by Zora in a play entitled *The First One* (submitted to the *Opportunity* magazine contest in 1926), where the legend of Ham was comically developed to show the ridiculousness of Biblical strictures against racial mixing. In September 1934, Zora submitted a story, "Fire and Cloud," to *Challenge* magazine, edited by Dorothy West. This terse and tightly woven story shows Moses sitting on his newly made grave on Mount Nebo, "his eyes leaping the Jordan and traveling over to Canaan." Just as the animals were to speak so wisely and with such humanity in *Their Eyes Were Watching God* (1937), the lizard in this story speaks words that are full of truth, for Moses and the lizard are the only characters in this story. As Moses reflects on his leadership in "The Fire and the Cloud," we see foreshadowings of the monumental work of the imagination which was to follow a full five years after in *Moses, Man of the Mountain*. To the lizard's question in "Fire and Cloud," "Do none of these hosts love their deliverer?" Moses answers:

> "Who shall know? Lizard, forty years ago I led a horde of slaves out of Egyptian bondage and I held them in the wilderness until I grew men. Look now upon the plain of Moab. A great people! They shall rule over nations and dwell in cities they have not builded. Yet they have rebelled against me ever. A stiff-necked people. They murmur against me—anew because I have held them before the Jordan for forty days. . . . I have not striven with God, with the wilderness, with rebellion, and with my own soul for forty years to bring them to a new bondage in the land beyond the Jordan. They shall wait for strength." (p. 11)

Later in the story, as Moses gazes down upon the tented nation beneath him and weeps over Israel, the ironic editorial commentary is, "But Israel, unknowing, sang and danced, hammered its swords, milked its cows, got born and died." When reminded by the lizard that where his hosts have triumphed, he, Moses, will be called "Kings of Kings," the leader replies, "I have already known the palaces of the Pharaohs, lizard, but I was not happy in the midst of them." Moses demonstrates the quality here which marks him so strongly in the novel, the humility, the reluctance to separate himself from the common people, and an austerity of personal lifestyle, all qualities associated with Moses and venerated in Afro-American leaders.

To demonstrate the frequent recourses to the Moses story in the Afro-American imagination, in that same issue of *Challenge* in which Hurston's story "Fire and Cloud" appeared, a hitherto unnoticed letter to the editor written by Arna Bontemps appeared. Bontemps wrote:

> I am not convinced about the "younger writers." We're [writers of the 20's] not washed up, not by a jugful. . . . We left Egypt in the late twenties and presently crossed the Red Sea. Naturally the wandering in the wilderness followed. The promised land is ahead. Why Langston [Hughes] has just recently been spying it out for us, and the grapes are promising. Furthermore we will be able to go over and possess it. Now if the younger writers can take our crowns, here is their chance, and here is our challenge. But they will have to take them. We have just achieved our growth. Nobody knows our strength. (p. 29)

Moreover, we remember in this connection the frequent references to Harriet Tubman as the Moses of her people. Like Harriet, Moses crosses over, and one of the most eloquent passages in the novel *Moses, Man of the Mountain* recounts the metamorphosis of a committed leader whose new identity gives him no choice but to follow this divinely appointed path of leadership. Not only the cadence and the rhythms but the content of the passage prefigure the lives and words of Malcolm X and of Martin Luther King. This leader, like the black preacher, had heard his call and forged a new identity as a member of an oppressed group with ties and responsibilities to the other members. He would henceforth draw his sustenance from the past experience of the group. Like Frederick Douglass after the beating he gave his cruel overseer, his new determination to be free and emancipated was nothing less than a resurrection of his spirit. He would henceforth act in accord with his new goals regardless of the price. No longer afraid to die, he was now a free man. As Stephen Butterfield says in *Black Autobiography in America,* that self is "not an individual with a private career but a soldier in a long historic march toward Canaan."[7] The personal and the mass voice are one.

Outside observers noted that the pantheon of Old Testament figures, especially Moses leading his people out of Egypt, defined the values of the slave world. After his arrival in Alabama, a Northern army chaplain wrote of the slaves, "Moses is their ideal of all that is high, and noble, and perfect in man, while Christ was regarded "not so much in the light of the spiritual Deliverer, as that of a second Moses." While the white preachers were stressing, in their sermons to slaves, the epistles of Paul and the need for humility and obedience, both the spirituals' and the Black preachers' call was for the more militant heroics of the Old Testament, with hope for delivery in *this* world. According to Levine, Colonel Thomas Wentworth Higginson "concluded from the songs of his black soldiers that their Bible was constructed primarily from the Book of Moses in the Old Testament and of Revelations in the New." The Colonel concluded that their memories of Jewish history was a "vast bewildered chaos of Jewish history and biography," all instinctively attributed to Moses.[8]

The Colonel, in all of his arrogance of judgement, would have been extremely amazed to know that his black soldiers were dealing with African and not Jewish biography and history. Finally, Levine reported that many Northerners who came South to lift the veils of ignorance from the eyes of Afro-Americans were deeply disturbed by the Old Testament militant emphasis of their religion.[9]

Although negative images of the black preacher have always existed, there is no denying the centrality of the black preacher as a unifying force, often as an agent of protest. Moreover, he has often been a force in the community which traditionally imparted hope, which has helped the community to seek communal strategies and tactics, and which has urged endurance amid hardship and despair. Rawick's *American Slave* points to the intense relationship between the preacher and the congregation, a relationship similar to that experienced in the West African extended family compound. Moses is such a figure, and this book uses the language and the folklore of the rural south to tell his story. Zora says in her Introduction, "Africa has her mouth on Moses. All across the continent there are legends of the greatness of Moses" (p. 7). In this book Moses is more than chief preacher and teacher; he is the original conjurer and two-headed doctor whose staff changes to a snake and who has the power to change water to blood, to bring a plague of frogs on Egypt, leprosy on Miriam, and death on Aaron. Hurston recognized these hoodoo powers as the hidden, perhaps lost, substratum of the Southern black church, that Moses combines his function as chief hoodoo houngan with that as Afro-American preacher/leader.

Other writers have recognized the eclectic and multi-faceted qualities of slave religion which included sacred folk beliefs. Lawrence Levine in his *Black Culture and Black Consciousness* reported the remarks of Thomas Smith of Georgia, who held that the power used by Moses to turn his rod into a snake before Pharaoh still existed among Afro-Americans:

"Dat happen in Africa duh Bible say. Ain dat show dat Africa wuz a lan uh magic powuh since duh beginnin uh history? Well den, duh descendants ub Africans hab duh same gift tah do unnatchul ting."[10]

In addition, Levine reports in this same connection that Mary Livermore, who left New England to tutor on a plantation in Virginia, reported that Uncle Aaron, the plantation's black preacher, was also a conjurer who could raise spirits and use a charm he wore to become invisible when he was threatened.

Hurston staked a novel on the assumption not only that Moses was a black culture-hero but also that we must look to Africa for an understanding of him. As the quintessential leader, W. E. B. DuBois had observed in *The Souls of Black Folk* (1903), the priest or medicine man was the chief surviving institution brought by the African slaves with them. He continued, saying that this leader functioned as "Leader of the sick, interpreter of the unknown, and comforter of the sorrowing."[11] Moses, then, emerges as a hero, unlike the trickster, but both as priest and chief houngan who confronts power and authority directly.

In the novel, Moses, as a boy in the palace, learned from old Mentu, the stableman, the ways of animals: "It was very amusing to the boy to hear the comments of the birds and beasts on human conduct and appearances." In fact, they were human in Mentu's interpretations. The conversation with a lizard follows, very much like the one in Hurston's earlier story "Fire and Cloud." Mentu warns Moses against the common run of priests who have learning without wisdom, like a "load of books on a donkey's back." Moses, he said, must have understanding. Later, Moses knows deep sorrow when old Mentu, his mentor, dies saying, "Please give me the funeral and the tomb of a priest. . . . [T]hat is what I wanted to be. But I wanted to be a great one—not just another one to light fires and burn incense. I couldn't make it from where I started. You have the power to insist—bury me as a priest" (p. 79). Finally, Mentu says, "You are right to listen to proverbs. They are short sayings made out of long experience" (p. 80).

In his own personal life, Moses is shown to obey the moral imperatives of the slave narrator in accounts subscribed "written by his own hand." Those imperatives included, as Butterfield points out, temperance, honesty, worship of God, and respect for hard work. Flavius Josephus had written in 93 A.D. that Moses had refused to have honors bestowed upon him, preferring to keep to the habit of a private man, and in all circumstances to behave as one of the common people and without distinction from the multitude, but having it known that he did nothing but think of them.[12] Genovese has remarked on the asceticism that has provided the decisive ingredient in the mobilization of every popular uprising from the peasant revolts of medieval Europe to the working-class movements of our own day. In addition, Genovese recalled Engel's observation on this matter: "This austerity of behavior, this insistence on relinquishing all enjoyment of life . . . is a necessary transitional stage without which the lowest strata of society could never start a movement."[13] The subjugated, it seemed, must strip themselves of everything that would reconcile them to the existing society. Moreover, unlike the followers of Moses in the Hurston novel who yearned for the "sweet-tasting little pan-fish" which they had had in Egypt, they must renounce all pleasures that would make their subdued position in the least tolerable.

In the novel, Moses soon encounters the pains of leadership. Speaking firmly of the need for unity and obedience to their own leaders and the necessity for respecting yourself if you want others to respect you, Moses hears the men scornfully pointing to their fellow slaves saying, "I don't intend to let no Hebrew boss me around." The Afro-American analogy is clear: "He ain't no better than I am. I don't mean to take nothing off him at all." Thereupon they turn on Moses, calling him the straw boss and asking, "How come you want to help us? How much are you getting out of it?"

Protesting that he doesn't want to be anyone's boss, and that bossism is just what he is trying to do away with, the worker answers:

> "We're mighty proud to hear all of them sentiments out of you. Cause some of us was scared you was trying to be our boss. And since we ain't heard tell of nobody putting *you over us,* so far as I'm concerned, I'd rather have an enemy overseer that beat me and sent me home with a sore back than one of them friends that might kill me and bury me in the sand." (p. 95)

He brags later, "Did I tell that Prince something. I told his head a mess" (p. 96). Hurt at the lack of appreciation of his motives, Moses reflected "that the will to humble a man more powerful than themselves was stronger than the emotion of gratitude. It was stronger than the wish for the common brotherhood of man. It was the cruelty of chickens fleeing with great clamor before superior force but *merciless* towards the *helpless*" (p. 95). Later Moses reflects:

> "You got to go to life to know life. God! It costs you something to do good! . . . if you want that good feeling that comes from doing things for other folks then you have to pay for it in abuse and misunderstanding. It seems like the first law of nature is that everybody likes to receive things but nobody likes to feel grateful. And the *very next* law is that people talk about tenderness and mercy, but they love *force.* If you feed a thousand people, you are a nice man with *suspicious* motives. If you kill a thousand you are a hero. The only time you run a great risk is when you serve them."

On October 15, 1931, well before the publication of "Fire and Cloud" in 1934, Zora wrote a letter to Mrs. Mason about what she called "our Negro Leaders." In the letter she complained, "Godmother, as I see it unless some of the young Negroes return to their gods, we are lost. . . . [T]he old bunch have neither gift nor honor." She continued, charging that many were around Tin Pan Alley imitating the Jews and stealing from other Negroes, "cleaning themselves with their tongues like a cat by saying, 'Other people do it.' " Further, she concluded that they get on the backs of the poor Negro and ride his misery to glory. More trenchantly, in this letter there is the further lament that the things our leaders are fighting for are privileges for the intellectual, not benefits for the humble. "The battles being fought," she continued, "are for Pullman reservations, hotels, residences in white neighborhoods, and white wives for Negro doctors but oh so little to improve the lot of the man in the street." Lest this view seem too despairing, Zora concluded:

> I suppose you will get the idea from what I have said that I am thoroughly dis-illusioned about my leaders. That is correct. But that is not serious. I am on fire about my people. I need not concern myself with the few individuals who have quit the race via the tea table.[14]

Even against this rather jaundiced backdrop, Zora retained an idealism developed later in *Moses, Man of the Mountain,* a positive scenario for black leadership.

Moses' leadership in the novel contains as much humor as sad reflection on the limitations of the slave mentality. In Midian, Moses is able to chase away Jethro's cousin Zeppo, who is accustomed to visiting with his large family and eating heavily, in his words, "a little something to give an appetite." Moses lifts his powerful right hand and rains a plague of frogs on Zeppo's family. Zora recounts that Zeppo "sent back a note that obviously taxed his small education to write." It read like this:

> DEAR COUSIN JETHRO:
> I take my seat and take my pen in hand to write you a letter. I want to know where is your raising that you ain't got no more manners than to let frogs be hopping all over people when they come to visit you? I have been a good and faithful cousin to you. I have always been kind enough to drop whatever I was doing and accept your invitation to bring my family and pass a few days with you and eat meat. But I know when I been insulted and I'll never accept another invitation to pass a week with you, not even if you ask me. But if you insist I will not refuse the meat you offer me. You can send it by my messenger when he comes.
>
> Your loving cousin,
ZEPPO
>
> P.S. I'll bound you all them frogs was the work of that son-in-law of yours, Moses. Nobody else could have done it.

So Jethro wrote back a letter like this:

> DEAR COUSIN ZEPPO:
> All the manners I ever had you done et it up long ago. So I reckoned there just ain't no more. You will have to refuse my offer of beef because I am not slaughtering today. All my cows have a bone in their legs. All of my beds are full of folks so you can't snore in my ears no more.
>
> Your loving cousin,
JETHRO (p. 147)

Even Moses' wife Zipporah strays so much from his ideal of simplicity that it is said of her that "she all dressed up so till it would take a doctor to tell her how near she is dressed to death. . . . She ain't got a finger nor a toe left uncovered. If all them necklaces she got on don't choke her to death I'd sure like to know the reason why."

Jethro agrees that Moses is a great priest whom Jehovah went out of his way to make: "His kind may never be seen no more on earth. He could call sinners to repentance, he could preach the socks off of sin if only he would. . . . The man's just running over with spirit" (p. 159). The spirit notwithstanding, when Moses goes up to the mountain, the people fall back to their old Egyptian gods. Remembering the old religious rituals back home, they talk of the breakdown and stomp to follow. One follower remembers what nice people "them Egyptians were to work for. You couldn't find better boss men nowhere." Another says, "Didn't I always say we was better off in slavery than wandering all over the wilderness following after some stray man that nobody don't know nothing about. Tell the truth, didn't I always say that?" Moses finally has to tell the overambitious Aaron, "I wish *I* could buy *you* for what *you* are really worth and sell *you* for what *you* think you're worth. I sure would make money on the deal." Later, hungry, they regret following Moses and remember the nice sweet-tasting little pan-fish they had for five cents every day in Egypt. Moses had finally discovered another sad truth that leaders encounter: that "no man can make another free. Freedom was something internal. . . . All you could do was give the opportunity for freedom and the man himself must make his own emancipation" (p. 345).

Despite the many West African cultures from which the slaves came, it is clear that they shared a common world view on the requirements of leadership. Moses, their culture hero, apparent everywhere in the Diaspora, was the embodiment of this view. His closest counterpart in the Afro-American society was the black preacher. Slave preachers, who were whipped, branded, sold, or worse for their less carefully guarded sermons, displayed the requisite courage and heroism. DuBois in *Souls of Black Folk* called the black preacher the most unique personality developed by the Negro on American soil. "The combination of adroitness with deep-seated earnestness, of tact with consummate ability, gave him his preeminence, and helps him maintain it." Zora Hurston herself had written a letter to James Weldon Johnson shortly after the publication of *Jonah's Gourd Vine*, where the preacher as poet is the dominant theme, expressing her deep resentment of the *Time* reviewer's comment that John Pearson's climactic sermon "is too good, too brilliantly splashed with poetic imagery to be the product of any one Negro Preacher":

> He means well I guess, but I never saw such a lack of information about us. It just seems that he is unwilling to believe that a Negro preacher could have so much poetry in him. When you and I (who seem to be the only ones even

among Negroes who recognize the barbaric poetry in their sermons) know that there are hundreds of preachers who are equaling that sermon weekly. He does not know that merely being a good man is not enough to hold a Negro preacher in an important charge. He must also be an artist.[15]

These preachers were, like Moses, the natural leaders in the community, leaders who were wise and eloquent, whose phrases were epic in grandeur, in clarity of statement, in earnestness of address, and in deep pathos of language. Their message, often like the message of the ancient Jewish prophets, was that not their original enslavement but their continued enslavement was the result of their continued collective disunity. This emphasis on the necessary foundations of black collectivity has been echoed down through the years by legitimate black preacher authorities, heirs to that ancient African leadership model.

Critics of this book speak of the novel's glories, but they equivocate about the novel that it might have been had Zora followed this or that critical evaluative canon. Even Zora herself wrote that she had not achieved all that she had set out to do. From our angle of vision, it seems that what she did achieve was a tour de force which ambitiously and successfully merged Afro-American folklore—its wit and its humor (God don't talk to everybody that comes slew-footing down the road)—with the universal folk hero, popularized in the Judeo-Christian tradition. Moreover, the work makes a definitive statement about the role of leadership, its sacrifice ([L]eaders have to be people who give up things. They ain't made out of people who grab things) and its loneliness ("He stood in his high, lonely place and led") and its imperative to make former slaves feel free and noble:

> This freedom, Moses who had denied himself many pleasures says, is a funny thing. . . . It ain't something permanent like rocks and hills. It's like manna; you just got to keep on gathering it fresh every day. If you don't, one day you're going to find you ain't got none no more. (p. 327)

Moses, the African leader in Zora's novel, in his fierce love of freedom and justice, had spent his forty-odd years of work to bring his Afro-American bondmen to this view. In this noble endeavor to which he was born, the fictional Moses joins other actual militant leaders in Afro-American history like David Walker, Ida Wells, Frederick Douglass, Harriet Tubman, and Sojourner Truth.

In the conclusion, Moses reflected that he "had meant to make a perfect people, free and just, noble and strong, that should be a light for all the world and for time and eternity" (p. 344). In this novel, Moses appears not as a Hebrew but as an African genius and leader not thrown away, but collected bone by bone in a much underrated novel by an unforgettable artist, Zora Neale Hurston.

Notes

1. Blyden Jackson, "Some Negroes in the Land of Goshen," *Tennessee Folklore Society Bulletin*, 19 (December 1953), p. 105.

2. Sigmund Freud, "Moses and Monotheism," in Vol. XXIII of *The Complete Works* (London: The Hogarth Press, 1964), p. 15.

3. Sir James Frazer, *Folklore in the Old Testament*, Chapters in *Myth, Legend, Custom in the Old Testament* (New York: Harper and Row, 1969), p. 224.

4. Freud, p. 15.

5. Zora Neale Hurston, *Moses, Man of the Mountain* (1939; rpt. Chatham, New Jersey: The Chatham Bookseller, 1957), p. 8. Parenthetical page references hereafter are to this edition.

6. Flavius Josephus, *Antiquities of the Jews*, trans. William Whiston, rev. by Rev. Samuel Burder, Vol. I (Boston: S. Walker, 1833), p. 64.

7. Stephen Butterfield, *Black Autobiography in America* (Amherst: Univ. of Massachusetts Press, 1974), p. 2.

8. Lawrence Levine, *Black Culture and Black Consciousness: Afro-American Folk Thought from Slavery to Freedom* (New York: Oxford Univ. Press, 1977), p. 50.

9. Ibid.

10. Ibid.

11. W. E. B. DuBois, *The Souls of Black Folk* (1903; rpt. New York: Fawcett, 1963), p. 144.

12. Flavius, p. 99.

13. Eugene Genovese, *Roll Jordan Roll: The World the Slaves Made* (New York: Vintage Books, 1976), p. 276.

14. Zora Neale Hurston to Mrs. Rufus Osgood Mason, October 15, 1931 (Alain Lock papers, Howard University).

15. Robert Hemenway, *Zora Neale Hurston: A Literary Biography* (Urbana: Univ. of Illinois Press, 1977), p. 193.

DUST TRACKS ON A ROAD: AN AUTOBIOGRAPHY (1942)

◆

Zora Hurston Sums Up
[Review of *Dust Tracks on a Road*]

PHIL STRONG

Zora Neale Hurston's father was the preacher and chief factotum of Eatonville, Fla., one of the few villages of, for, and by Negroes in the United States. The old man was a powerful preacher, and also a powerful man and husband; as a slave, says Zora, with the charming practicality which marks the manner of the whole book, he would have fetched a high price for stud stock. He could flatten people to the door either with his big fists or his hell-fire eloquence.

Zora had a good deal of her father's violence and more of her tiny mother's sensitivity, intelligence, and determination. These got her through school after a bitter struggle, then through Howard University and Barnard, and finally made her what she is, an outstanding anthropologist in the field of Negro folklore and other Negro cultures. She has surveyed everything from Afro-American songs to voodoo and left a mark on modern American music and reasonable accounts of the over-romanticized magics of the Haitians.

This book is more a summary than the autobiography it advertises itself as being. It is a delightful one and wise one, full of humor, color, and good sense. It is told in exactly the right manner, simply and with candor, with a seasoning—not overdone—of the marvelous locutions of the imaginative field nigger. Miss Hurston explains that there are white niggers and black niggers; being a nigger is a matter of character rather than color among the Negroes.

After Zora's mother died her father married a fat shrew who wanted to make the social jump of being the preacher's wife. The stepmother was jealous of the children and drove them from home, one by one, including Zora who was still in her earliest teens. The girl held "maiding" jobs, but very briefly because of her fondness for books and children. These tastes conflicted with her allotted labors virtually to the exclusion of the latter and Zora moved on and on. Finally, she caught on as maid to the leading lady in a tour-

Reprinted from *Saturday Review of Literature* (28 November 1942): 6–7.

ing comic opera company, learned manicuring, and manicured her way through Howard.

She had learned that if one wanted to go to school the thing to do was to go to school, so she went on to Barnard, became Fanny Hurst's secretary and a favorite of Franz Boas's, and thereafter made her way in research on fellowships and the five books which precede this one. She might have taken either of two attitudes from these experiences; either an arrogant, self-made Negro attitude, or the conventional bitter and downtrodden one. She takes neither because she does not see that she was under any special disadvantage, and in the end she has no reason for bitterness. This text indicates that anyone who tries to down-tread Zora Neale Hurston had better wear thick-soled boots.

The race-consciousness that spoils so much Negro literature is completely absent here. Miss Hurston is less impressed by her own color than most Aryan redheads. She gives in one chapter to "My People" perhaps the most sensible passage on the subject that has ever been written. She agrees with Booker T. Washington that if the stuff is in you it is likely to come out and that if it isn't it doesn't make any difference whether you are white, black, green, or cerise. Some people, she says, have made a whole career out of moaning, "My people! My people!" She thinks they would have been better engaged in some useful labor. The only thing she claims for the Negro is perhaps a little more capacity for fancy and enthusiasm than the average white man possesses.

The most amusing chapter is Miss Hurston's delightfully frank treatise on love. It makes sense, but few people have had the reckless heroism to come out with it. She has had one "great" love and still has it; she doesn't know yet how it is going to come out, since the chosen gentleman is jealous of her work, as well as of all other gentlemen discovered in even remote proximity to Zora. Miss Hurston, with a prescience of trouble, has tried to break herself of the man several times without success. Occasionally she feels like being in love with someone else, incidentally—and is, briefly. When these unfortunate swains remind her of tender passages she is all too often feeling like "a charter member of the Union League Club" (this may be a slander) and the recalled endearments are "the third day of Thanksgiving turkey hash."

The conclusion is:

> Love is a funny thing; love is a blossom—
> If you want your finger bit poke it at a possum.

It may be judged that the book is rich in humor and that is true; it is real humor—the humor of character, from the old deacon who prays, "Oh, Lawd, I got something to ask You, but I know You can't do it," to Zora's own feud, nourished through the years and beyond all scholarship and honors, with her gross stepmother. The old lady, at last reports, was in the hospital with some malignant growth on her neck—Miss Hurston says, quite frankly and honestly, that she wishes the woman had two necks.

She has, too, a philosophic feeling for the statement of her friend, Ethel Waters, "Don't care how good the music is, Zora, you can't dance on every set."

It is a fine, rich autobiography, and heartening to anyone, white, black, or tan.

[Review of *Dust Tracks on a Road*]

W. Edward Farrison

This is not a great autobiography, but it is a worthwhile book. It is the story of a Negro woman whose talents, professional training, and opportunities have enabled her to view many phases of life steadily and understandingly, and it is fully possessed of human interest. Everything in it is interestingly presented, whether fact or fancy, and there is much of both in it. Perhaps more illustrative of the latter than the material in the chapter entitled "Figure and Fancy" is the account of the twelve visions of destiny first referred to near the end of the preceding chapter on "The Inside Search." There are some references to these visions here and there in the remainder of the book, but not all of them are ever singularized. They remain not only indistinct but elusive, though perhaps this is as matters should be since they were only visions.

Miss Hurston's life story, as she has told it, may be divided into three parts. The first is her childhood and its world, to which the first five chapters of the book are devoted. The second is the story of her struggles and her achievement of some success as a research student and an author. To this six chapters are devoted. Finally, there is in the last five chapters some record of her mature experiences with people and things and of her reflections on them.

Everywhere in the first part details are vividly and zestfully, if often briefly, portrayed. There are details not only of the author's own life as a child but also of the life around her. In setting forth these details she usually left more to the reader's imagination than Mr. J. Saunders Redding did in several places in *No Day of Triumph*, which is partly autobiographical, but in some places she did not leave very much more. Two instances of what may be called an over-supply of details may be found on the last two pages of the chapter on "My Folks."

Although Miss Hurston has insisted that the story of her success is no Cinderella story, it does resemble that heroine's story to an appreciable extent, as Miss Hurston is too much of the student of life to have missed noting. Certainly, there was no fairy overseeing her destiny; but almost always, it seems, when she gravely needed sympathy and assistance, she found herself in contact with those who were willing as well as able to help her. Proof of this

Reprinted from *Journal of Negro History* 28.3 (July 1943): 352–55. © 1943 The Journal of Negro History. Reprinted by permission of the journal.

fact is found in her acknowledgment of a large number of benefactors of one kind or another, from "the Second in Command," the matron under whom she spent a part of her childhood in a school in Jacksonville, Florida, to the patron on Park Avenue in New York (for whom Langston Hughes eventually proved to be insufficiently "primitive"). Unlike Cinderella, however, Miss Hurston possessed both intelligence and genius enough always to seize opportunity by the forelock.

In setting forth her reflections on people and things Miss Hurston wrote frankly and often amusingly, as she did in presenting matters of fact. But from such chapters as "My People! My People!," "Religion," and "Looking Things Over" one can hardly miss getting the impression that she has left much to be thought over and said clearly in the future. There is, to be sure, considerable truth in her arguments concerning the race problem—as there usually is on the several sides of all troublesome questions. This truth, however, can make a much greater claim to interest because of the author's manner of expression than because of novelty, even when her views are casually presented, as some are by way of comment on an incident which took place in a Washington barber shop where she worked as a manicurist while she was a student at Howard University.

As a child Miss Hurston was brought up to strict observance of the Baptist forms of Christianity. As a social anthropologist she has studied the history of religions, and her views have been broadened by her studies. Apparently, she has come to recognize the good as well as the merely conventional in many faiths but is yet without a rationale for her personal beliefs. The mixture of agnosticism, positivism, and pantheism in the last few paragraphs of the chapter on religion can hardly be considered that.

Dust Tracks on a Road is not a long narrative. With its easy, colloquial style it moves along so rapidly that one need not take much more than an evening to read it. Even so, the book is as long as it is because in it Miss Hurston has done at least a noticeable amount of hash-warming. She has represented much of the folk material she had previously used in *Jonah's Gourd Vine* (1934) and *Mules and Men* (1935). Hash-warming, of course, is not necessarily bad; it depends very much upon the original quality of the hash and the skill of the cook, and in this instance the cook was indeed skillful enough to keep the dish from tasting absolutely stale. Anyway, respectable examples of this kind of literary cookery are easy to find among authors much older than Miss Hurston including the late James Weldon Johnson.

Those who are interested in matters of usage, especially those of the purist persuasion, will find many objectionable little things in Miss Hurston's diction and style. Indeed, there are many matters of usage which could have been advantageously as well as easily improved. This, however, does not apply to the racy folk idioms and figures which Miss Hurston has used so freely. Whatever these may want of "correctness" or refinement is compensated by their simplicity, freshness, and vigor. Moreover, they are an integral part of Miss Hurston's style, which is, presumably, intentionally familiar; and it can hardly be divested of them without losing much of its gusto and individuality. All things considered, thus far Miss Hurston has rendered a good account of herself; but there still lies, one hopes, a long stretch of untracked road ahead of her. Perhaps one may take it that the familiar serial promise "To be continued" is implied at the bottom of her last page.

Zora Neale Hurston's *Dust Tracks:* Autobiography and Artist Novel

PHILLIP A. SNYDER

This is all hear-say. . . . I am of the word-changing kind.[1]

DUST TRACKS

"Don't you want me to go a piece of the way with you?" offered the child Zora Neale Hurston to the white travelers who passed her Eatonville house in their automobiles and carriages on the road to Orlando (*Dust Tracks,* 34). This interrogative invitation reflects the invitation that she, through her writing, continues to make to her many readers. Like the vanishing hitchhiker of folk-lore fame, Zora seems to charm her way into our vehicles, amusing us with her self-assurance and regaling us with her wide narrative repertoire for part of the way, only to disappear just when we think we are getting to know her fully but, we eventually realize, well before we reach our destination or truly understand and appreciate our passenger's identity. We are left with a vague sense of having made fleeting contact with someone wonderful and other-worldly, someone who seems real enough but who always slips from our grasp despite our attempts to keep her seat-belted in our scholarly cars for the dura-tion of the journeys we want her to make with us. As a textual trickster, a shape-shifting African-American Hoodoo woman writer and scholar, the hitchhiking Hurston refuses to ride in anyone's vehicle exclusively or to take a trip according to someone else's itinerary.

Nevertheless, like Alice Walker, who made her famous 1973 pilgrimage to the segregated cemetery in Fort Pierce, Florida, the Garden of Heavenly Rest, to place an appropriate marker over Hurston's previously unmarked grave, most of us who read Hurston's writing still want to make our own pil-grimages "in search of our mother's gardens" and to erect our own memorial epitaphs over Hurston's literary remains as a way of encompassing the signif-icance of her life and work.[2] However, again like Walker, we find it impossi-

This essay was written specifically for this volume and is published here by permission of the author.

ble to determine the exact locus for that memorial because Hurston's life and work will tolerate no final resting place, however festooned with flower or granite or scholarly tributes, for Hurston's life and work celebrate travel over arrival, motion over stasis, possibilities over probabilities, dialogic over monologic, and infinity over totality.

Accordingly, Hurston left us with perhaps the most felicitous title ever for an autobiography, *Dust Tracks on a Road,* a title that privileges the traces, rather than the substance, of a self and a life and that, in a gesture that anticipates poststructural theory, defers the closure of the absent signified, Hurston's actual self and life, in favor of the play of the signifier, the textual dust tracks she has made on her life's road. As Roland Barthes reminds us, "The *I* which writes the text . . . is never more than a paper-*I*."[3] Indeed, the title turns more on the trope of metonymy than on metaphor, for Hurston's autobiography seems much more interested in figures of association than in figures of equivalence; the dust tracks associated with Hurston mark her absence, of course, not her presence, and mock our attempts to track her down using their vanishing traces no matter how persistently we cruise along the roads where we expect to pick up her elusive, hitchhiking figure. As Barthes also notes, "The logic regulating the Text is not comprehensive . . . but metonymic; the activity of associations, contiguities, carryings-over coincides with a liberation of symbolic energy." Thus, *Dust Tracks* functions poorly when read as an equivalent (re)presentation of Hurston's self and life but functions well when read as a fictive narrative associated with that self and life, an autobiographical act that is as much production as product, as much nurture as nature, as much convention as creation, and as much imagination as memory.

Indeed, Hurston's autobiography takes place on an open road, with a multitude of speaking subjects making the textual tracks along it, constantly intersecting both themselves and other, alternate routes; paradoxically, her autobiography undercuts the search for identity at the same time it undertakes that search, and it partakes of traditional autobiographical conventions at the same time it innovates and fictionalizes them. As both autobiography and artist novel, *Dust Tracks* invites multiple readings of the figure we call Zora Neale Hurston, none of which can support itself suitably enough to be called definitive because there is no limit to the theories with which we can construct our readings and (de)construct other readings. The interaction among the various readings creates a kind of Hurston network we can access and engage infinitely while our conversations with her texts and with each other multiply and intersect, especially as the dusty roads of Hurston's day give way to our contemporary theoretical superhighways.

AUTOBIOGRAPHY

What if there is no me like my statue? . . . My real self had escaped him. (*Dust Tracks,* 26, 188)

Hurston's question here articulates a fundamental dilemma for many autobiographers, particularly her contemporaries and predecessors. Most of them, naively believing in their ability to (re)present an authentic self and life through writing, still acknowledged the difficulties inherent in such an endeavor, being particularly anxious regarding the possibility of creating a textual "statue" of themselves that did not truly correspond to their unique internal vision of themselves. Today we take the impossibility of this kind of autobiographical project for granted, accepting the inevitability of the "real" self's escape and even questioning whether such a unique, coherent, definitive self exists at all. We assume that the autobiographical self and life will escape not only the readers of autobiography but also the autobiographers themselves. As critic Terry Eagleton notes,

> Since language is something I am made out of, rather than merely a convenient tool I use, the whole idea that I am a stable, unified entity must also be a fiction. Not only can I never be fully present to you, but I can never be fully present to myself either.[5]

We refuse to privilege autobiography as an authoritative discourse that provides a unique insider's look at a self and a life unmediated by the many constraints of language expression. Hurston's choice of metaphor to (re)present her autobiographical project, a sculptured self-portrait, indicates her sense of herself as an artist who creates an artificial "double" for public consumption and acknowledges her understanding that she must use all the same tools and materials for the construction of her double that she would for any other creative artifact. The lines between autobiography and fiction thus become unavoidably blurred for her as well as for her readers. Recent studies of *Dust Tracks* reflect the ambiguity and complexity inherent in Hurston's autobiography and bear witness to the variety of approaches to the text based on different theoretical assumptions about autobiography, although virtually all of these studies are based on a naive view that accepts the existence of an authentic self and life and acknowledges the relevance of the autobiographical pact; collectively, they demonstrate the healthy, active condition of Hurston scholarship. While they address many issues, these recent *Dust Tracks* studies tend to focus on the problematics of the following general topics, most often as they interrelate: textual production and publication, historical accuracy, autobiographical narrative technique, and self-construction in terms of gender and race.

Claudine Raynaud's " 'Rubbing a Paragraph with a Soft Cloth': Muted Voices and Editorial Constraints in *Dust Tracks on a Road*,"[6] undoubtedly the best article on the publication of *Dust Tracks*, traces the changes from the first-draft manuscript to its first publication through the more recent editions, which include supplementary information in an effort to restore some of the material that Hurston and her editors excised. As Raynaud's article demonstrates, a study of the omitted sections emphasizes the complexity of her resistance to the white publishing world, and the ways in which she eventually complied. It stresses how the creation of her fictive self is not solely a self-conscious textual strategy, but also a product of her historical position as a black female writer.[7]

Raynaud discusses the manuscript history of *Dust Tracks;* the various editorial interventions; the language alterations to silence many of Hurston's voices—the erotic voice, the black woman's voice, the voice of excess, and the political voice; and the alterations of structure and meaning. Her article compares the problematics of *Dust Tracks*'s publication, especially the tension between Hurston and her white editors and intended white audience, with the production of nineteenth-century slave narratives, concluding that the same mediating forces are at work: "The editor (the publisher, the guarantor, the patron) carries on, acting as authenticator; he or she actively competes with the author for control over the production of the text."[8]

Certainly the erasure under which Hurston wrote *Dust Tracks* was defined largely by the various editorial intrusions that attempted to set her autobiography in a congenial context for profitable public consumption by the dominant white culture; as Raynaud persuasively argues, this assertion of editorial authorization and control seriously compromised an already problematic autobiographical text.[9] However, while Raynaud acknowledges that autobiography consists of a "fiction of the self," her assumptions about autobiography also seem to suggest that autobiographical "authenticity" according to an author's "original intent" or "self-conscious textual strategy" may be possible to some degree, that, in theory at least, autobiography may not necessarily be mediated by the inescapable influence of outside cultural forces.[10] On the contrary, autobiography always depends on the complex cultural constraints of the sign systems that circumscribe the constructional codes by which autobiographical production takes place; indeed, these external cultural codes determine the very idea of autobiography. Without the editorial intrusions Raynaud rightly critiques in her article, *Dust Tracks* might have been a different text, but it would not have escaped the mediation of external cultural constraints, nor would Hurston's expression have been completely self-conscious or self-controlled.

Many articles on *Dust Tracks* note, at least in passing, the various authorial inconsistencies and omissions that raise some significant questions regarding the relative sincerity and authenticity of Hurston's autobiographical pact with herself and her readers to tell the "truth" in her autobiography as honestly and openly as she can. Numerous studies have shown *Dust Tracks* to be a highly unreliable account of Hurston's life and work. For example, Harper's 1991 edition of *Dust Tracks* includes a fairly extensive Hurston "chronology" in the appendix, as if to set the historical record straight as a way of completing and correcting the autobiography that precedes it. Further, Robert E. Hemenway's *Zora Neale Hurston: A Literary Biography,* the standard Hurston biography, functions as a kind of historical and biographical counterpoint to Hurston's autobiography, as his well-researched, scholarly treatise covers the same ground as *Dust Tracks* but with much more comprehensive detail. In a strange twist on Raynaud's concept of the editor-author competition for authority over the autobiographical African-American text, Hemenway competes with Hurston for authority over her self and life. Hemenway's biography purports to be the complete *histoire* (history) of Hurston's incomplete *récit* (narrative) of her life and work; the obvious sincerity of his biographical pact with his readers contrasts the apparent insincerity of her autobiographical pact, and his commitment to truth telling overshadows her preoccupation with "lying sessions." In short, the biography, inscribed as "fact," seems to expose the relative inadequacy of the autobiography, inscribed as "fiction," at the same time it tries to explain the possible reasons behind that inadequacy. However, historical "facts" always become so subordinated within the imaginative constructs that order and assign them meaning that they lose much of their authoritative, truth-telling power, so Hemenway's biography may be as "fictional" with respect to the narrative codes governing its construction as *Dust Tracks.*

The inadequacies Hurston critics cite regarding *Dust Tracks* tend to revolve around Hurston's refusal to unify her autobiography structurally and thematically or to reveal everything truthfully or to acknowledge fully the racial dimensions of her self and life. In his chapter "Ambiguities of Self, Politics of Race" Hemenway makes the following assessment:

> *Dust Tracks* can be a discomfiting book, and it has probably harmed Hurston's reputation. Like much of her career, it often appears contradictory. Zora seems to be both an advocate for the universal, demonstrating that this black woman does not look at the world in racial terms, and the celebrant of a unique ethnic upbringing in an all-black village. . . . When Zora selects a story from the repertoire of her life and narrates it for her audience, *Dust Tracks* succeeds. It fails when she tries to shape the narrative into a statement of universality, manipulating events and ideas in order to suggest that the personal voyage of Zora Neale Hurston is something more than the special experience of one black woman.[11]

Hemenway's assessment of Hurston's dilemma—"How can Zora Hurston express herself as both one of the folk and someone special?"[12]— depends on his particular view of Hurston's attraction to universality, which he depicts as revolving around her repudiation of race and her assertion of individuality. Ironically, African-American autobiography has tended to align notions of universality with race, not with individualism, as each exemplar of the genre has functioned simultaneously as a (re)presentation of the whole African-American experience and of the individual who exemplifies in particular the general patterns of the race. In *Dust Tracks,* Hurston constructs an autobiography that proposes to be radically symbolic in its polyphonic presentation of its autobiographical subject, a figure of multiple forms and many cultural connections, who unsuccessfully strives to disavow these forms and connections by constantly reiterating its individual uniqueness. Hurston's dilemma between individualism and racial identity here dramatizes the identity crisis inherent in autobiography: the self that strives to be one within the confines of the text always projects multiple, contradictory selves instead.

Paola Boi's "Zora Neale Hurston's *Autobiographie Fictive:* Dark Tracks on the Canon of a Female Writer," Kathleen Hassall's "Text and Personality in Disguise and in the Open: Zora Neale Hurston's *Dust Tracks on a Road,*" and Raynaud's "Autobiography as a 'Lying' Session: Zora Neale Hurston's *Dust Tracks on a Road*" all explore the narrative techniques Hurston uses to display her multifaceted textual self; they differ in their theoretical approaches to *Dust Tracks* as autobiography but share a preoccupation with those performative aspects of the text that "signify" Hurston's self and life.[13] Boi's article, the most theoretically sophisticated of the three, addresses the following questions: What is the function of the autobiographical text within the whole production of a writer? How can we reconcile the internal formal structures of literary language with their external, referential, and public effects? Can we consider autobiography a distinct unit of referential meaning? Is internal meaning an outside reference?[14]

Boi's poststructural discussion of *Dust Tracks* as *autobiographie fictive* in light of these questions cannot be synthesized easily because of its already dense complexity, but some of her key points include the following:

> —Boi notes that Hurston's *autobiographie fictive* concerns "the various self-representations and metaphors that the writer projects, the relationship between these images and the reader produced *through* the written text."
> —With reference to the definition of African-American "signifying" as articulated by Henry Louis Gates Jr. in *The Signifying Monkey,* Boi argues that "*Dust Tracks* originally derives from a 'matrix of literary discontinuities,' in which the author signifies upon communication as a literary discourse, upon herself as a black writer, and upon autobiography as a literary genre."
> —With reference to the numerous pluralities, gaps, masks, traces, ambiguities, and the like evident throughout *Dust Tracks* as a hybrid example of imaginative autobiographical discourse, Boi concludes that "The imprint of [Hurston's] artistic self, *la trace de l'écriture,* runs parallel to her personal trace—elusive, hidden, inscrutable, flashing from the pages only in glimpses or guesses. . . . Self-revelation becomes an act of self-deception, an attempt to think of truth as originating from its opposite."

—Thus, according to Boi, "Hurston's text is self-destructive, displaced by an infinite series of images, metaphors, and rhetorical reversals that keep it suspended between truth and its own negation. . . . Signifying, the lying contest, the bright exercise of similes and metaphors—these are Hurston's weapons of feminine and literary power."[15]

Boi's brilliant analysis of *Dust Tracks* as an infinitely transgressive autobiographical text that subverts the limited literary and cultural contexts in which most readers and scholars have placed it redefines the very grounds for its analysis and displaces readings that call its complexities inadequacies and its pluralities fragments. Likewise, Hassall and Raynaud examine the dynamics of Hurston's signifying narrative to shift the discussion away from a naive, simplistic view of autobiography toward a view that acknowledges autobiography's complexity as a highly mediated discourse. Hassall describes Hurston as a performance artist in the folk tradition from which Hassall traces Hurston's strategies for disguising herself through fictionalized self-invention: "By generating enigmatic, inconsistent, multifarious performance Hurstons, she thwarted attempts to define her, and some of her secrets are still her own."[16] Raynaud also discusses the influence of folklore on *Dust Tracks,* particularly the narrative power of the "lying session" convention, arguing that Hurston allows the community voice to dominate the personal voice and so "subverts the confessional goal of autobiography."[17] Hurston, claims Raynaud, thus presents a suspicious autobiographical pact: "Everything in *Dust Tracks* points to the subversion of the autobiographical mode, which becomes invested with competing discourses—folkloric material, tall tales, residual structure from the spiritual autobiography."[18] Unlike Boi, Raynaud and Hassall naively base their analyses of *Dust Tracks* on their assumption of a sincere autobiographical pact that Hurston violates and on the existence of an authentic autobiographical self that she persists in hiding or disguising; they, like most scholars of *Dust Tracks,* miss the point Boi articulates so persuasively regarding the dialogic nature of Hurston's multiple selves in *Dust Tracks:* "Hurston does not have a monolithic truth to offer the reader on a silver platter to be consumed decorously; her authenticity is attested to by her ambiguity itself."[19]

Most articles on *Dust Tracks* address the influence of gender and race on Hurston's self-portrait and acknowledge her ambivalence regarding her gender and racial connections, particularly in her assertion of a unique individuality that purports to have transcended somehow the limitations of gender and race. In "Becoming 'Colored': The Self-Authorized Language of Difference in Zora Neale Hurston," Priscilla Wald discusses Hurston's presentation of the "stock scene of racial discovery,"[20] in particular Janie's "mirror stage" drama from *Their Eyes Were Watching God,* in which Janie recognizes herself as black for the first time by viewing a photograph of herself among a group of white children. Wald describes this "stock scene" as defining the marginal black self solely by contrast with the dominant white other and, thus, as constructive of a double-consciousness that produces multiple selves, subjective and objective, which characterize Hurston's self-expression. In "My Statue, My Self: Autobiographical Writings of Afro-American Women," Elizabeth Fox-Genovese summarizes the multiple connections that create African-American women's autobiography:

> The account of the black woman's self cannot be divorced from the history of that self or the history of the people among whom it took shape. It also cannot be divorced from the language through which it is represented, or from the readers of other classes and races who not only lay claim to it but inscribe it in a culture that for each of us is only partially our own. For black women autobiographers, the gap between the self and the language in which it is inscribed looms especially large and remains fraught with struggle.[21]

According to Fox-Genovese, *Dust Tracks* should be read in this manner regardless of Hurston's attempts to assert a self-representation detached from cultural constraints; Fox-Genovese ascribes Hurston's difficulty with the African-American autobiographical mode in *Dust Tracks* to the "deadlock between her commitment to her roots as a black woman in a black community and her commitment to transcending all social and gender roots in her craft."[22] Nellie McKay, in " 'Crayon Enlargements of Life': Zora Neale Hurston's *Their Eyes Were Watching God* as Autobiography," uses Janet Varner Gunn's theory of autobiography as an "outside in, not inside out" discourse to explore the relationship between "author Hurston, the writerly self, and fictional Janie, the speakerly self, creating a common text delineating a black female self-in-writing."[23] McKay questions the traditional "sovereignty of the private 'I' " and bases her study of Hurston on Gunn's theory:

> Autobiography, Gunn suggests, is not the mask that hides the true self, but the revelation of an unalienated, *displayed* or representative self joined to the world through an understanding of shared humanity. Instead of "the private act of a self writing, autobiography becomes the cultural act of a self reading" against the background of time, place, race, class, gender, and the other variables that define individual members of particular groups.[24]

Other writers addressing gender and race in *Dust Tracks* include Eva Lennox Birch on how gender and race impact autobiography in *Dust Tracks* and in Buchi Emecheta's *Head above Water;* Gabrielle P. Foreman on the influence early African-American women's autobiographies had on Hurston; James Krasner on the interaction of male and female autobiographical modes in Hurston; Lucinda H. MacKethan on the inheritance of "mother wit" in

Hurston; Deborah G. Plant on the influence of the African-American folk sermon on Hurston; and Cheryl A. Wall on Hurston's narrative strategies for empowerment.[25] These studies of the cultural contexts within and from which Hurston constructed her self and her life in *Dust Tracks,* particularly as related to gender and race, all refute the notion that Hurston could create an autobiography that could be both written and read free from the cultural constraints that circumscribe that autobiography; in fact, these constraints are what make Hurston's self and life possible, for without them there would be no *Dust Tracks* for Hurston or for her readers.

ARTIST NOVEL

I am her friend, and her tongue is in my mouth. (*Dust Tracks,* 178)

Hurston's status as a (re)presentative African-American woman artist may be unparalleled for her influence on the many contemporary African-American women writers who hearken back to her as their pioneering role model and inspiration; their work features correspondences to Hurston's that sometimes seem to speak as with Hurston's tongue or to walk as in her tracks. Constructed according to a traditional bildungsroman and *künstlerroman* initiation and development pattern, *Dust Tracks* functions as an exemplar of the genre for twentieth-century African-American women writers, especially when set alongside Hurston's other, more famous artist novel, *Their Eyes Were Watching God,* in its appropriation of traditional male codes and its simultaneous assertion of revisionary female codes. Accordingly, *Dust Tracks* adheres to the following generic structure:

—Protagonist, a child of sensibility, grows up in the country or a provincial town.
—Protagonist experiences constraints, especially from the family and particularly from the father.
—Protagonist's schooling is inadequate.
—Protagonist leaves repressive atmosphere and goes to the city.
—Protagonist's real education begins.
—Protagonist has two love affairs, one that debases and one that exalts.
—Protagonist begins soul-searching and accommodating the self to the modern world.
—Protagonist leaves adolescence and finds maturity; the initiation is complete.
—Protagonist returns home and demonstrates newfound maturity.[26]

This conventional pattern also depends on the presence of the following ideals: (1) the ideal of self-formation through educational, cultural, and sexual experiences; (2) the ideal of individual uniqueness against a broad cultural background; (3) the developmental focus on a single life; and (4) the implied potential for completing the developmental ideal.[27] In addition, as Carl D. Malmgren notes, the initiation and development pattern for the artist-apprentice includes special "marking" features designed to distinguish the artist-apprentice as singular and unique:

1. The artist's name—the name itself or the act of naming sets the artist apart from the ordinary, everyday world.
2. His appearance, demeanor, carriage—certain physiological oddities serve as signs of the artist's difference, queerness, uniqueness.
3. His parentage—the artist's parents invariably reflect his contradictory traits, his divided self, his dubious heritage.[28]

Dust Tracks certainly depicts Hurston's self as unique from her miraculous birth onward and her life as a progressive struggle toward independent self-actualization and mature artistic expression; in addition, by appropriating white male developmental ideals, *Dust Tracks* asserts both Hurston's right and potential as an African-American woman to succeed, even according to the traditional pattern from which she has been excluded because of her gender and race. Ironically, she wants to make her emancipation proclamation in the form of a conventional autobiography only so she can free herself from that convention by demonstrating her ultimate developmental transcendence. For example, Hurston acknowledges her mentors from the various subcultures in which she finds a place so she can then demonstrate her eventual independence from them, and she leaves certain gaps in her narrative, such as her refusal to describe her marriages in detail, so she can circumvent the generic expectations of her readers, white and black. By estranging her textual self from the gendered and racial communities that have been oppressed by the overall developmental and initiation pattern she follows, Hurston attempts to (de)center *Dust Tracks* from both the mainstream and the margins. By signifying off the traditional constructional codes of the bildungsroman and *künstler-roman*, Hurston sets the tone for further appropriations and revisions, opening the way for the autobiographical narratives that come after hers.

The logocentric power of white, male, upper-class discourse to construct a self-privileging world—socially, institutionally, and artistically reinforced as naturally or divinely ordained—is the cultural story against which the narratives of Zora, Janie, Celie, and Sethe run counter in *Dust Tracks, Their Eyes Were Watching God, The Color Purple,* and *Beloved.*[29] Their personal narratives display an emancipating discourse that constructs an alternative cultural history and system built by other voices speaking from the margins of that dominant culture: African-American, female, and lower class. Like their predecessors Zora and Janie, both Celie and Sethe want front-porch, story-telling status, a material locus from which to enact a future, as well as a past, for themselves and their sisters. The front porch (re)presents an idealized material culture whose logos is diversity, whose ethos is community, whose politics is liberation, and whose economics is a benign capitalism of exchange; it is a place where, in Bjørnar Olsen's words, "power can be inscribed," but it is also a place "outside the power of language"[30] because its discourse is based on a polyphonic performance in which everyone takes part and no single voice remains privileged for very long. Virginia Woolf rightly calls for a room of one's own; Zora, Janie, Celie, and Sethe also call for a move onto the front porch and for a feminist transformation of that porch as a locus for productive discourse.

At the intersections of this autobiography and these three novels, as on a figurative front porch, the isolated voices of their respective protagonists harmonize into a powerful, dialogic discourse community they do not fully realize alone. Like Celie and her sister, Nettie, who are not able at first to actually correspond with one another because of Mr. _____'s secret hoarding of Nettie's letters, all four protagonists speak and write correspondingly under the repressive threat of exposure and erasure; they jointly perceive a material, textual self that incorporates both the self-assertion and self-denial present in Celie's own self-depiction in her first letter to God: the crossed-out "I am."[31] Nevertheless, all four also tell a story that coheres in its common emancipation theme, enabling each to come out from under racist, masculinist, capitalistic erasure and expose the dynamics of her repression under an alien discourse of race, gender, and class. Zora, Janie, Celie, and Sethe all speak and act against this discourse, seeking both independence and success from within its strictures, to seize the material ground of their own liberation. Zora desires an economic and intellectual independence; Janie wants a cooperative, peartree marriage and a place among the men at the checkerboard or on the front porch; Celie yearns for sexual and economic liberation with "Folkspants, Unlimited" in sizes to fit everyone; and Sethe seeks familial forgiveness and a reason to believe in a future.

Most of all, however, these protagonists desire to narrate, because their lives, like Scheherazade's from *Arabian Nights*, depend on the stories they tell. Silence signifies death to them, while speech and writing signify life; the self, as they demonstrate, must be told to have significance. Like a "talking cure" or a confession, the narratives they construct about their selves and their lives—their autobiographies, in effect—liberate them from the external, objectifying imprisonment of Michel Foucault's guard-tower notion of the critical gaze because they construct an alternative, inward edifice of textuality in which the self articulates, critiques, and acts out its own drama of signification, which opposes the outside totalization of "discipline and punish."[32] Zora, Janie, Celie, and Sethe want to overturn what Susan Gubar calls the Pygmalion myth of male creativity, in which logocentrism equals phallocentrism and women are reduced to "blank pages":[33] men write, while women are written upon. In this sense, the telling becomes more important than the living; in fact, the telling may *be* the living. As Tzvetan Todorov writes of Odysseus—"There are two Odysseuses . . . one has the adventures, the other tells them"[34]—so we could write of Zora, Janie, Celie, and Sethe. We could also write of them and their individual quests that they, like Odysseus, do not pursue final destinations but journeys marked by various ports of narrative call, such as the places from which they speak: "Home is not [Odysseus's] deepest desire," Todorov argues; "his desire is that of the narrator . . . [who] desires to tell."[35] What absences Zora, Janie, Celie, and Sethe experience once they actually arrive at their homes—Zora's isolated and insistent individualism, Tea Cake's death, Shug Avery's departure, and Beloved's exorcism—they mediate by the presence of narrative, privileging the signifier and deferring the signified. As Janie says, "Dis house ain't so absent of things lak it used tuh be. . . . It's full uh thoughts."[36]

Their Eyes Were Watching God, as Janie's autobiography, thus constitutes the courtroom testimony Hurston briefly reports Janie giving near the end of the novel; it fills that empty space left in the narrative by the trial's capital witness not being allowed to speak for herself in the novel's penultimate scene. Janie's back-porch narrative to her friend Pheoby also confronts indirectly the gossipy, front-porch condemnation she intuits at the beginning of the novel as she walks down the road, finally returning home after burying her husband Tea Cake. Her neighbors, themselves repressed daily by race, gender, and class, all become, in the evening, powerful front-porch sitters and talkers whose discourse attempts to totalize and destroy Janie. In Hurston's words,

> It was the time to hear things and talk. These sitters had been tongueless, earless, eyeless conveniences all day long. Mules and other brutes had occupied their skins. But now, the sun and the bossmen were gone, so the skins felt powerful and human. They became lords of sounds and lesser things. They passed notions through their mouths. They sat in judgement.[37]

Janie's neighbors and Pheoby thus (re)present, respectively, yet another jury and judge she must face with her testimonial narrative in defense of her life; this time, however, as Susan Glaspell might say, it is an informal jury of her peers, not a formal collection of 12 white men presided over by a manipulative judge who must find her innocent or guilty. Ironically, it is a racist, sexist system of justice that frees Janie the first time; her own peers, had they been allowed to testify in court, would have certainly condemned her. Hurston writes, "They were all against her, she could see. . . . They were there with their tongues cocked and loaded . . . the only killing tool they are allowed to use in the presence of white folks."[38] Their dissatisfaction with the court's affirmation of Janie's innocence affects her almost as much as a guilty verdict would have, because, as Hurston writes, "It was not death [Janie] feared. It was misunderstanding."[39] Janie's desire for understanding fuels her narrative and undercuts the significance of white "justice"; like the splendid funeral she arranges for Tea Cake, Janie's narrative attempts to produce for her discourse community an authentic, readable representation of both her life and her love for her husband. This is why the court's verdict has limited power to emancipate Janie; she must be set free within her own community—within her own race, gender, and class. Her narrative is calculated to redefine that community's codification of social-sexual mores and to proselytize Pheoby as her spokesperson. At the end of her story, Janie gives the following instructions:

> Ah know all dem sitters-and-talkers gointuh worry they guts into fiddle strings till dey find out whut we been talkin' 'bout. Dat's all right, Pheoby, tell 'em. Dey gointuh make 'miration 'cause mah love didn't work lak they love, if dey ever had any. Then you must tell 'em dat love ain't somethin' lak uh grindstone dat's de same thing everywhere and do de same thing tuh everything it touch.[40]

This same ideology of individualism within the community underscores *The Color Purple*. Walker has acknowledged her debt to Hurston in many ways, especially by becoming herself a proselytizing "Pheoby" to match Hurston's "Janie" and also by signifying her own version of emancipation off of Hurston's; it is almost as though, by inscribing Hurston's absent tombstone and cultivating her spiritual mother's textual garden, Walker somehow hopes to recover the past and restore part of the African-American female canon we have lost. The novel's dedication and postscript, like bookends, circumscribe its production in this tradition of spiritual recovery: first, the dedication, *"To the Spirit:* / Without whose assistance / Neither this book / Nor I / Would have been / Written," and then the postscript, "I thank everybody in this book for coming. / A.W., author and medium."[41] Walker writes herself into existence at the same time Celie and Nettie write themselves, all three writing under the masculinist prohibition ascribed to the rapacious, incestuous stepfather Fonzo at the opening of the novel: "You better not never tell nobody but God. It'd kill your mammy."[42]

Their epistolary productions mediate the separation enforced by Fonzo and Mr. _____ because Nettie and Celie continue to write, despite the impossibility of receiving responses, to assert and reassert one another's existence through language. As Nettie promises Celie when they part, "Nothing but death can keep me from [writing]."[43] They resurrect themselves, each other, and their "mammy," as Walker resurrects Hurston; they even recover God from racism and sexism by their revisionary notions of divinity. However, their productions do not affect the community until they speak out of their silences, inviting other voices into their emancipation discourse, Shug and Samuel primarily but later even Mr. _____, who himself is (de)constructed and (re)written out of his violent sexism. Celie describes their front-porch conversations as a production of friendship and company: "He ain't Shug," Celie writes, "but he begin to be somebody I can talk to."[44] Celie's and Nettie's dual narratives construct a truly African-American text, which explores, as Henry Louis Gates Jr. describes it, the hyphen between the words *African* and *American:*[45] the hyphen is a "wild zone" of textuality where most anything is possible, a place whose traces are inscribed in Adam's and Tashi's facial scarification, a place where we, as readers, are invited to come face-to-face with them as other.

Like Adam and Tashi, Sethe and Paul D and Beloved are written upon, but their scarification (re)presents a different kind of trace—slavery, dehumanization, genocide, infanticide, disintegration, and so on—traces that the novel *Beloved* attempts to revise. Their bodies as texts signify their experience and their struggles to read it. Sethe's back scars parallel the narrative of externally determined self-identity that the Garners and the Schoolteacher try to inscribe on her psyche; her choice is whether to accept their "origin of meaning" or to (de)construct it to produce her own transcription. Here the reader, not the author, is privileged with the power of signification, so Sethe's back can become a chokecherry tree and Paul D's neck scars a necklace. There is no definitive, "correct" meaning, only paradox. As Toni Morrison explains to Bill Moyers, Sethe's killing of Beloved cannot be reduced by authorial intent or by simplistic ideologies of right and wrong: "Someone gave me the line for it at one time which I have found useful. 'It was the right thing [for her] to do, but she had no right to do it.' "[46] Thus Sethe cannot be freed from her guilt by Beloved's resurrection because Beloved does not intuitively understand and forgive as Sethe expects her to do; instead, she demands explanation and recompense from her mother, asserting herself as the other that cannot be totalized by maternal bonding. Sethe is freed only by becoming her own "best thing" in the telling of *Beloved* and also by becoming part of a present-tense story,[47] which privileges the future and not the past. Beloved is exorcised, first by Paul D and then by Ella's group of women, all of whom also reclaim Sethe and Denver by forcing them out from inside a haunted house onto the front porch of community.

Zora, Janie, Celie, and Sethe tell powerful, harrowing stories, and despite the taboo articulated thrice at the end of *Beloved*—"This is not a story to pass on"[48]—these *are* stories meant to be passed on, or as Paul D suggests, stories that should be placed beside one another. Like Janie and Hurston, who have passed their stories on to Pheoby and to Walker and, like Celie and Walker, to Sethe and Morrison, who have set their stories beside Janie's and Hurston's, we pass this autobiography and these three novels on to one another in classes and in conferences regardless, but still respective, of our own race, gender, and class. In this way, the discourse of the other—here, African-American, female, and lower class—can liberate us as well, inviting us onto the front porch of dialogic, even deconstructive, textual production.

As Timothy Yates reminds us, "Deconstruction opens text to new readings, situated in new areas of signification, examining meaning in terms of that which systems have obscured under writs of prohibition, precisely because they depend on them."[49] According to the philosopher Emmanuel Levinas, we look at one another, as if face-to-face, to celebrate our difference, not to assert our own autonomy by an unethical reduction of the other into the same. Levinas writes, "Experience, the idea of infinity, occurs in the relationship with the other. The idea of infinity is the social relationship."[50] Together, in such communal exchanges as these, we lay bare the repressive devices of our culture and of ourselves to confront one another's proclamations of self-emancipation as open texts inviting further reading on into infinity: stories to pass on.

INFINITE JOURNEYS

I know that nothing is destructible; things merely change forms. . . . I am one with the infinite and need no other assurance. (*Dust Tracks*, 202, 203)

Hurston's notion of the infinite here may not correspond exactly with Levinas's, but it nevertheless suggests her strong preference for infinity over totality in contemplating her present and her future as one of the "word-changing kind" (*Dust Tracks*, 19). As readers of Hurston's work, we transform her writing continually according to the reading practices we value without ever really bringing that writing to some fixed form of interpretation. In reading *Dust Tracks*, we seek a theory with the power to engage the elusive autobiographical figure of Zora Neale Hurston without (re)producing it, for we understand that such a (re)production would be unacceptable, even if it were not already impossible, because it would privilege totality over infinity and violate the ethics of our encounter with the other. As Foucault explains, "In writing the point is not to manifest or exalt the act of writing, nor is it to pin a subject within language; it is rather a question of creating a space into which the writing subject constantly disappears."[51] Our assurance, like Hurston's, should reside in our acceptance of the constant textual transformations that occur within the open spaces of our multiple readings of Hurston, whose autobiographical journey we attempt to trace through her dust tracks on a road.

Notes

1.   Zora Neale Hurston, *Dust Tracks on a Road* (1942), fwd. Maya Angelou (New York: Harper, 1991), 19. All references are to this edition and will be incorporated into the text.

2. Alice Walker, *In Search of Our Mother's Gardens: Womanist Prose* (New York: Harcourt, 1983).

3. Roland Barthes, "From Work to Text," in *Image—Music—Text,* trans. Stephen Heath (New York: Noonday, 1977), 161.

4. Ibid., 158.

5. Terry Eagleton, *Literary Theory: An Introduction* (Minneapolis: University of Minnesota Press, 1983), 130.

6. Claudine Raynaud, " 'Rubbing a Paragraph with a Soft Cloth:' Muted Voices and Editorial Constraints in *Dust Tracks on a Road,*" in *De/colonizing the Subject: The Politics of Gender in Women's Autobiography,* ed. Sidonie Smith and Julia Watson (Minneapolis: University of Minnesota Press, 1992), 130.

7. Ibid., 35.

8. Ibid., 56.

9. Ibid., 57

10. Ibid., 56, 35.

11. Robert E. Hemenway, *Zora Neale Hurston: A Literary Biography,* fwd. Alice Walker (Urbana: University of Illinois Press, 1977), 276–77.

12. Ibid., 283.

13. Paola Boi, "Zora Neale Hurston's *Autobiographie Fictive:* Dark Tracks on the Canon of a Female Writer," in *The Black Columbiad: Defining Moments in African-American Literature and Culture,* ed. Werner Sollors and Maria Diedrich (Cambridge, Mass.: Harvard University Press, 1994), 191–200. Kathleen Hassall, "Text and Personality in Disguise and in the Open: Zora Neale Hurston's *Dust Tracks on a Road,*" in *Zora in Florida,* ed. Steve and Seidel Glassman and Kathryn Lee (Orlando: University of South Florida Press, 1991), 159–73. Claudine Raynaud, "Autobiography as a 'Lying' Session: Zora Neale Hurston's *Dust Tracks on a Road,*" in *Black Feminist Criticism and Critical Theory,* ed. Joe Weixlmann and Houston A. Baker (Greenwood, Fla.: Penkevill Publishing, 1988), 111–38.

14. Boi, "Dark Tracks," 92–93.

15. Ibid., 193, 194, 196–97, 199.

16. Hassall, "Text and Personality," 171.

17. Raynaud, "Autobiography," 113.

18. Ibid., 131.

19. Boi, "Dark Tracks," 196.

20. Priscilla Wald, "Becoming 'Colored': The Self-Authorized Language of Difference in Zora Neale Hurston," *American Literary History* 2 (Spring 1990): 79.

21. Elizabeth Fox-Genovese, "My Statue, My Self: Autobiographical Writings of Afro-American Women," in *The Private Self: Theory and Practice of Women's Autobiographical Writings,* ed. Shari Benstock (Chapel Hill: University of North Carolina Press, 1988), 82–83.

22. Ibid., 83.

23. Nellie McKay, " 'Crayon Enlargements of Life': Zora Neale Hurston's *Their Eyes Were Watching God* as Autobiography," in *New Essays on "Their Eyes Were Watching God,"* ed. Michael Awkward (Cambridge, England: Cambridge University Press, 1990), 51.

24. Ibid., 52.

25. Eva Lennox Birch, "Autobiography: The Art of Self-Definition," in *Black Women's Writing,* ed. Gina Wisker (New York: St. Martin's, 1993), 127–45. Gabrielle P. Foreman, "Looking Back from Zora, or Talking Out of Both Sides of My Mouth for Those Who Have Two Ears," *Black American Literature Forum* 24 (1990): 649–66. James Krasner, "The Life of Women: Zora Neale Hurston and Female Autobiography," *Black American Literature Forum* 23 (Spring 1989): 113–26. Lucinda H. MacKethan, "Mother Wit: Humor in Afro-American Women's Autobiography," *Studies in American Humor* 4.1–2 (1985): 51–61. Deborah G. Plant, "The Folk Preacher and Folk Sermon Form in Zora Neale Hurston's *Dust Tracks on a Road,*" *Folklore Forum* 21.1 (1988): 3–19. Cheryl A. Wall, "*Mules and Men* and Women: Zora Neale

Hurston's Strategies of Narration and Visions of Female Empowerment," *Black American Literature Forum* 23 (Winter 1989): 661–80.

26. Jerome H. Buckley, *Season of Youth: The Bildungsroman from Dickens to Golding* (Cambridge, Mass.: Harvard University Press, 1974), 17–18. Karl D. Malmgren, " 'From Work to Text': The Modernist and Postmodernist *Künstlerroman*," *Novel* (Fall 1987): 6. Randolf P. Shaffner, *The Apprenticeship Novel: A Study of the "Bildungsroman" as a Regulative Type in Western Literature with a Focus on Three Classic Representatives by Goethe, Maugham, and Mann* (New York: Peter Lang, 1984), 17–19.

27. G. B. Tennyson, "The Bildungsroman in Nineteenth-Century English Literature," in *Medieval Epic to "Epic Theater" in Brecht,* ed. Rosario Armato and John Spalek (Los Angeles: University of Southern California Press, 1968), 136.

28. Malmgren, "From Work to Text," 6.

29. Zora Neale Hurston, *Their Eyes Were Watching God* (1937; rpt., Urbana: University of Illinois Press, 1978). Alice Walker, *The Color Purple* (New York: Pocket, 1982). Toni Morrison, *Beloved* (New York: Plume, 1987). All references are to these editions and will be incorporated into the text.

30. Bjørnar Olsen, "Roland Barthes: From Sign to Text," *Reading Material Culture: Structuralism, Hermeneutics and Post-Structuralism,* ed. Christopher Tilley (Cambridge, England: Blackwell, 1990), 197.

31. Walker, *The Color Purple,* 11.

32. Michel Foucault, *Discipline and Punish: The Birth of the Prison* (New York: Pantheon, 1978).

33. Susan Gubar, " 'The Blank Page' and Issues of Female Creativity," *Critical Inquiry* (Winter 1981): 243–63.

34. Tzvetan Todorov, *The Poetics of Prose,* trans. Richard Howard, fwd. Jonathan Culler (Ithaca, N.Y.: Cornell University Press, 1977), 62.

35. Ibid., 63.

36. Hurston, *Their Eyes,* 284.

37. Ibid., 9–10.

38. Ibid., 275.

39. Ibid., 279.

40. Ibid., 284.

41. Walker, *The Color Purple,* i, 253.

42. Ibid., 1.

43. Ibid., 26.

44. Ibid., 241.

45. Henry Louis Gates Jr., *The Signifying Monkey: A Theory of Afro-American Literary Criticism* (New York: Oxford University Press, 1988), 47.

46. Bill D. Moyers, *A World of Ideas II,* ed. Andie Tucher (New York: Doubleday, 1990), 62.

47. Morrison, *Beloved,* 273.

48. Ibid., 275.

49. Timothy Yates, "Jacques Derrida: 'There Is Nothing Outside of the Text,' " *Reading Material Culture: Structuralism, Hermeneutics, and Post-Structuralism,* ed. Christopher Tilley (Cambridge, England: Blackwell, 1990), 276.

50. Emmanuel Levinas, *Collected Philosophical Papers,* trans. Alphonso Lingis (Boston: Marinus Nijhoff, 1987), 54.

51. Michel Foucault, "What Is an Author?" in *Textual Strategies: Perspectives in Post-Structuralist Criticism,* ed. Josué Harari (Ithaca, N.Y.: Cornell University Press, 1979), 142.

SERAPH ON THE SUWANEE:
A NOVEL
(1948)
◆

Freud in Turpentine
[A Review of *Seraph on the Suwanee*]

FRANK G. SLAUGHTER

"Seraph: One of an order of celestial beings conceived as fiery and purifying ministers of Jehovah," says Webster. Arvay Henson, the heroine of the long novel of the Florida sand barrens and turpentine forests, probably never heard of a seraph, but she set out to be one nevertheless. Arvay never heard of Freud either, but she's a textbook picture of a hysterical neurotic, right to the end of the novel.

Arvay had reckoned without her "Id" which shortly asserted itself on the appearance of Jim Meserve, dark, handsome turpentine boss from the Alabama River. Before Jim, Arvay had gotten rid of impetuous suitors by having a fit, but the first time she put one on for Jim Meserve, he eyed the performance in critical appraisal, recognized the rather primitive symbolism involved in such hysterical convulsions, and cured it pronto, with a drop of turpentine in one of Arvay's lovely eyes. After that, of course, she was his slave, no matter how much she might protest. Married to Jim Meserve, Arvay's troubles should have been over, but they were only beginning. For Jim was a man with an eye on the future and Arvay was a girl with her eyes on the past. Being neurotic, Arvay could not make up her mind to forget the past and take the exciting ride on a comet that Jim Meserve promised. And when her first child was an idiot, Arvay's guilt over her illicit and hidden passion for a visiting preacher, plus an episode among the turpentine trees with Jim on the afternoon before her wedding, pretty well snowed her under for awhile.

Upon such an uncertain background it was inevitable that this chronicle of an unstable woman's search for happiness would be filled with ups and downs. Happy and unhappy by turns, Arvay still helped Jim build a new life for them in southern Florida, but always there was the neurotic's yearning for the scenes of her childhood. And with her children grown, and Jim increasingly occupied with business, Arvay's inferiority finally drove her to a break and return to the Suwanee. There, in a sort of self-psychoanalysis, she learns the truth about herself, and begins to realize her destiny.

Reprinted from *New York Times Book Review* (31 October 1948): 24. © 1948 New York Times Company. Reprinted by permission.

The author knows her people, the Florida cracker of the swamps and turpentine camps intimately, and she knows the locale. One gets the impression that she took a textbook on Freudian psychology and adapted it to her needs, perhaps with her tongue in her cheek while so doing. The result is a curious mixture of excellent background drawing against which move a group of half-human puppets.

A Woman Saved
[Review of *Seraph on the Suwanee*]

HERSCHEL BRICKELL

The author of this simple, colorfully written, and moving novel of life among the Florida Crackers is a born writer who, in such of her preceding works of fiction as *Jonah's Gourd Vine,* has proved herself a person of exceptional talent. Her own career has been filled with variety and interest; she set out to be a geologist, turned to anthropology instead when told that there was no future for a woman in geology, and has won distinction as a folklorist in such books as *Mules and Men.*

Her present theme is that of a woman saved, brought finally out of her feeling of insecurity that has crippled her life, by the wholehearted affection of a real man. Hence the title. The hero, Jim Meserve, plays the part of a "fiery and purifying minister of Jehovah," with sufficient success to make him seraphic.

Arvay Henson was a pretty, slight, neurotic young girl, with a talent for music and a fixation on a handsome preacher married to her sister, when Jim turned up at the "teppentime" camp where she lived and fell in love with her. Jim was a hard-working go-getter, who wanted the best for his wife, and their first step upward was to move to the citrus country.

The first child was an idiot, true to the Cracker blood, and this of course gave Arvay a fresh wound. Then there were two more, an attractive and intelligent girl and a handsome boy talented in music; but not even this kind of family, plus Jim's continued financial success, cured Arvay of her lifelong difficulty, made her whole.

At long last, Jim, barely saved from the attack of a rattlesnake in a symbolic scene, tells his wife of his disappointment in her, and goes away, leaving her to find herself. She does, and the story ends on a note of hope for the future, with true love triumphant but not in any conventionally sentimental sense.

Miss Hurston's wonderful ear for the vernacular, for the picturesque phrase and the poetical turn of words that so often is a part of the conversation of the unlettered, makes the novel one that may be read with instant sur-

Reprinted from *Saturday Review of Literature* (6 November 1948): 19.

prise and delight, somewhat aside from its intrinsic merits as a piece of fiction. Her own prose at times inclined to be stiff and somewhat graceless, but she makes the fullest possible, and very effective, use of the great richness of speech among her people.

Anyone who grew up in the South will find himself encountering on every page the familiar expressions of his childhood, half forgotten, and invoking nostalgia, like a language that has been put away in the subconscious, being no longer heard nor used. That fascinating word "tureckly," for example, which means exactly the opposite of its parent, "directly...."

All Miss Hurston's fiction has had warmth of feeling, a happy combination of lustiness and tenderness, that gives it an appeal too often missing from much of the day's bloodless writing, which is sexless in spite of its frequently overpowering sexiness.

The Courageous Undertow of Zora Neale Hurston's *Seraph on the Suwanee*

Janet St. Clair

Seraph on the Suwanee, Zora Neale Hurston's apparently regressive last novel, has few friends among critics. Hurston has been almost unanimously faulted for turning her back on her own racial heritage and feminist convictions in this novel: unlike the vibrant and courageous Janie Starks of *Their Eyes Were Watching God*, Arvay Henson Meserve, the whining white protagonist of *Seraph*, seems to evade the responsibilities of individuality and self-knowledge by cravenly clinging to the demeaning refuge of domestic obedience. The entire work, it is commonly conceded, is riddled with weaknesses, inconsistencies, and authorial capitulation and cowardice. There is some truth to the charges. But both Hurston and her protagonist have been unfairly judged.

Although the weaknesses of the novel are real, the inconsistencies are the result of a subversive feminist substory that has so far gone unrecognized, a narrative of resistance and self-discovery that exists not between the lines but solidly on every page. It is the story of Arvay's faltering efforts to reject both oppression and, more importantly, the mental submission to oppression. Her persistent attempts to preserve her integrity through withdrawal, resistance, and suspicion are motivated by a tenacious belief in her own intrinsic worth and in her rights to individual freedom and social respect. Because she is consistently denied access to the power of both word and deed, her progress is slow. But in the end she finds freedom, meaning, a sense of community, and the potential for continued growth in her discovery of an active, inclusive, unconditional love. In finally refusing passively to allow people to take from her and instead deciding freely to give, she claims the confidence, power, and self-respect that nourish her determination and ability to shape her own place, locate her own authority, and direct her own way.

Seraph on the Suwanee has been virtually ignored by all but authors of full-length studies of Hurston, and even they generally scurry across its surface in consternation. Feminist critics are chagrined because the protagonist finally chooses to find fulfillment in home and family, consigning herself to a "waste-

Reprinted from *Modern Language Quarterly* 50.1 (March 1989): 38–57. © 1990 University of Washington. Reprinted by permission of the publisher.

land" of "dead values, lost ambition and thwarted goals."[1] Critics of black literature are disappointed because Hurston abandons her racial heritage and her literary commitment to black folk culture in creating white protagonists. Arvay's courage does seem blurred by her creator's apparent cowardice: Hurston ostensibly capitulates to the antifeminist sentiment of the conservative postwar forties. Published in 1948, *Seraph on the Suwanee* reflects the oppressive traditionalism of the so-called reconversion period when the capable and independent figure of the wartime woman worker is "transformed into the naïve, dependent, childlike, self-abnegating model of femininity in the late forties."[2] Hurston's novel, superficially accommodating itself to the repressive and sexist exigencies of the time, is apparently about a recalcitrant wife who learns, under the patient tutelage of her kind and wise husband, to accept graciously her appointed place as gentle hearthside angel. In fact, at first glance the novel seems little more than an embarrassingly anachronistic genteel romance, so poorly constructed that it cannot even stay on its own formulaic track. And it is, as almost every critic of Hurston grieves, about white people, a fact that seems to confirm for some readers Hurston's shabbily disguised "contempt for the Negro race."[3]

Critics of Hurston should know her principles, processes, and publications well enough to avoid a facile dismissal of this novel. Her career is characterized by resistance to oppression, affirmation of self-discovery and fulfillment, and celebration of her cultural origins. Far from being the "reactionary, static, shockingly misguided and timid" fiasco that Alice Walker claims it is,[4] *Seraph on the Suwanee* reiterates Hurston's characteristic themes. Arvay's final expansive assertion of feminine authority and maternal power has a dimension of heroism that transcends Janie Starks's final withdrawal to the isolated confines of her upstairs room, and Arvay's repudiation of tyranny and constriction and her proud declaration of personal worth underscore the universality of the political struggles of American blacks. Hurston's text, as usual, is liberation; but in this case her discourse is distorted by an ambivalence so complex and an expression so awkward that critics, discomfited and bewildered, have shunted the novel off the canonical track.

The confusion is understandable. *Seraph on the Suwanee* is an almost schizophrenic story that at once tells and untells itself, threatening to cancel itself altogether as it simultaneously works both for and against a dominant culture that demands self-cancellation of its women. Writing from the triply marginalized position of woman, black, and champion of an aesthetically disdained folk tradition, Hurston ostensibly denies all three of these identities in her story of an upwardly mobile white family under inflexible male control. But the yarn unravels as fast as Hurston spins it: the details of the story, by continually undermining the narrative privileges granted to the conventions of the dominant culture, rescue the novel from charges of cowardice and capitulation. The overt story line does present women as "brainless, thoughtless, inferior, helpless wretches . . . to be subjugated to the will and whim of men."[5] And it "is not even about black people" (Walker, p. xvi). But the voice of oppression and its subversion has neither gender nor color. And *Seraph on the Suwanee* is finally the thinly veiled story of a woman who resists victimization, throws off oppression, chooses the burden that she will carry, and takes it up with courage, dignity, and delight.

It is the failure to recognize this subversive subtext that results in critical consternation. And yet, clumsy as Hurston's sabotage of white male authority is, it is surprising that her subterfuge has gone undetected. Mikhail Bakhtin's discussions of hidden polemic and double-voiced discourse have long held special significance for critics of women's and black literature: not saying what one means and saying what one does not mean are common techniques for conveying antagonistic or subversive intentions.[6] Feminist critics have typically instructed readers to look for the messages encoded in women's silences, denials, and evasions; meaning is often found at the junction of expression and repression. Henry Louis Gates's central critical mission is "identifying levels of meaning and expression" that seem "buried beneath the surface" of black literature.[7] And Hurston's own manipulations of language have been noted by several critics. In one of Gates's discussions of "Signifying," or talking around a subject in indirect argument, he observes, "Zora Neale Hurston is the first author of the tradition to represent signifying itself as a vehicle of liberation for an oppressed woman. . . ."[8] His extensive commentary on her studied uses of language in *Their Eyes Were Watching God* further suggests that the apparent carelessness of construction in *Seraph* warrants a closer examination (*SM*, pp. 196 ff.).

Hurston herself seems to offer ample invitation to look beneath the surface: the many parallels between her life and Arvay's imply the unreliability of apparent authorial condemnation of the protagonist, and the unabashed use of black idiom, frequently lifted directly from such works as *Mules and Men* and *Their Eyes Were Watching God*, seems clearly to hint that things are not as black and white as they immediately seem. Yet *Seraph* is marred by a confusion of purpose that suggests just as clearly that the author's own ambiguous motives and ambivalent attitudes undermined whatever conscious control she may have had. According to Robert Hemenway, her biographer, Hurston was fed up with racial polemics and badly in need of money when she wrote *Seraph;* the first source of distress might have distorted her vision, and the second perhaps tempted her consciously (but not unconsciously) to forsake her principles. In a letter to her editor at Scribner's, she expresses her exasperation with people like Arvay who carry inferiority "like a raw sore on the end of the index finger," but in the same letter she rails against a man in her life who tries to thwart her growth and restrict her freedom, just as Jim restricts Arvay (Hemenway, p. 312).

The subversive undertow of *Seraph on the Suwanee* exists on every page, although Hurston's conscious courage (or cowardice) in its development is problematic. It is this feminist manifesto roiling just beneath the vapid and saccharine surface that lends the novel interest. Growing out of Hurston's own spirit and appealing to common sense and social decency, this submerged narrative concerns an oppressed woman who ferociously conceals and protects an embryonic sense of self until she gains the space and safety to nurture it and bring it to light and life. The two irreconcilable stories constantly clash, each struggling to take control of the text, just as Arvay struggles to reclaim control of her life from Jim and the seemingly invincible social forces that support him. Every character and incident is rent by dualities; every narrative assertion self-destructs. Nothing is as it seems; nothing retains its shape. Jim Meserve is presented as an enthusiastic, resourceful, and virile lover, but his cruelty, selfishness, arrogance, and condescension reveal him to be a self-involved, sexist bully who manipulates the ideals of romantic love to ensure his own uncontested power. Arvay is presented as a weak, contrary, backward, and passive whiner, but she resists both external and internalized oppression in her uncertain struggle toward reconciliation of self and circumstances.

The story begins like a Victorian romance: the "rakishly" handsome and aristocratic hero sweeps into town, spots the unrecognized Cinderella, and whisks her to her glorious reward in the matrimonial bed. Jim Meserve "stir[s] the hearts of practically every single girl in town,"[9] but it is Arvay, the slight and eccentric little blue-eyed blonde, bullied by her big sister and discounted by her father, who unwittingly wins his approval. Her self-effacing insecurity recalls that of young Zora herself, whose autobiography, *Dust Tracks on a Road*,[10] portrays a girl intimidated by her father's preference for her sister and agonizingly insecure about her attractiveness. Arvay sees marriage as a liberation from domestic oppression, public humiliation, and sexual anxieties, and worships Jim as a man "clothed in all the joys of Heaven and earth" (p. 24). Astonished, flattered, and finally reassured by Jim's public demonstrations of solicitude, she allows herself literally to be swept off her feet and into the carriage that will speed her to the paradise of holy wedlock.

A pretty story, tailored for its time. Hurston no doubt hoped that it would sell, but it is certainly not one that she could buy. The hero is as brutal as any man in her fiction, and his courtship of Arvay is loaded with images of restraint. He wastes no time in establishing his power and her subservience. Their first meeting begins against her will when "she felt her elbow being caught by a man's long and strong fingers" as she walks to church (pp. 13–14); the rest of her day with him is characterized by similar instances of force. The oppressive truths of Arvay's marriage are foreshadowed as Jim variously "held Arvay's arm so that she could not advance" (p. 17) and "grabbed her by her arm and jerked her backwards" (p. 32). Despite the "gray veil of apprehension" (p. 16) through which she perceives his charming smiles, Arvay submits to the familiar intimidation that passes as care. "I have to . . . give you my good protection to keep you from hurting your ownself too much," Jim arrogantly explains (p. 15). He brags of knowing just how to handle her, then deliberately drops turpentine in her eye to demonstrate the proper taming of a shrew, and insolently assures her "deeply impressed" father that "a woman knows who her master is all right, and she answers to his commands" (pp. 30–31).

Jim lays proprietary claim to Arvay, flatly declaring, "I'm picking you" (p. 24). He makes it equally clear that he expects—indeed tolerates—no thinking. "Women folks don't have no mind to make up nohow," he explains. "They wasn't made for that. Lady folks were just made to laugh and act loving and kind and have a good man . . . and have him as many boy-children as he figgers he'd like to have . . ." (p. 23). Throughout his professions of absolute dominion and demands for vulnerability and subservience, the narrative voice unflinchingly purports to side with Jim. The facts of the discourse, however, consistently undermine that support. The discrepancy is central to the novel's significance: it is absurd to think that such oppressive arrogance represents the opinions of Zora Neale Hurston, the woman who left two husbands and at least one lover because they threatened her freedom and individuality.

The disguised polemic intensifies as Jim seeks to seal this contractual imbalance of power that will characterize their marriage: he rapes Arvay. But even this is presented in such romantic terms that Hemenway can claim that Jim "rescues Arvay from a teenage withdrawal into repressed sexual hysteria by engaging to marry her, then raping her, then marrying her" (p. 309). The novel appears to support Hemenway's chilling interpretation of "rescue" by idealizing Arvay's violent rape as the act of a hero who means well, knows best, and subsumes the pain, terror, humiliation, and guilt into romantic rapture and sexual ecstasy. The virgin's preposterous response to this unexpected attack transforms the outrage into an even more outrageous complicity: "Arvay opened her mouth to scream, but no sound emerged. Her mouth was closed by Jim's passionate kisses, and in a moment more, despite her struggles, Arvay knew a pain remorseless sweet" (p. 45). A few minutes later: "It seemed a great act of mercy when she found herself stretched on the ground again with Jim's body weighing down upon her" (p. 47).

But again the story undoes itself, revealing the cruel power play behind the romantic rhetoric. The rape was motivated by Jim's conversation with Joe Kelsey, his long-married "pet Negro" (p. 54). Worried about the "hold-back to her love" that Jim detects in Arvay, he appeals to Joe for advice. "Make 'em knuckle under," Joe tells him. "From the very first jump, get the bridle in they mouth and ride 'em hard and stop 'em short. They's all alike, Boss. Take 'em and break 'em" (p. 41). Jim rapes Arvay two days later. Then, fearing he will be stopped by her parents before he can get her away, he "grabbed up Arvay . . . and ran staggering for the gate . . . growling like a tiger which had just made a kill and was being challenged" (p. 48). She is his prize, the image clearly implies, his to devour. A few minutes later, on their way to the courthouse, Jim gloats about how "the job was done up brown," and puts the structure of their imminent marriage into terms they both understand. "Sure you was raped," he replies when she accuses him of the violation, "and that ain't all. You're going to keep on getting raped . . . every day for the rest of your life" (p. 50).

The genteel romance plot begins to erode after their marriage; its simplicity and duplicity are clearly inadequate vehicles for Hurston's unmediated exposure of social oppression. Jim continues to be presented as the hero, however, defending his timid wife against her own worst impulses, while Arvay is increasingly portrayed as the thorn in Jim's side, unappreciative of his tender care and determined to ensure her own unnecessary misery. Her insecurities seem irrational remnants of an irrelevant past: her sister, Larraine, with their father's help, had oppressed her as a child, taken the best for herself, and left Arvay persuaded that "she was born to take other people's leavings" (p. 22). Like Zora herself, who in girlhood had lived a rich fantasy life to make up for her lack of "someone who felt really close and warm" and who had "made particular friendship with one huge tree and always played about its roots" (*DT*, pp. 258, 64), Arvay had found happiness playing alone at the foot of her spreading mulberry tree and living "a sweet and secret life inside herself" (p. 10). Increasingly, Arvay protects herself by assuming the role of martyr and outcast, resigning her threatened self to injured isolation and romantic fantasies of altruistic immolation. The narrative voice presents the martyred, maidenly Arvay with a sort of benevolent condescension, as if adolescent stages, however absurd, must be indulged; but after her marriage, her insecurity and withdrawal are revealed as unjustified, perverse, destructive, and divisive.

Throughout the passing years in the story, Jim is developed as the enterprising businessman, expansive and fun-loving friend, and tireless provider, while Arvay is portrayed as the increasingly dour, withdrawn, narrowminded, and apathetic drain on his effervescent good will. But although she seems to invent threats to her security with such tedious regularity that "the reader gets as sick of the whining heroine as Hurston got when she wrote the novel" (Howard, p. 136), Jim gives her cause for withdrawal. She had envisioned marriage as an escape from the oppression that "had done something to [her] soul across the years" (p. 8), but optimism is blighted under Jim's shortsighted governance. Far from alleviating her insecurity, marriage to Jim exacerbates it as he repeatedly shames, ridicules, threatens, and rejects her. Humiliated and rebuffed, Arvay "hungered and retreated inside of her self"; her only recourse in the face of his insensitivity is to "huddle with her eternal fear and wait" (p. 58).

There is little reason to trust the narrative voice that insistently reiterates Arvay's responsibility for Jim's dissatisfaction: the apparent complicity serves only to reveal the insidious duplicity of the situation. Jim Meserve's solicitous words collide violently with his insensitive, tyrannical deeds. Arvay is constantly faulted for suspicion, small-mindedness, and martyrdom. Inarticulate and stripped of both authority and voice, she must fight for her identity in total isolation, alienated not only from her self and her husband, but even from the biased narrative voice and the reader who accepts fraudulent word over obvious deed. The coercive lies by which Jim retains absolute control are clear, however, to readers who will see. During their courtship he brags about his ability to understand her insecurity, and after their marriage he repeatedly reassures her, "You don't have to worry about a thing" (p. 65; cf. p. 87). But despite his insistence that she neither worry nor think, he forces her to do both under impossible conditions, for he refuses to tell her his expectations yet requires her to acquiesce in his will. Although she blossoms into cooperative gratitude at the slightest reassurance, he consistently abandons her to a limbo of ignorance, neither leaving her alone nor allowing her to participate as a partner.

Jim deliberately excludes her from knowledge of his activities, his feelings, and even his whereabouts. He blames his secretiveness on her: she seems uninterested, she will not understand, she will not approve, she will resist. But his rationale is as faulty as it is unfair: Arvay, although hurt by the exclusions, always comes around to Jim's way of thinking. She accepts and learns to love the swamp property, never says a word against the whiskey still, adjusts graciously to the news that Angie, their daughter, has married secretly, and assents to Jim's lengthy and frequent trips to the coast. She knows that she is slow to adjust to change, and asks only for "a chance to collect herself" (p. 188) and "get used to the idea" (p. 174), but her modest requests are seldom respected. Her outlets for creative family involvement are choked at every turn; feeling "like a dammed-up creek," she is constantly "torn with anxious fears," "always wondering what Jim wanted her to do" (pp. 221, 68, 237). She worries that he will leave her, but her fears are grounded. Even early in their relationship Jim decides that "there was not sufficient understanding in his marriage," and he can think of no "help for it except by parting from Arvay" (pp. 92–93). He stays, not to protect her, as he proclaims, but for the selfish reasons that he acknowledges to himself: he would miss her "doing around in the kitchen fixing him the kind of a supper that she figured he might choose and fancy" (p. 93), and so he wants to prevent "some other man" from finding out "what he knew about Arvay, and be soothing his trashy head on Arvay's soft and comforting bosom" (p. 94). He feels free to take comfort from Arvay, but denies her the solace of knowing that he depends upon her because "that way wouldn't do me no good" (p. 177).

Yet Jim is always presented as the victim. He attributes his misery to Arvay's shortcomings, and the reader is invited to sympathize with the great and manly patience with which he endures his secret pain. Using an analogy that Hurston has borrowed directly from *Mules and Men*,[11] he accuses Arvay of being "unthankful and unknowing like a hog under an acorn tree. Eating and grunting with your ears hanging over your eyes, and never even looking up to see where the acorns are coming from" (p. 230). Using a phrase lifted directly from *Their Eyes Were Watching God*,[12] he tells her, "I see one thing and can understand ten. You see ten things and can't even understand one" (p. 229). But it is clearly Jim who is deficient in both appreciation and understanding. He affectionately calls her his "Little-Bit" (pp. 57, 61), Zora's own nickname (*MM*, p. 193), and repeatedly promises her the benefit of his "strong arm of protection" (p. 123), but it is he from whom she must protect herself. It is almost as if Hurston, bitter at the insistent sniping of black critics, weary of the interminable battle for her own creative and personal independence, and fed up with what must have seemed deliberate and spiteful misunderstanding of her work and her self, has offered in *Seraph on the Suwanee* a negative image of both her life and Janie's in *Their Eyes Were Watching God.* The story is still that of a woman who seeks only her own integrity and liberty, but this time it subtly exposes those who will blindly or dishonestly insist that black is white and white is black.

Arvay is blamed for passivity and apathy, but every attempt she makes at self-assertion is instantly quashed by this man who continually condemns her lack of action. Both Jim's viciousness and Hurston's subversive gloss become more apparent as he deliberately strips Arvay of power and enforces abject submission. Early in the relationship he simply ignores or ridicules her efforts at self-affirmation, delighted that "she did not know her own strength" (p. 94). As time passes, however, he maintains his power through increasing brutality. His cruelty and the shocking incongruity between word and deed are especially apparent in the rape scene following the football game in Gainesville. Arvay, seeing Felicia Corregio at the game, is crushed and quite naturally suspicious upon discovering that she has again been excluded from something that "the rest of the family seemed to know" all about. She tries "to feel and act happy" despite feeling "so out of place," but hours elapse and still neither Jim nor her children offer her the courtesy of an explanation (p. 183). Intensely uncomfortable, she follows Jim through the day's activities, participating as best she can, but she finally asks to leave the dance early. Jim refuses. For once, she insists on having her feelings respected, and Jim rushes her away in a molten fury. Thwarted for the first time, he drives maniacally home, storms into the bedroom where Arvay has fled for refuge, and attacks her verbally and physically for the temerity of being upset by his habitual insensitivity. "Where I made my big mistake was in not starting you off with a good beating just as soon as I married you," he snarls (p. 189). He blocks her exit from the room, rips her clothes off, forces her to stand naked and trembling before his sneering appraisal, then rapes her. He looks down on her "as if she were a chair" and stretches full length upon her "in the same way that he might have laid himself down on a couch" (pp. 188, 190). The images are apt: his right, he believes, is to take comfort and rest from her; hers is to be crushed under his weight. Arvay, driven to distraction by her "bondage" to this man whom she adores, hysterically vows to free herself through suicide and ends her uncharacteristic outpouring of emotion "on a high and agonizing scream of desperation." Jim, coolly noting that she is utterly broken and enslaved by her love for him, is finally pacified, and "with a kind of happy arrogance, snuggled his head down on her breast . . . and went off into peaceful sleep" (pp. 191, 192).

The attitudes that Jim reflects in *Seraph on the Suwanee* are typical of fiction of the conservative postwar forties, where "women are bitches whenever they disagree or try to assert themselves; they are burdens whenever they are passive and subservient."[13] But it would be unnatural and unbelievable if Arvay did not retreat from such degrading and unrelenting disapproval. The subversive truth about tyranny will not be silenced simply by social endorsement: despite the apparent complicity of the narrative voice, anguish and outrage are evident in Arvay's adamant resistance to cancellation. Wholly unsupported in her unarticulated quest for independent identity, she feels guilty and worthless for her inability to please Jim, defensively insisting, "I try to do what's right" (p. 103). But wholesome defiance and resentment operate beneath the shame and insecurity to protect her integrity until she is strong enough to overcome his emotional control and her own self-imposed enslavement to him. Denied a middle ground, her spirit is eroded by oppression on the one hand and isolation on the other. She tries to resist his "compellment," recognizing that submission to his influence makes her "just about as near nothing as anybody could be," but love and need keep her "tied and bound down in a burning Hell" of self-effacing subjugation (pp. 154, 138, 191). Refusal to yield completely to this duplicitous and morally demeaning union permits her, nevertheless, to retain at least the potential for self-realization and dignity.

Meanwhile, identity is held in suspension: although Hemenway is partly right in charging that she "can never define the self apart from her husband" (p. 313), Arvay realizes that there will be no self to define if she submits to the degree that Jim requires. She manages to find great joy in her family but only at the expense of great suffering. Arvay frequently retreats to her childhood "temple of refuge" and resents Jim for having "tricked her out of her refuge" when, in her youth, she had suspected that "she had never been counted or necessary" (pp. 173, 174). It is true that she sometimes revels in self-pity, but her actions do not reveal the sniveling, sullen, and self-pitying crosspatch that the narrative voice portrays: she is a woman without allies who never stops trying to fit in, to be accepted, and to fight off her justifiable sense of exclusion, insignificance, and oppression.

Arvay's faults are forever in the narrative spotlight, while Jim is presented as hovering around solicitously, trying "every way that he [knows] how" to help Arvay in "finding her way" (p. 103). He, the narrative voice, and the complacent reader are always acutely aware of her deficiencies, but oblivious of Jim's. The snake incident, after which Jim self-righteously determines to leave Arvay, encapsulates the cruelty, childishness, selfishness, condescension, and insensitivity that characterize him throughout the novel's subversively feminist substory. According to the narrative line, Jim courageously picks up the rattlesnake to impress Arvay and finally win her love, urgently requires her assistance when the snake constricts around his torso, discovers, as Darwin Turner sympathetically notes, "that he cannot depend upon her when he needs help,"[14] despairs of ever molding her into an adequate mate, and sorrowfully leaves her.

Jim's version is as full of holes as Hurston's herpetology. To claim that a diamond-back rattler is capable of constriction would strain even the most liberal interpretation of poetic license, but no stretch of the imagination can validate Jim's construction of the incident. In his eyes the entire event is Arvay's fault. Only an arrogant, immature show-off would frivolously pick up an eight-foot rattler in the first place, but he would be even more foolish to expect a woman to interpret his action as a heroic display of true love if she so fears and hates snakes that she balks even at worms. Yet this is what Jim does, and what he expects. Arvay sees his "bragging, triumphant face" and interprets correctly: Jim was "like a little boy turning cartwheels in front of the house where his girl lived," ignoring in his self-congratulatory vanity the obvious fact that "this was nothing to be fooling with" (p. 222). When Jim loses control and the snake coils around his waist and begins to free its head as its constriction loosens Jim's grip, Arvay is immobilized by terror—her standard and predictable reaction, as Jim well knows, to snakes.

Later, having been saved by the handyman who had left him holding the snake in the first place, Jim begins methodically to blame Arvay for every aspect of the incident. It is even her fault that he picked up the rattler, because he "was a man in love" acting "full of manhood" in order "to win admiration . . . and compliments" from her (p. 229). But Arvay, according to his interpretation, "pitched in and helped the rattlesnake out" (p. 230). He refuses to let her speak in her own defense and denies her right even to hold opinions. Throwing open his bathrobe to display "a band of raw-red abraded flesh," he charges, "Your kind of love, Arvay, don't seem to be the right thing for me," as if she were responsible for his injury (p. 233). He tells her he is leaving her in the morning, and he adds, reproachfully, "I'm tired of waiting for you to meet me on some high place and locking arms with me and going my way" (p. 233). He gives her one year to "come to the same point of view" as his (p. 234). Not once does he even hint at an acknowledgment of his errors; after more than twenty years of marriage, he can still see only hers.

Finally, Jim does Arvay a genuine service. He leaves her. At this point, the subversive subtext begins to claim authority. Freed at last from the potentially lethal constriction of Jim's kind of love, Arvay knows only that "there was some hidden key to re-open the door of her happiness" and that she must find it by herself (p. 235). The key, of course, is the rediscovery, acknowledgment, and respect of her self; and because she is left alone, she has the time, space, and safety for the search. Not only must she find and nourish the valuable and affirmative aspects of her identity; she must also relinquish and bury the deforming fears, insecurities, and suspicions to which she has clung so long.

Earl, Arvay's idiot firstborn, serves as an image of the deformed and illogical consciousness that restricts her growth and potential. The baby's "exceptionally small" mouth, with thick bottom lip "thrust out at the world," reflects the inarticulate, aggrieved face that Arvay presents; his ferocious appetite mirrors her incessant hunger. His "string-like fingers" make Arvay wonder "if her son would ever be able to use his tiny hands," or whether he, too, would be helpless, empty-handed, unable to handle life. Like his mother, the child seldom cries or makes demands, seeming to live in "a world within himself," but he, too, is unnaturally fearful and easily alarmed (pp. 61, 62). Feeling his defenselessness, Arvay coddles and protects him as she does her own insecurity because "the poor, pitiful thing ain't got nobody to care for him but me" (p. 113). Finally, Earl is destroyed by his own sexuality: he is shot by his neighbors after he attacks Lucy Ann Corregio. Arvay is destroyed by her sexual maturity, too, in a sense: once raped by Jim, she is no longer permitted an identity of her own. After more than twenty years of marriage, Jim again viciously strips her, rasps, "You're my damn property, and I want you right where you are, and I want you naked," and leaves her standing, shivering, "with her legs close together," ineffectually defending herself against invasion and violation (p. 190). But Earl himself is full of destructive potential; and like Arvay's deformed mentality, which invites and expects oppression, he is destroyed so that productive life can resume. Although her anguish at his death is acute, she finally realizes "that she must come back to her family somehow" (p. 137). She comes to the same conclusion when she returns to Sawley for her mother's death and burial.

Arvay has long yearned for "something or someone to come and drive away the lonesome feeling" from her heart (p. 119). Once she admits that this elusive "something" has been within her all the time that she herself is the sole "someone" responsible for its liberation, she can renounce oppression and begin to develop independence. She watches her mother die clutching at the meager property that Carl and Larraine, "hanging around just like turkey buzzards," have systematically attempted to wheedle or swindle her out of (p. 244). Maria, Arvay's mother, has suffered a lifetime of disrespect, deprivation, and despair because she had never envisioned or demanded anything better. Displaying her few functional gifts from the Meserves as if they were trophies too good for "one of them nothing kind of human beings" such as herself to use, she expends her dying strength protecting these tangible emblems of her worth from the parasitic, scavenging Middletons (p. 246). Watching her weary mother die in inarticulate self-denigration and regret, Arvay feels the necessity, as Zora Neale Hurston had at her mother's death, "to speak for her. She depended on me for a voice" (DT, p. 95). The words both women formulate are for themselves as well as for their mothers: no joy can accrue to one who accepts victimization.

This lesson is reiterated when Arvey confronts the squalor, avarice, igno-rance, and jealousy of the filthy "ton of coarse-looking flesh" and the "soiled, heavy-set man" who are her sister and brother-in-law (p. 241). As characters, Larraine and Carl are weakened by caricaturization; as symbols of the petty, grasping, self-serving, and suspicious elements in Arvay, however, they are enormously instructive to her. Their defensive hostility toward her and their insolent rejections of her well-intentioned gestures parallel her defensiveness with Jim. Just as Jim expresses annoyance with Arvay's claim that he "had never taken her for his equal" (p. 115), Arvay is hurt and baffled by Carl's antagonistic charges of being treated like "some old throwed-away dog" by his uppity rich sister-in-law (p. 251). Just the day before, Arvay had "tossed her head defiantly" in her big house in Citrabelle and "rhymed out that she was a Cracker bred and a Cracker born, and when she was dead there'd be a Cracker gone" (p. 238). Carl and Larraine's empty, defiant pride is calculated to protect, just as Arvay's has been, but Arvay sees from her new perspective that there is small virtue in such hollow defiance. Finally feeling safe enough to surrender her habitual defenses, she begins to see that "she had not really been trying to find the answer. . . . As always, she had been trying to defend her background and justify it . . ." (p. 238).

Arvay's liberation parallels her growing understanding of how her damaging self-centeredness has blighted her natural capacity for love. Accepting the community's condolences and assistance with wonder and amazement of her new, more expansive vision, she "came away from her mother's funeral changed inside" (p. 262), sensing her own inherent worth and recoiling from the narrowness and insecurity that have blinded her to it through the years. Admitting that "the fault could be in her" for her chronic failure to win warm responses, she joyfully purchases boxes of delicacies not only for her family, but for Jeff as well, the handyman who has treated her with such frigid insolence since her separation from Jim (p. 263). Condemned for so long to coddling a strangled sense of freedom and identity within the constrictive limits of her own alienation, Arvay begins to experience a burgeoning sense of liberty in a communal context: her reconciliation of her self and her world begins with her renunciation of both external and internal oppression.

But her insights must survive outside hostility and inner disillusion-ment. Returning to her mother's house with generous gifts and even more generous plans for relocating Carl and Larraine in Citrabelle, Arvay finds the house ransacked and gutted, pictures of the Meserve family mutilated, fruit trees ready to be set afire with trash, and her sister's family gone. Temporarily injured, she offers the box of groceries to a neighbor, then goes out to her mulberry tree, her "sacred symbol" (p. 269) of life, protection, and regenera-tion, to think. The tree, its spreading branches barren of leaves, stands starkly against the February sky.

But soon now, three weeks at the most, tender green leaves would push out of those tight little brown bumps. . . . Fuzzy little green knots . . . would turn out to be juicy, sweet, purple berries before the first of May. But most of all, this tree would become a great, graceful green canopy rolling its majesty against the summer sky. (p. 268)

The tree, Arvay's "cool green temple of peace" since her childhood (p. 34), clearly represents her own spirit. It has always been there, strong, protective, eternal, and nourishing. Arvay had allowed herself to lose contact with it, choking it with the trash of her fear, anxiety, and defensive false pride, but a new surge of vitality is at hand.

As Arvay's capacity to find and define herself grows, so does her ability to lay claim to her inherent unifying might. She has always dimly understood the sublime power of love, but she must abandon the shoddy security of withdrawal and the crippling restraints of fear and suspicion before unselfish love can become her guiding principle. Standing between the tree that symbolizes her self and the road that symbolizes the world is her house, bequeathed to her by her defeated mother. Ramshackle, fetid, crawling with vermin, it represents to Arvay all the protective negativity that had "blinded her from seeing and feeling through the years" (p. 269). In burning it to the ground, she destroys the constriction of spirit that chokes her happiness. Finally effecting the "cleansing of her sacred place" (p. 34), she feels a calmness and unity of spirit that she has never experienced before; the reconciliation of Arvay and her world is achieved.

Reaction and rumination had only kept Arvay continually on the defensive, angry, resentful, and mistrustful. Her decision to act and her bold assumption of responsibility for her actions have brought her peace. When the neighbor offers to remember Arvay in her prayers, she replies, "Do that, Miss Hessie, and I'll do all in my power to take care of things my ownself. No need of wearing God out" (p. 273). She vows to win back her husband if she can: "If she failed, it was not going to be because she never tried" (p. 277). Arriving back home, she sets about her preparations immediately "with hope and determination" (p. 277). Self-involvement falls away as she immerses herself in cooperative action, and fears about the outcome of her quest no longer send her into retreat.

Critics have overlooked the significance of her transformation; her decision to return to the well-meaning but sexist bully who denies her selfhood is seen as Arvay's or Hurston's failure of will, Arvay's or Hurston's failure of insight, or Hurston's failure in characterization. It is in fact a splendid ending for this subversive novel of the forties. The novel creates the story of the seraph that the title promises, as well as that of a woman who affirms her individual identity, restores the unity of her family on a new and durable foundation, and replaces the crippling elements of old cultural ties with a new sense of community that strengthens all its members. Arvay affirms her separate identity by *choosing* her own direction and refusing any longer to be victimized. If her choice is to return to Jim, it is because that is where she expects to find her happiness and realize her potential. She has always loved Jim, her family, and married life; she has no good reason not to return.

Indeed, Arvay's enormous expansion in self-confidence and personal equilibrium is powerfully illustrated in her ability to express unconditional love for her husband. She is utterly uninterested in changing Jim; accepting him as he is, she strives only after her own growth and happiness, trusting that her efforts will lead naturally to the well-being of others. She had accused him of his insensitivities several times during the course of their marriage; in her newfound wisdom she knows that resolution and joy do not lie in that direction. As far as her efforts are concerned, his conduct is irrelevant; her affair is to discover "what she could do and be, and that was going to be a gracious plenty" (p. 304). She acknowledges the truth of Jim's accusations against her without charging him with his own considerable insufficiencies, but she absolves herself of self-destructive guilt, too, in recognizing that she "had taken good care of Jim in every way" and that he will never realize how desperately she has battled "in order to stand beside him" (p. 302). In the end, Arvay submits to the power of love and the logic of order, not to Jim's unreasonable demands.

Arvay chooses to love and care for Jim but to do so without the self-denigrating illusions that had kept her bound to his whims and her own anxieties. She knows that he is childish, inflexible, and egotistical, and she allows him his delusions. Arvay plays her wifely role with flattery and affected femininity, tranquilly granting the demands of Jim's undisciplined ego, knowing that her accommodation of his fragility does not compromise her integrity (p. 292). She indulgently notes "how like little boys" the men on the boat act (p. 301), but it is for her "a wonderful and powerful thing to know" that her vulnerable husband requires her care; her new dignity, equilibrium, and self-respect place her beyond the threat of oppression (p. 307). Wholly embracing the role of mother now that her children are dead or grown, Arvay has become like the sea, mother of all life, the placid water that had "to cut and gnaw [its] way out" of deep underground caves (p. 295). But Jim, she knows, will stay the same. It is not for her to expect him to meet her "on some high place"; his life is his to live just as hers belongs to her (p. 233). As he hauls his catch out of the vast sea, she watches as he takes only what will profit him and casts the rest overboard as waste. There is a price to pay for her choice, of course, and she pays it; her willingness to pay asserts her belief in the dignity of her decision. Returning to Jim, Arvay courageously affirms the freedom of choice; the necessity of commitment, and the value of her chosen role as nurturer.

The tidy symbolic representation of Arvay's difficult transition from the protective harbor, through the perilous bar, and out to open sea at glorious sunrise is perhaps a bit overdrawn, and the necessity of her doing it while standing "just back of [Jim] and look[ing] fearfully over his shoulder" (p. 291) seems a disconcerting concession for both Arvay and Hurston. Arvay, however, is willing to give her husband his due: he recognizes her potential from the start and continues to believe in it despite the disappointments of their marriage. But Arvey effects her own rebirth. Accepting full responsibility for herself, granting that "all that had happened to her, good or bad, was a part of her own self and had come out of her," she begins to discover life's "many mysteries" by finding a way of "stretching and extending with her surroundings" (pp. 309, 291). She becomes what she does because infinity was in her all the time, a truth that even Larraine and Carl had sensed while she was still a child. Her own realization is a long time coming, but it comes with a conviction. "Seems like I been off somewhere on a journey," she confides to Jim as they gaze at the sea, "and just got home" (p. 293).

Seraph on the Suwanee is not a great novel: it is marred by structural weaknesses, embarrassing characterizations, technical flaws, and an apparent uncertainty of moral purpose. This ethical ambivalence, however, lends the novel a redemptive fascination. Zora Neale Hurston was a woman of courage, vision, and commitment, but her motives were often unclear. Her entire career, speckled with concessions to the white establishment, illustrates the lengths to which she would go to get published. She certainly seems to comply with America's postwar effort to restore innocence through conformity and traditionalism. Yet *Seraph on the Suwanee* destroys the very stereotypes it affects to endorse. The unanswered question is whether Hurston consciously controlled the novel's subversive undertow. The constant tension between her professional aspirations and her individual convictions is well known, but so is her ability to "signify," to manipulate language for her own ends. As one of her characters in *Mules and Men* observes, some stories "got a hidden meanin'. . . . Everybody can't understand what they mean" because most people cannot "seek out de inside meanin' of words" (pp. 162–63).

"De inside meanin' " is there, intentionally or not. The times required a tale of a hearthside angel; the author required a tale about the renunciation of bondage. *Seraph on the Suwanee,* the story of Arvay's reconciliation of personal conviction and social realities, may have been Hurston's own deliberate but uncertain attempt at a similar reconciliation. Since each thematic thread both wrecks and informs the other, it is difficult to determine the exact degree of courage and cowardice in both the author and protagonist. Fannie Hurst once described Zora Neale Hurston as "a figure in bas relief, only partially emerging from her potential into the whole woman."[15] The same might be said for Arvay Henson Meserve. Creator and protagonist agree, however, that "submission tazzled you all up inside" (p. 22). As a story and as a creative effort, *Seraph on the Suwanee* illustrates that truth with certainty.

Notes

1. Karla F. C. Holloway, *The Character of the Word: The Texts of Zora Neale Hurston,* Contributions in Afro-American and African Studies, 02 (New York: Greenwood Press, 1987), p. 44.

2. Maureen Honey, *Creating Rosie the Riveter: Class, Gender, and Propaganda during World War II* (Amherst: University of Massachusetts Press, 1984), pp. 1–2.

3. Chidi Ikonné, *From DuBois to Van Vechten: The Early New Negro Literature, 1903–1926,* Contributions in Afro-American and African Studies, 60 (Westport, Conn.: Greenwood Press, 1981), p. 184.

4. Foreword to Robert Hemenway, *Zora Neale Hurston: A Literary Biography* (Urbana: University of Illinois Press, 1977), p. xvi.

5. Lillie P. Howard, *Zora Neale Hurston,* TUSAS, 381 (Boston: Twayne, 1980), p. 144.

6. See, for example, Mikhail Bakhtin's "Discourse Typology in Prose," trans. Richard Balthazar and I. Titunik, in *Readings in Russian Poetics: Formalist and Structuralist Views,* ed. Ladislav Matejka and Krystyna Pomorska (Cambridge: MIT Press, 1971), pp. 176–96.

7. *The Signifying Monkey: A Theory of Afro-American Literary Criticism* (New York: Oxford University Press, 1988), p. xx; hereafter cited *SM.*

8. *Figures in Black: Words, Signs, and the "Racial" Self* (New York: Oxford University Press, 1987), p. 241.

9. *Seraph on the Suwanee* (New York: Charles Scribner's Sons, 1948), p. 7. Unless otherwise noted, page numbers in the text refer to this work.

10. Philadelphia: J. B. Lippincott, 1942; hereafter cited *DT.*

11. Philadelphia: J. B. Lippincott, 1935; rpt. New York: Negro Universities Press, 1969, p. 176; hereafter cited *MM.*

12. Philadelphia: J. B. Lippincott, 1937; rpt. New York: Negro Universities Press, 1969, p. 111.

13. Thelma J. Shinn, *Radiant Daughters: Fictional American Women,* Contributions in Women's Studies, 66 (New York: Greenwood Press, 1986), p. 69.

14. *In a Minor Chord: Three Afro-American Writers and Their Search for Identity* (Carbondale: Southern Illinois University Press, 1971), p. 115.

15. "A Personality Sketch," in *Zora Neale Hurston,* ed. Harold Bloom, Modern Critical Views (New York: Chelsea House, 1986), p. 23.

THE SANCTIFIED CHURCH:
THE FOLKLORE WRITINGS OF
ZORA NEALE HURSTON
(1984)

♦

Reflections of the Sanctified Church as Portrayed by Zora Neale Hurston

MARION A. THOMAS

Although Zora Neale Hurston's portrayal of the sanctified church was written sixty years ago, her description is still valid and merits careful consideration by anyone interested in the Holiness-Pentecostal movements of the late nineteenth and early twentieth centuries. Specifically, she refers to the Saints of God in Christ and the more well-known Church of God in Christ, founded and incorporated as a chartered denomination in Memphis, Tennessee, in 1897 by Elders C. H. Mason and C. P. Jones. "This church," writes Vinson Synan, "was the first Southern holiness denomination to become legally chartered. . . . Consequently, many white ministers of independent holiness congregations received ordination from Mason, making his organization interracial" (80). In Los Angeles, from the beginning of the Azusa Street Pentecostal revival of 1906 until 1914, blacks and whites worshiped together.

The sanctified church Hurston describes is an African-American institution begun in "protest against the high-brow tendency in Negro Protestant congregations as the Negroes gain more education and wealth" (103). For Hurston, the elements and style of worship in the sanctified church are more African than Christian. The sanctified church is "a revitalizing element in Negro music and religion. It is putting back into Negro religion those elements which were brought over from Africa and grafted onto Christianity as soon as the Negro came in contact with it . . ." (Hurston 105).

Many of the elements and much of the style of worship observable in the sanctified church were to be found among certain classes of white believers in the days of the camp meetings in the 1800's. Led by itinerant preachers, these meetings were held in open fields and usually lasted seven or eight days. Bishop Asbury of the Methodist Church reported a large number of these meetings in his journal of 1811, and a Presbyterian minister of the period wrote of

Reprinted from *Black American Literature Forum* (currently *African American Review*) 25.1 (Spring 1991): 35–41. © 1991 Indiana State University. Reprinted by permission of the publisher.

the glare of the blazing campfire falling on a dense assemblage . . . and reflected back from long ranges of tents upon every side; hundreds of candles and lamps suspended among the trees, together with numerous torches flashing to and fro, throwing an uncertain light upon the tremulous foliage, and giving an appearance of dim and indefinite extent to the depth of the forest; the solemn chanting of hymns swelling and falling on the night wind; the impassioned exhortations; the earnest prayers; the sobs, shrieks, or shouts, bursting from persons under intense agitation of mind; the sudden spasms which seize upon scores, and unexpectedly dash them to the ground; all conspired to invest the scene with terrific interest, and to work up the feelings to the highest pitch of excitement. (qtd. in Sweet 229)

Other reports of these camp meetings tell of people falling, running, jumping, and jerking. Under his preaching, in 1903, A. J. Tomlinson, a mystical Quaker, reported that, in some areas, "the Spirit worked in many ways, with many saints' shouting, weeping, clapping their hands, jerking[,] and hand shaking. . . . people fell on the floor, and some writhed like serpents, while others seemed to be off in a trance for four or five hours" (Synan 86).

Similar behavior occurred during the Azusa Street revival, which was attended by African Americans, whites, Chinese, and Jews. "Falling under the power, speaking in tongues, shouting[,] and jumping" were characteristic reactions to the passionate preaching of black preacher William J. Seymore. Such congregational activity was understood to denote the participants' having attained a deep sense of sin, hell, and judgment with the subsequent joy of forgiveness and anticipation of heaven. However, Synan reports that some found it disturbing that "white people were imitating the unintelligent, crude Negroisms of the Southland and laying it on the Holy Ghost" (110).

CONVERSION AND VISION

Hurston observes that conversion and vision in the sanctified church are "almost always" linked (85). Because converts may be unwilling to believe that conversion has taken place, they must be in a position of being offered visible proof of its having occurred. Hurston cites the example of a woman who "fell under conviction in a cow lot," and asked God for a sign: " 'Now, Lord, if you done converted my soul, let dat cow low three times and I'll believe.' A cow said, 'Mooo-oo, moo-oo, moo-ooo-oo—and I knowed I had been converted and my soul set free' " (86).

A key element in seeking visions is to open oneself up to the possibility of previously unexperienced phenomena, which are often induced by isolation and fasting. Hurston reports a Deacon Ernest Huffman as saying:

One day, bout noon, it was de 9th day of June, 1886, when I was walkin in my sins, wallerin in my sins, dat He tetched me wid de tip of His finger and I fell right where I was and laid there for three long days and nights. I layed there racked in pain under sentence of death for my sins. And I walked over hell on a narrer foot log so I had to put one foot right in front de other, one foot right in front de other wid hell gapped wide open beneath my sin-loaded and slippery feet. And de hell hounds was barkin on my tracks and jus before dey rushed me into hell and judgment I cried: "Lawd, have mercy," and I crossed over safe. But still I wouldn't believe. Then I saw myself hangin over hell by one strand of hair and de flames of fire leapin up a thousand miles to swaller my soul and I cried: "Jesus, save my soul and I'll believe, I'll believe." Then I found myself on solid ground and a tall white man beckoned for me to come to him and I went, wrapped in my quilt, and he 'nointed me wid de oil of salvation and healed all my wounds. Then I found myself layin on de ground under a scrub oak and I cried: "I believe, I believe." Then Christ spoke peace to my soul and de dungeon shook and my chains fell off, and I went shouting in His name and praising Him. I put on de whole armor of faith and I speck to stay in de fiel until I die. (88–89)

Visions, Hurston observes, play a role not only in conversion but also in the call to preach. In such cases, the "vision seeks the man. Punishment follows if he does not heed the call, or until he answers" (87).

But visionary experience, for Hurston, is not limited to explicitly religious contexts. It also shares linkages to African-American folklore and to the "lying" sessions she describes in *Mules and Men* and *Their Eyes Were Watching God*. Hurston herself, deeply influenced by her cultural background as the daughter of a Baptist pastor, claims in her autobiography that, from the age of about seven, she began having a series of twelve visions, depicting twelve stages of her life, which recurred "at irregular intervals" (*Dust Tracks* 56–60).

Among the reasons for the identification of religious visions with African-American religious practice is the minimal emphasis sanctified church leadership places on academic study and systematic theology. When little emphasis is placed on objective knowledge, importance is often accorded visions, the subjective confirmation of conversion, and the call to preach. The Church of God in Christ, unlike its counterpart the (white) Assemblies of God, has not developed a network of Bible colleges to train its preachers. According to Harold A. Carter, there are black preachers who feel that the "call" is a substitute for training (19–30).

It is noteworthy that the division between white and black Pentecostal believers which took place in 1914 occurred mainly because of incipient racism and differences of administrative policy rather than over styles of worship. Nevertheless, Hurston affirms that "Negro religion" has a sustained intensity and vividness that is lacking in (white) "Christianity." This is seen most clearly in the spirituals, shouting, and preaching.

THE SPIRITUALS

> The real spirituals are not really just songs. They are unceasing variations around a theme.
>
> Contrary to popular belief their creation is not confined to the slavery period. Like folk-tales, the spirituals are being made and forgotten every day. . . .
>
> The idea that the whole body of spirituals are "sorrow songs" is ridiculous. They cover a wide range of subjects from a peeve at gossipers to Death and Judgment. . . .
>
> There never has been a presentation of genuine Negro spirituals to any audience anywhere. (*Sanctified* 79–80)

The spirituals, Hurston contends, are not pat compositions which a group of singers practices for presentation to an audience. Speaking of the irregular harmony, dissonances, falsetto voices, and changes of key that characterize the real "Negro spiritual," Hurston maintains that ". . . each singing of the piece is a new creation" which grows out of deep feeling and emotion. "Glee clubs and concert singers put on their tuxedos, . . . get the pitch[,] and burst into magnificent song but not *Negro* song" (80).

African-American song, and formal speech, is characterized by "audible breathing [which] is part of the performance[,] and various devices are resorted to to adorn the breath taking. Even the lack of breath is embellished with syllables" (81). On occasions when the congregation in an African-American sanctified church sings "white hymns," it tends to sing them more slowly than the printed music indicates. As someone has said, black singers want to "get all the juice out of the words." It is not unusual to hear black congregants add an extra hum or moan to printed music, whereas even in cultures and locales where white congregations sing hymns slowly (in Poland, for example), the singers adhere to the musical directions.

SHOUTING

Shouting is a response to various kinds of rhythm, to passionate preaching or singing. It may be silent or vocal, and the person may run, jump, fling arms violently, and, after two or three minutes of intense activity, just collapse. Hurston asserts that "there can be little doubt that shouting is a survival of the African 'possession' by the gods. In Africa it is sacred to the priesthood or acolytes, in America it has become generalized" (91).

As I have already indicated, shouting is not unique to the African-American sanctified church; it was characteristic of the nineteenth-century camp meetings attended by whites and blacks. Furthermore, as blacks move up the socioeconomic ladder, their form of worship becomes less wedded to

African tradition. Some defenders of this "possession" by the gods (with its etymological link to the word enthusiasm) claim that it helps to relieve tension and frustration, and can thus be therapeutic. It is significant that among some modern charismatics (black and white, of various denominations), dancing and jumping before the Lord are quite acceptable. What is unique in the sanctified church is the intensity with which the movement occurs.

PREACHING

The African-American sanctified preacher has an incomparable manner of praying and preaching. He is a master of dramatization, using his vivid imagination and giving vent to deep emotions, preaching with his whole being. Hurston believes that black speech forms are particularly well-suited to the sanctified preacher, and she records a sermon by C. C. Lovelace at Eau Gallie, Florida, given on May 3, 1929, from which I excerpt a section:

> I heard de whistle of de damnation train
> Dat pulled out from Garden of Eden loaded wid cargo goin to hell
> Ran at break-neck speed all de way thru de law
> All de way thru de prophetic age
> All de way thru de reign of kings and judges
> Plowed her way thru de Jordan
> And on her way to Calvary when she blew for de switch
> Jesus stood out on her track like a rough-backed mountain
> And she threw her cow-catcher in His side and His blood ditched de train.
> He died for our sins.
> Wounded in the house of His friends.
> Thats where I got off de damnation train
> And dats where you must get off, ha!
> For in dat mor-ornin', ha!
> To dat judgment convention, ha!
> When de two trains of Time shall meet on de trestle
> And wreck de burning axles of de unformed ether
> And de mountains shall skip like lambs
> When Jesus shall place one foot on de neck of de sea, ha!
> One foot on dry land
> When His chariot wheels shall be running hub-deep in fire
> He shall take His friends thru the open bosom of a unclouded sky
> And place in their hands de hosanna fan. . . .
>
> (Sanctified 102)

Similar speech forms are found in the creation sermon "Behold de Rib" in *Mules and Men,* and while the use of graphic symbols in these sermons may be compared with those in James Weldon Johnson's "The Creation" (from

God's Trombones), Hurston's use of the black vernacular contrasts with Johnson's standard English, through which he carried his appeal beyond the African American community. The *ha!* is a well-known device in black preaching: "Instead of permitting the breath to drain out, when the wind gets too low for words, the remnant is expelled violently" (*Sanctified* 82).

Besides exercising freedom with respect to grammar, breathing, and mannerisms, the black preacher makes striking use of tone and intonation, including varieties of chanting tones and rhythms such as *moaning, mourning, whooping,* and other ploys designed to produce a "spiritual atmosphere" which will encourage audience involvement and emotional response. From the preacher's point of view, the higher the pitch of excitement, the better the sermon.

Call-and-response is one of the most characteristic features of black preaching, the audience "bearing the preacher up" by punctuating his sermon with "Amen," "That's right," "Have mercy," "Make it plain," etc. If the preacher feels he is not arousing his listeners, he is likely to ask, "Can I get a witness out there?" The reason behind Hurston's failing to include typical congregational responses in her report of the sermon cited above is not clear, although she does allude to the practice at several points in *The Sanctified Church,* and she makes clear the "pity" the "folk Negro" feel for "white" preaching: "They say of that type of preacher, 'Why he don't preach at all. He just lectures'" (106–07).

On the other hand, sanctified preaching, impressive though it may be, has been accused of producing great "heat" but comparatively little "light." Henry H. Mitchell observes that, whereas

> the slack preaching tradition has been very strong in the area of free, healing expressions and celebration[, i]t has been very weak in making the climax relevant, either to the sermon text or to the reinforcement of Black growth and enablement. It has been much stronger in its capacity to steel and strengthen determination than in its capacity to relate to what that determination should be. (189)

This has left much of the present generation, especially young people, ill-prepared to face the tough, complex, social, economic, and spiritual issues of today. Seventy per cent of present-day black Americans do not attend church with any regularity.

Hurston's celebration of African-American experience in *The Sanctified Church* is to be applauded, but combining some of the strengths of the "highbrow" church with the best elements of the sanctified church need not result in a denial of African patrimony. If black sanctified preaching is too emotional and manipulative, what Hurston calls "the high-brow tendency in Negro Protestant congregations" can be too intellectualized, too detached. As Mitchell also observes,

To destroy escalation of emotion in climactic utterance is by implication to do away with emotions of less intensity as well, and to decree a flat, even, uninteresting level of involvement. But people live by emotion. Emotions move people, while ideas which do not generate some emotion are powerless to change anybody's life. (194)

Notes

Carter, Harold A. *Myths That Mire the Ministry.* Valley Forge: Judson, 1980.

Hurston, Zora Neale. *Dust Tracks on a Road.* 2nd ed. ed. Robert E. Hemenway. Urbana: U of Illinois P, 1984.

———. *The Sanctified Church.* Berkeley: Turtle Island, 1981.

Mitchell, Henry H. *Black Preaching.* Philadelphia: Lippincott, 1970.

Sweet, William W. *The Story of Religion in America.* Grand Rapids: Baker, 1979.

Synan, Vinson. *The Holiness-Pentecostal Movement in the United States.* Grand Rapids: Eerdmans, 1971.

MULE BONE:
A COMEDY OF NEGRO LIFE
(1991)

◆

Why the *Mule Bone* Debate Goes On
[Review of *Mule Bone*]

HENRY LOUIS GATES JR.

Controversy over the play *Mule Bone* has existed ever since it was written by Langston Hughes and Zora Neale Hurston in 1930. Not only did an authors' quarrel prevent the play from being produced, but its exclusive use of black folk vernacular has also provoked debate. In 1984, when the play became part of the publishing project of Dr. Henry Louis Gates Jr., the editor of Hurston's complete works, he sent a copy of it to Gregory Mosher, then the artistic director of the Goodman Theater in Chicago. When Mr. Mosher moved to the Lincoln Center Theater in New York, he brought the play with him, and eventually the theater decided to mount it. Dr. Gates and George Houston Bass, the literary executor of the Hughes estate, edited the play and served as consultants to the production. *Mule Bone* is being published this month to coincide with its world premiere Thursday at the Ethel Barrymore Theater on Broadway. Dr. Gates, the John Spencer Bassett Professor of English at Duke University, was elected to the board of Lincoln Center Theater last spring.

For a people who seem to care so much about their public image, you would think blacks would spend more energy creating the conditions for the sort of theater and art they want, rather than worrying about how they are perceived by the larger society. But many black people still seem to believe that the images of themselves projected on television, film and stage must be policed and monitored from within. Such convictions are difficult—even painful—to change. And never more so than in the case of *Mule Bone,* the controversial 1930 Langston Hughes–Zora Neale Hurston play that is only now being produced for the first time, almost 60 years to the day after it was originally scheduled to open.

Why should a folk comedy about the residents of a small Florida town in the 1920's cause such anxiety? Because of its exclusive use of black vernacular as the language of drama.

Reprinted from *New York Times* (10 February 1991): 5. © 1991 the New York Times Company. Reprinted by permission of the publisher.

In analyzing the discomfort *Mule Bone* has aroused over the decades, the playwright Ntozake Shange has said that Hurston's language "always made black people nervous because it reflects rural diction and syntax—the creation of a different kind of English."

"Are we still trying to figure out what is real about ourselves that we know about that makes it too dangerous to say it in public?" she asked.

Ms. Shange was speaking at a 1988 forum at Lincoln Center at which the play was read and the merits of staging it debated—"in a post-Tawana Brawley decade," as the theater's artistic director, Gregory Mosher, put it. Few occasions have brought together more prominent black actors, directors, writers and critics than that November reading: the actors Ruby Dee, Paul Winfield, Giancarlo Esposito and Joe Morton, and the playwrights Ed Bullins and Ron Milner were among the nearly 100 people present, along with Hughes's biographer, Arnold Rampersad, the literary executor of the Hughes estate, George Houston Bass, who died last September, and myself.

As each speaker commented, often passionately, it seemed incredible that the debate was occurring in the first place. Why would anyone believe there are still aspects of black culture that should be hidden because they are somehow "embarrassing"?

Mule Bone is a revelation of life "behind the veil," in the words of W. E. B. DuBois. It portrays what black people say and think and feel—when no white people are around—in a highly metaphorical and densely lyrical language that is as far removed from minstrelsy as a Margaux is from Ripple. It was startling to hear the play read aloud and enjoyed by actors who weren't even alive when it was written. The experience called to mind sitting in a black barbershop, or a church meeting—any one of a number of ritualized or communal settings. A sign of the boldness of Hughes (1902–1967) and Hurston (1891–1960) was that they dared to unveil one of these ritual settings and hoped to base a new idea of theater on it. Would the actors and writers in the late 1980's find poetry and music in this language, or would it call to mind minstrelsy, vaudeville and Amos 'n' Andy? Was it Sambo and Aunt Jemima, or was it art?

Sixty years after *Mule Bone* was written, many black Americans still feel that their precarious political and social condition within American society warrants a guarded attitude toward the way images of their culture are projected. Even a work by two of the greatest writers in the tradition cannot escape these concerns, concerns that would lead some to censorship, presumably because of "what white people might think," as if white racists attend black plays or read black literature to justify their prejudices. While the causes of racism are legion, literature hardly looms large among them.

Yet much of the motivation for the creation of what is now called the Harlem Renaissance—that remarkable flowering of black literature and the visual arts that occurred during the 20's, when *Mule Bone* was conceived—was implicitly political. Through the demonstration of sublime artistic capacity, black Americans—merely 60 years "up from slavery," as Booker T. Washington described it—could dispel forever the nagging doubts that white Americans might have about their innate intellectual potential. Then, the argument went, blacks could easily traverse the long and bumpy road toward civil rights and social equality.

Given this burdensome role of black art, it was inevitable that debates about the nature of that art—about what today we call its "political correctness"—would be heated in black artistic circles.

These debates have proved to be rancorous, from that 20's renaissance through the battles between social realism and symbolism in the 30's to the militant black arts movement in the 60's. More recently, there have been bitter arguments about sexism, misogyny and the depiction of black women and men in the works of Alice Walker, Toni Morrison, Michele Wallace and Ms. Shange, as well as controversies about the writings of such social critics as Shelby Steele and Stanley Crouch. "The Negro in Art: How Shall He Be Portrayed?"—the subject of a forum published by DuBois in *The Crisis* magazine in the mid-20's—can be identified as the dominant concern of black artists and their critics for the last 70 years.

Black art in the 20th century, then, is a pivotal arena in which to chart worries about "political correctness." The burden of representing "the race" in accordance with explicitly political programs can have a devastating impact on black creativity. Perhaps only black musicians and their music, until rap arose, have escaped this problem, because so much of what they composed was in nonverbal forms and because historically black music existed primarily for a black market. Categorized that way, it escaped the gaze of white Americans who, paradoxically, are the principal concern of those who would police the political effects of black art.

But such fears were not for the likes of Zora Neale Hurston. In April 1928 she wrote Hughes about her interest in a culturally authentic African-American theater, one constructed on a foundation of black vernacular: "Did I tell you about the new, the real Negro theater I plan? Well, I shall, or rather we shall act out the folk tales, however short, with the abrupt angularity and naivete of the primitive 'bama Nigger." It would be, she assured him, "a really new departure in the drama."

Hurston and Hughes did more than share the dream of a vernacular theater. They also established themselves as creative writers and critics by underscoring the value of black folk culture, both in itself and as the basis for formal artistic traditions. But the enormous potential of this collaborative effort was never realized, because, as Hughes wrote on his manuscript copy of the play's text, "the authors fell out."

Exactly why they "fell out" has never been clear, but the story of this abortive collaboration is one of the most curious in American literary history. For whatever reason, Hurston would copyright *Mule Bone* in her own name and deny Hughes's role in its writing.

The action of their play turns on a triangle of desire between a guitarist, Jim Weston (played by Kenny Neal), and an unnamed dancer (Dave Carter Eric Ware), who are best friends as well as a musical duo, and their growing rivalry for the affections of Daisy Taylor (Akosua Busia). Directed by Michael Schultz, *Mule Bone* has a score by Taj Mahal, who has set five Langston Hughes poems to music and composed four songs for the Lincoln Center production.

Eventually, the two friends quarrel and Weston strikes Carter with the hock bone of an "ole yaller mule." He is arrested and his trial forms the heart of the play. The trial, and most of the second act, takes place in the Macedonia Baptist Church, converted into a courthouse for the occasion, with Mayor Joe Clark (Samuel E. Wright) presiding. The resolution of the case turns upon an amusing biblical exegesis: Can a mule bone be a criminal weapon? If so, then Weston is guilty; if not, he is innocent.

Using Judges 18:18, Carter's "attorney" (his minister, played by Arthur French) proves that since a donkey is the father of a mule, and since Samson slew 3,000 Philistines with the jawbone of an ass, and since "de further back you gits on uh mule de more dangerous he gits, an' if de jawbone slewed 3,000 people, by de time you gits back tuh his hocks it's pizen enough tuh kill 10,000." Therefore, "I ask y'all, whut kin be mo' dangerous dan uh mule bone?" Weston is banished from the town, which was based on Hurston's own Eatonville, Fla. The final scene depicts the two friends' reconciliation after both reject Daisy's demand that her husband get a proper job.

What is so controversial about all this? Hughes and Hurston develop their drama by imitating and repeating historical black folk rituals. Black folklore and Southern rural black vernacular English served as the foundation for what they hoped would be a truly new art form. It would refute the long racist tradition, in minstrelsy and vaudeville, of black characters as ignorant buffoons and black vernacular English as the language of idiots, of those "darkies" who had peopled the American stage for a full century before *Mule Bone*.

This explains why they subtitled their play *A Comedy of Negro Life* and why they claimed that it was "the first real Negro folk comedy." By using the vernacular tradition as the basis of their play—indeed, as the basis of a new theory of black drama—Hurston and Hughes sought to create a work that would undo a century of racist representations of black people.

It is clear that Hurston and Hughes believed the time had come to lift the veil that separates black culture from white, allowing black art to speak in its own voice, without prior restraint. Had they not fallen out, one can only wonder at the effect that a successful Broadway production of *Mule Bone* in the early 1930's might have had on the development of black theater.

A Difficult Birth for *Mule Bone*
[Review of *Mule Bone*]

FRANK RICH

If ever there was a promising idea for a play, it is the enigmatic story of what went on when two giants of the Harlem Renaissance briefly collided in 1930 to collaborate on "a comedy of Negro life" they titled *Mule Bone*.

The writers were the poet Langston Hughes and the anthropologist, folklorist and novelist Zora Neale Hurston. Both were in their late 20's, and both had the same dream of a new truly African-American theater. Their goal was Broadway, which they hoped to liberate from the stereotypical minstrel musicals (the many progeny of *Shuffle Along*) and sentimental problem dramas (*Green Pastures, Porgy*) that then distorted the black experience on the mainstream stage. Yet *Mule Bone* was never finished and never produced because, as Hughes put it, "the authors fell out."

What went wrong? No one knows for sure, despite the fascinating and painstaking efforts of both writers' authoritative biographers, Arnold Rampersad (Hughes) and Robert E. Hemenway (Hurston), to piece the events together. Everyone agrees, as Henry Louis Gates Jr. has written, that the fight was "an extremely ugly affair" that at the very least involved a battle over authorial credit and the neurotic machinations of a wealthy white patron. Hurston's present-day publisher, Harper Perennial, has just brought out a first edition of the uncompleted text of *Mule Bone* in which all the relevant biographical accounts and documentary evidence have been assembled, and the volume leaves no doubt that whatever the provocation, the Hughes-Hurston conflict was the stuff of high drama.

The same, sad to say, cannot be said of *Mule Bone* itself, at least as mounted by Lincoln Center Theater at the Barrymore Theater on Broadway, six full decades after Hurston and Hughes set their sights on the Great White Way. This is an evening that can most kindly be described as innocuous—not an adjective usually attached to either of its authors—and it is not even a scrupulously authentic representation of what Hughes and Hurston wrote, fragmented and problematic as their aborted collaboration was. Indeed,

Reprinted from *New York Times* (15 February 1991): 1. © 1991 The New York Times Company. Reprinted by permission of the publisher.

there's something disturbingly disingenuous about the entire production. This *Mule Bone* is at once so watered down and bloated by various emendations that one can never be entirely sure if Lincoln Center Theater is conscientiously trying to complete and resuscitate a lost, unfinished work or is merely picking its carcass to confer a classy literary pedigree on a broad, often bland quasi-musical seemingly pitched to a contemporary Broadway audience.

On occasion—rare occasion—this rendition does make clear what Hurston and Hughes had in mind, which was to bring to the stage, unfiltered by white sensibilities, the genuine language, culture and lives of black people who had been shaped by both a rich African heritage and the oppression of American racism. The play was adapted from an unpublished Hurston story recounting one of the many folk tales she had collected during her anthropological exploration of Eatonville, Fla., the black town where she was born. In the story, two male friends come to blows over a turkey, with one knocking out the other with a mule bone and ending up in a trial that turns on an issue of biblical interpretation. In the play, the object of dispute is a woman named Daisy, not a turkey—the change is believed to have been Hughes's—but the anecdote remains in any case an excuse for an explosion of vernacular speech, blues poetry and extravagantly ritualized storytelling.

Perhaps if the writers had had the chance to finish *Mule Bone* and to see it with an audience, they would have tightened or rethought what was a work in progress. Perhaps even if they had completed their mission, *Mule Bone* would still seem as dated today as other ambitious American plays of its exact vintage, such as Eugene O'Neill's "Mourning Becomes Electra." We'll never know. As the text stands, it often feels like a rough draft in which two competing voices were trying to reach a compromise. Among the more arresting sections are a boisterous trial scene featuring dueling Baptist and Methodist congregations and a late-evening confrontation in which the antagonists compete for their woman's hand with hyperbolic metaphors. When the men try to court Daisy by bragging about how long a chain-gang sentence they would serve to win her over, *Mule Bone* surely succeeds in creating startling, linguistically lush folk comedy that nonetheless reflects the tragic legacy of slavery.

Those scattered passages, as well as sporadic well-turned lines, make the Barrymore vibrate, but they are surrounded by slack sequences and contemporary interpolations. *Mule Bone* opens with an embarrassing prologue by George Houston Bass, the literary executor of the Hughes estate until his death last year, in which Hurston herself awkwardly appears as a character on stage and gives the audience a primer on her career. At other isolated junctures five Hughes poems have been set to music by Taj Mahal, and sweet as the music and words are, the songs are not particularly well sung and always bring a flaccidly constructed show to a self-defeating halt. Dianne McIntyre's rudimentary, thigh-and-knee-slapping choreography lends only perfunctory animation.

As staged by Michael Schultz, who is certainly capable of tougher work, the whole enterprise has a candied Disneyesque tone, more folksy than folk. *Mule Bone* entirely lacks the striking visual style and gut-deep acting with which George C. Wolfe and his collaborators so precisely distilled the tough-minded voice of Hurston and the passions of her characters in "Spunk" last year. ("Spunk" also dramatized three Hurston stories in less time than *Mule Bone* takes to dramatize one.) Here the production design is mostly hokey, the performances often aspire to be cute, and even the fisticuffs are not played for keeps. While the authors intended *Mule Bone* to be funny, this production confuses corny affability with folk humor.

No wonder, then, that a number of precocious children roam the stage. The company is also profusely stocked with distinguished actors who have a lot of time on their hands while waiting for an occasional cue: Reggie Montgomery, Frances Foster, Robert Earl Jones, Arthur French. Though the three principal performers—Eric Ware, Kenny Neal, Akosua Busia—are at best likeably amateurish, their efforts are balanced by the assured center-stage turns of such old pros as Leonard Jackson, as a fuming man of the cloth, and Theresa Merritt, who gets to shimmy to a traditional blues recalling her Broadway performance as August Wilson's Ma Rainey. But it is all too typical of the evening that Ms. Merritt's song, the sole rousing musical interlude, is abruptly truncated before it can reach a soaring conclusion. It's almost as if this maiden production were determined to make *Mule Bone* prove on stage what it has always been in literary legend—a false start that remains one of the American theater's more tantalizing might-have-beens.

A Discovery Worth the Wait
[Review of *Mule Bone*]

In the Broadway production of *Mule Bone,* the characters gathered on the teeming porch of Joe Clark's general store in Eatonville, Fla., tease and cajole each other, laughing at the small-town follies at the heart of this 1930 comedy written by Langston Hughes and Zora Neale Hurston.

Given the familiarity with which the all-black cast of 30 inhabit their roles, it seems as though these folks have been sitting on that porch forever. But *Mule Bone* is coming to the stage 60 years after writer Hurston and poet Hughes, the royal couple of the Harlem Renaissance in the 1920's, collaborated on the project. Featuring a half-dozen songs added by blues composer Taj Mahal, *Mule Bone,* subtitled *A Comedy of Negro Life,* opened earlier this month for a limited run. While some critics found the material thin, others acknowledged its place in America's cultural history.

Indeed, *Mule Bone* is one of the curiosities of this Broadway season—a Rip Van Winkle awakened to entertain audiences in a Spike Lee era. Based on a Hurston short story, the play was intended to liberate the stage of its time of the black stereotypes which were then popular—the cavorting "darkies" of minstrel shows, vaudeville and musical revues. In April of 1928, Hurston described her concept to Hughes as "real Negro theater . . . we shall act out the folk tales, however short, with the abrupt angularity and naivete of the primitive "bama Nigger.' "

After sketching a couple of drafts of the three-act play, the collaborators had what has been called a "mysterious falling-out" and the production was canceled. The play lay neglected in a drawer until 1983, when Henry Louis Gates Jr., the noted Duke University English professor, brought the unfinished manuscript to Gregory Mosher, then the artistic director at the Goodman Theater in Chicago, who, intrigued, brought the script with him when he moved to Lincoln Center in 1985.

However, in the decades since the play was written, playwrights from Lorraine Hansberry (*Raisin in the Sun*) to August Wilson (*Fences*) had liberated

Reprinted from *Los Angeles Times* (24 February 1991): 4. © 1991 Los Angeles Times. Reprinted by permission of the publisher.

the "stage darkie" far beyond the scope of the *Mule Bone* creators' intent—so much so that Hurston's "primitive" figure might now appear offensive to blacks and whites alike. In a "post-Tawana Brawley decade," as Mosher describes it, what could be gained from a play in which blacks insulted each other in a rural dialect? Was *Mule Bone* simply a socially regressive museum piece better left dormant? The caricatures of Deacon Hambo, Old Man Brazzle, Lum Boger, Teets and Bootsie, among others, appeared, verbally at least, akin to characters in white-written works such as "Song of the South," which had raised questions of their own.

Lincoln Center Theater undertook the current production only after the play was hotly debated at a 1988 reading, a discussion that revealed the sensitivity heightened by racial tensions. Some argued that hewing to "political correctness" could be devastating to black creativity, whether one was talking about *Mule Bone* or the portrayal of male characters in Alice Walker's *The Color Purple.*

Prof. Gates later stated in a *New York Times* essay that "60 years after *Mule Bone,* many black Americans still feel that their precarious political and social condition within American society warrants a guarded attitude toward the way images of their culture are projected. Even a work by two of the greatest writers in the tradition cannot escape these concerns, concerns that would lead some to censorship, presumably because of 'what white people might think.' . . ."

The producers felt confident enough that the authenticity of the material would override these concerns. Michael Schultz, who after a distinguished tenure with the Negro Ensemble Company, had worked in television and film (*Cooley High, Car Wash*), was enlisted as director; writer George Houston Bass provided a new prologue and epilogue; and Taj Mahal set Langston Hughes' poems to music to fill in the slots where the creators had indicated there should be traditional folk songs.

Still, there were concessions to "what white people might think" in the editing of the play. The word "nigger" was deleted from the dialogue, as were all sexist allusions to women as chattel.

Other more troubling issues of "political correctness" remained. Was the play worthy of a production simply because the title page featured the names, as Gates noted, of "two of the greatest writers" of the black tradition, despite its limitations as theater? Might it not be historically important but theatrically feeble?

After all, these townfolk were in service to a leisurely driven plot, the rivalry between Jim and Dave, a song-and-dance team, for the affection of the coquettish Daisy. When guitar-twanging Jim whacks his best friend over the head with "de hock bone of an old yaller mule," his trial divides the town's Baptists and Methodists who argue whether a mule bone can be considered a weapon, according to the Bible. In the play's vernacular, the minister's argument clinches Jim's conviction: "Since de further back on a mule you goes, do mo' dangerous he gits, by de time you gits clear back tuh his hocks he's rankpizen (poison)." This was hardly compelling material for a Broadway audience familiar with playwrights like Wilson whose emotionally rich *Piano Lesson* is set in the same decade as *Mule Bone.*

Mosher says that he was not bothered by the skimpiness of the script Gates sent to him. Apart from the importance of producing a "lost work" of the Harlem Renaissance, he says that he was captivated by the "richness of detail and uniqueness of spirit" of the story-telling—the first instance of African-Americans themselves turning a light on a world which was merely a shadow in most dramas written up to that time.

Though the play is about a people "60 years up from slavery," racial conflicts happen beyond the railroad tracks of Eatonville. Because Hurston's hometown was the first incorporated black municipality in the United States, the play's comic spirit could emerge untainted by the victimization occurring in other communities. The central social structure of *Mule Bone* is determined not by color but by divisions between rich and poor, the powerful and the powerless, Baptists and Methodists.

"But the point of the play is not social work," Mosher adds. "What Hughes and Hurston did was to come along and tap into an entire people's dream life. It addresses the subconscious of an entire community. It brings us no nearer to an understanding of problems of racism, but its effect on the imagination can be joyous."

At 39, Hurston had by then mastered in her numerous short stories the colorful dialogue of a small-town existence and embroidered it with humor. A decade younger, Hughes is credited with giving the play dramatic structure, most specifically in changing the plot so that the boys come to blows over a pretty girl rather than over a turkey, as happened in the original story. This was merely a vehicle which the authors then used to elaborate their cultural legacy. In this regard, *Mule Bone* might be considered as representative of a community's "dream life" as Thornton Wilder's *Our Town*—which captured the archetypes and vernacular of New England, even as it transcended them.

"And nothing happened in the first act of *Our Town* either!" says Mosher, who directed a revival of it on Broadway a few years ago. "It used to drive me crazy. Why would anybody want to come back for the second act? I wondered. And yet, like in *Mule Bone,* they're saying these things for the first time, unraveling this tapestry of life which, at least for me, is thrilling to behold and absorb."

While *Mule Bone* might strike some whites as an entertaining dip into African-Americana, the play appears to viscerally engage the blacks in the audience, attesting to its familiarity and authenticity. The enjoyment stems at least in part from the simplicity of a show in which the biggest crisis is whether or not to build a municipal jail—this before a multi-racial audience that has seen a frightening crime wave in their hometown.

"There are more burning issues out there," says director Michael Schultz, "but this wasn't meant to address those. I've always thought of this as 'a black valentine' to revel in. To say to both whites and to blacks, but blacks especially, 'this is part of your heritage, too.'"

Rousing the dream life concocted by Hughes and Hurston was no easy task, he adds. "And those guys were dead, they couldn't help." The burden fell mostly to the cast to flesh out the broadly comic, sketchily written characters and to add whatever resonance the play might have for a 1991 audience. The difficulty of casting was exacerbated by the fact that many actors simply couldn't handle the rural dialect. Says Schultz, "It had to do with how much in touch with their roots they were."

Theresa Merritt had no problem filling out the ample Katie Pitts, who sassily sings "Shake That Thing" in the show. "My people were from Emory, Ala., and there were Katie Pittses around there," she says. "You know, those women who [are a] little more worldly because they've been up to the sinful North and come back home."

Merritt herself journeyed up to the "sinful North" in the early '40's to pursue a singing career birthed in the Alabama Baptist camp meetings where, as a child, she learned to express herself singing before the congregation. The arc of the actress's career—from her Broadway debut in *Carmen Jones* (1943), to her featured role in August Wilson's *Ma Rainey's Black Bottom,* for which she was nominated for a Tony Award in 1985—reflects the transformation black theater has undergone as it has explored and refined the process begun by Hurston and Hughes.

For Merritt, as well as for other veterans, *Mule Bone* signifies a "comin' around again," as the actress puts it. "My early life was a lot like in *Mule Bone,* people sittin' around telling tall tales about ghosts in graveyards and who's sleeping around with whom. During the day, we'd sing hymns and then on Saturday night, the grown-ups listened to the jazz records they'd put on the Victrola. Jazz was sin music, not fit for children, so we'd have to sneak down. Years later, when I was asked to play Ma Rainey, I knew she'd sung 'Shake That Thing.' I didn't get to sing it then so I was delighted when they asked me to sing it in this show."

Unlike Merritt, 25-year-old Eric Ware had no memories of his own to draw upon in creating suave Dave Carter, who seduces Daisy with his hip-rolling shuffle. But he used certain historical references his grandmother from Greene, Ala., gave him—"She said they used to call a guy like Dave 'a jelly.'" But Ware says he drew inspiration from rides on the uptown IRT subway as well.

"Dave is fast-paced, nonchalant and cocky," he says, "and you can see that on the subway. There's that same physicality in a group of boys together and one of them is talking about what he did last night, and it's 'Hey!' or 'Ya-cha-cha!' It's that same enjoyment of telling the stories and the effect the words have on people." What anchors the show for a contemporary audience is the score played by an off-stage combo complementing the work of Kenny Neal, who plays the guitar-picking Jim.

Once Taj Mahal started reading the poems, he says, the music leaped from the page to his guitar. "I was shocked at how well versed Langston was in the blues," says Mahal. "My parents were always saying Langston this and Langston that, but I thought he was bourgeois, all that search for connectedness. The blues didn't care whether you were listening to it or not. It just had to sing its song."

His songs for *Mule Bone,* says Mahal, were intended to take the audience back to a certain period but also to give them the feeling that they were moving forward. "If you listen carefully," he says, "you can hear cultural relatives of the blues: r&b, soul, gospel, even a little bit of jazz and calypso. There's a certain crying blues you could put out there, but once I started reading through the poems, I started rocking."

Mahal says he saw the fusion between African-American storytelling and the blues in both Hughes' poetry and the play. The art of laughter was one of the black folk's gift to American culture. But, "it's the art of laughing to keep from crying. That's what the blues is about too."

THE COMPLETE STORIES
(1995)
◆

The Light at Daybreak: Heterosexual Relationships in Hurston's Short Stories

WILFRED D. SAMUELS

Describing Zora Neale Hurston as "a woman who wrote and spoke her mind," Pulitzer Prize–winning novelist Alice Walker confesses that "there is no book more important" to her than Hurston's *Their Eyes Were Watching God.* Traveling to Eatonville, Florida, the all-black town in which Hurston was born in 1891 and would spend the last years of her life before dying in poverty in 1960,[1] to find Hurston's unmarked and obscure grave in Fort Pierce, Florida, Walker places on it a headstone that identifies the former graduate of Barnard College, anthropologist, celebrated student of Franz Boas, and voice of the Harlem Renaissance as " 'A Genius of the South': Novelist, Folklorist, Anthropologist."[2] This was 1973.

Walker's eloquent resurrecting homage, the work of Hurston's biographer Robert Hemenway, and perhaps more important, the "(re)discovery" of African-American literature coupled with the feminist/womanist movement of the 1980s, helped to move Hurston from the shadow of the veil behind which she lies buried in a segregated cemetery into the mainstream of America's literary canon. The work of the former secretary, chauffeur, waitress, and domestic—particularly *Their Eyes Were Watching God*—is now the subject of panel discussions at MLA conferences, M.A. theses and Ph.D. dissertations, and critical volumes edited by distinguished scholars, white and black. HarperCollins has committed to publishing new editions of Hurston's collected works.

Often described as the most prolific black woman writer in America, Hurston's oeuvre includes four novels: *Jonah's Gourd Vine* (1934), *Their Eyes Were Watching God* (1937), *Moses, Man of the Mountain* (1939), and *Seraph on the Suwanee* (1948); two collections of folklore: *Mules and Men* (1935) and *Tell My Horse* (1938); two plays: *Color Struck* (1925) and *Mule Bone: A Comedy of Negro Life in Three Acts* (1931), which she wrote with poet Langston Hughes; and an autobiography: *Dust Tracks on a Road* (1942). Until recently, however, not much critical attention has been given to Hurston's short stories, the genre

This essay was written specifically for this volume and is published here by permission of the author.

her such labels as "limb of Satan," "lil' hasion," and "hellion."[8] At 11 years of age, she is a dancing banshee who must be reprimanded and reminded to "put yo' knees together" and behave like a lady (18). Like John Redding, however, Isis becomes various personages through her vivid imagination, which also takes her to the "horizon, for she still believed that to be [the] land's end" (19).

Drawn by the sounding brass and tinkling cymbal of a carnival marching band, the fluid and joy-filled Isis instinctively bolts out of her grandmother's circumscribing gate, dancing, imitating the dignity and grace of a Spanish dancer and creatively costuming herself with her grandmother's new red-and-white tablecloth for her shawl, a daisy thrust behind her ear.

> The Grand Exalted Ruler [of the sponsoring Grand Order of Odd Fellows] rose to speak; the band was hushed, but Isis danced on, the crowd clapping their hands for her. No one listened to the Exalted one, for little by little the multitude had surrounded the brown dancer. (22)

Not surprisingly, Isis's exhilaration is quelled only by her grandmother, whose appearance signifies yet another whipping to the gifted and life-filled child. Deciding to commit suicide rather than submit to her grandmother's abuse any longer, Isis is rescued by an older white couple who identify her as their "little gypsy" (23). They invite her to travel with them to their destination, the Park Hotel, located a short distance up the road from her grandmother's house. Although Isis readily agrees, her grandmother thwarts her plans once again, describing her as "de wustest lil' limb dat ever drawed bref" (24). However, the grandmother is easily muted by the white lady, who gives her five dollars to replace her now-ruined tablecloth, which is apparently more valuable to her than her granddaughter. The grandmother allows Isis to escort the couple, realizing a profit of four dollars for her shawl. The white woman explains, "I want brightness and this Isis is joy itself, why she is drenched in light! . . . I want a little of her sunshine to soak into my soul. I need it."

In "Drenched in Light," Isis, despite her grandmother's suppression, actively seeks to determine the outcome of the events in her life. Although cognizant of the punitive consequences her behavior will inadvertently elicit, she remains uninhibited. Even her decision to commit suicide rather than be whipped once again attests to the empowerment she desires. She yearns to validate her own voice and maintain and exercise control over her own body. Like Frederick Douglass, who resolves not to be broken by the whipping forced on him by the slave breaker, Mr. Covey, Isis is empowered in the end by her rejection of the demeaning abuse she suffers at the hands of her grandmother.

In contrast, John Redding submits to defeat, admitting to being beaten by both mother and wife. John remains a passive dreamer. He tells his father,

"Oh, yes, I'm a dreamer. . . . I have such wonderfully complete dreams. . . . They never come true." Consequently, John remains "soil lying helpless to move" himself (10), like the unyielding soil in which Claudia and Frieda plant marigold seeds in Morrison's *The Bluest Eye*. Song-filled Isis, on the other hand, erupts with the energy released by fulfilled plowed lands in Jean Toomer's *Cane*. John's father, Alfred, concedes as he laments, "Oh, yes, my boy, some ships get tangled in the weeds" (9).

However, Alfred takes a giant step beyond the sentimental, landing in the midst of the argument that will occupy Hurston's many narrators and characters, when he offers a different reason for John's quandary: the fundamental and complex issue of proprietorship. He tells his wife, Stella:

> Yas, dat's all you wimmen study 'bout—settlin' some man. You takes all de get-up out of 'em. Jes' let uh fellah mak uh motion lak gettin' somewhere, an' some 'oman'll begin tuh hollah, "Stop theah! where's you goin'? Don't fuhgit you b'longs tuh me." (8)

Thus, in his near-misogynistic view Alfred sees and defines Stella, and all women, as emasculating agents who in attempting to own and stabilize men—making them homebodies—prevent them from exercising what he presumes to be an almost instinctive independent mobility. Hurston's reversal is indeed noteworthy. Ironically, Alfred, in claiming that "dat's all you wimmen study 'bout," accuses Stella of behaving like men. This bent toward ownership is generally associated with masculine behavior, as is ascertainable from the behavior of Logan Killicks and Jody Starks, Janie's first and second husbands respectively in *Their Eyes Were Watching God*. Whereas Logan tells Janie, "You ain't got no particular place. It's wherever Ah need yuh" (52), Jody declares that Janie is "uh woman and her place is in . . . [the] home" (69). Certainly these men claim the prerogative of owning "their" women like they own their land or dry-goods store. When Jody explains the role he envisions for Janie, he makes this quite clear: "[M]ah wife don't know nothin' 'bout speech-makin'. Ah never married her for nothin' lak dat." Jody appropriates Janie's voice as he relegates her to the domestic place he has determined she should occupy.

This is what makes Isis such a significant first character for Hurston. Isis, though a child, flaunts a "magic and feistiness" generally associated with untrammeled black male behavior. She yearns for what Morrison describes as a form of male prerogative and privilege of being "free"—"not free in the legal sense, but free in his head."[9] Isis, like the Janie who eventually reclaims her voice, is not to be domesticated in the final analysis; each must adhere to the imperative of pulling in her own horizon—of calling in her soul to come and see. This feat is not only physically emancipatory but, perhaps more important, results in spiritual transformation. As argued by Lloyd Brown, who finds similarities between Hurston's ideas and the philosophical analysis

Simone de Beauvior offers in *The Second Sex,* both Hurston and de Beauvior conclude that "it is a female trait . . . to use dreams as a means of transcending rather than resigning to reality." Dreams allow the "imprisoned woman to transform her prison into a heaven of glory, her servitude into sovereign liberty."[10] What remains problematic, however, is yet another reversal. In "John Redding Goes to Sea" father and son are imprisoned by women; Isis's jailor, like Janie's guardian, is none other than her grandmother, a woman.

Robert Bone describes "Drenched in Light" as the story of "the portrait of the artist as a young girl."[11] It clearly resonates with Hurston's own quest, which she seems to verify in *Dust Tracks:*

> I kept on probing to know. . . . I had a stifled longing. I used to climb to the top of one of the huge chinaberry trees which guarded our front gate, *and look over the world.* The most interesting thing I saw was the horizon. . . . It grew upon me that I ought to walk out to the horizon and see what the end of the world was like. (36; italics added)

Like Isis and Janie, Hurston had discovered, at an early age, the importance of not only exploring the horizon beyond one's gate but doing so in a manner that leads to personal liberation. She desires to "look *over* the world," to gaze above and beyond, to exceed the limited space with which she has been provided. Only then, it seems, can she become the art and the artist, the very clay she uses to mold and shape her own life.

Thus, the perspective afforded by Hurston's Eatonville gate places her at the "center of the world"—her own world. Beginning with her first stories, she uses Eatonville as a backdrop for the stage on which she explores and engages the dynamics of everyday life that interested her. Here she had experienced dramatizations that seem more valuable than even the most sophisticated Greek tragedy or comedy.

Hurston's award-winning short story "Spunk" bears this out, with a community of men, resembling a Greek chorus, who gather at the local general store.[12] "Spunk" clearly validates the significance Hurston places on her intimate familiarity with her provincial milieu as well as continues her active interest in the place of misogynistic thought and behavior in heterosexual relationships in public social settings, such as the porch.

Like the Greek chorus, the men narrate and comment on the life and behavior of the tragic hero, intrepid Spunk Banks, who is admired for his raw masculinity. At the sawmill, Spunk is dauntless in his deft handling of the circle-saw. The men celebrate his strength, acknowledging that Spunk, who "ain't skeered of nothin' on God's green foot-stool—nothin' " (26), is more courageous than they are. "When Tes' Miller got cut to giblets on that circle-saw, Spunk steps right up and starts ridin'. The rest of us was skeered to go near it" (26).

What the men seem to admire most, however, is Spunk's brazen public behavior and relationship with Lena Kanty, Joe Kanty's wife. Spunk unabashedly flaunts her on his arm around town. When Spunk is challenged by a jealous and disgraced razor-wielding Joe Kanty, "a round-shouldered figure in overalls much too big" (26), he shoots him. Spunk argues that he shot Joe in self-defense because Joe attacked him from the back; he is tried and set free. But before he and Lena, the victor's prize, can fully consummate their relationship in their new home, Spunk is haunted by a huge black bobcat, which he believes is Joe's spirit that has come back from hell to haunt him. Spunk dies at work after falling on the circle-saw, convinced that Joe's spirit pushed him.

Despite Joe's passivity and cowardly behavior, and the obvious praise the men shower on Spunk, they are not accepting of Spunk's narcissistic behavior in the end. The men readily acknowledge his virility and death-defying action at the sawmill, but they are not willing to acquiesce totally to Spunk's exhibitionist behavior. Although they are embarrassed by Joe's wimpy behavior and goad him on to defend his (and their) honor as a man, they are simultaneously embarrassed by having someone like Spunk around, someone who makes them all appear unmanly.

Spunk exercises his proprietor's rights when he uses Lena to convince Joe, Lena's husband, that Spunk—not Joe—is her "boss." According to Spunk, "A woman knows her boss an' she answers when he calls" (28). Lena willingly complies, responding to Spunk like an animal to its master. Through his action and declarations, Spunk not only controls Lena and overshadows her wimpy husband but also appears to stand above the other men, who despite their boisterous laughter were already dwarfed by Spunk's reputation at the sawmill. Their already fragile position of privilege is further weakened and jeopardized by Spunk's narcissism. After all, Lena is legally married to Joe, and he should, according to moral forces in their community, have authority over her domain, whether he has and shows grit or not. What is to prevent Spunk from invading anyone else's domestic space? Walter confesses, "Ah like [Spunk] fine but 'tain't right the way he carries on wid Lena Kanty." Walter remains sympathetic to Joe in the end. He argues that "Joe wuz a braver man than Spunk."

> "Thas a fact," went on Walter. "Lookit whut he done; took a razor an' went out to fight a man he knowed toted a gun an' wuz a crack shot, too; 'nother thing Joe wuz skeered of Spunk, skeered plumb stiff! But he went jes' the same." (30)

Joe becomes the men's sacrificial lamb who, although he acts late in the game, defends his honor nevertheless. It is difficult to disagree with Walter. Joe might have attacked Spunk from behind, but not only has it been well established that Joe is the weaker of the two men and therefore no match for brawny Spunk, but his razor must have appeared limp before Spunk's army .45. Although they appear to celebrate Spunk's machismo, the porch sitters ferociously guard the benefits they enjoy in their patriarchal space—one in which woman is an object of ownership. The most sacred communal moral values, which punish Spunk for his transgression, leave them sitting on high, like communal elders and chiefs, on the store porch. Privileged, the men can accept and reject Spunk's behavior.

Ultimately, however, Spunk's downfall and violent death are due to his own hubris, which causes him to see himself as invincible. "He'd go after *anything* he wanted" (28). Restored and vindicated, the community cleanses itself through the funerary rituals. At the wake the "fallen giant" is humbled with only "a dingy sheet . . . [for] his shroud. The women ate heartily of the funeral baked meats and wondered who would be Lena's next. The men whispered coarse conjectures between guzzles of whiskey" (32).

In "Spunk" we find Hurston not only celebrating the lifestyle of rural blacks, a world dominated by a stringent morality, but exploring and filtering the rich and complex dynamic of a patriarchal "village," male sexuality, and heterosexual relationships. Both John Redding and Janie have quite romantic views about their sexuality. Both imagine the revelatory lessons in nature, such as the pollination process, as the blueprint for human sexuality. But the communal narrators in "Spunk" abandon such a rose-colored perspective, clearly offering a much different prism. In the end, the men come to realize that despite their socialization and subscription to any unwritten but practiced and accepted code of virility, they are still bound by the moral parameters of their community, irrespective of the obvious privileges they enjoy.

Nevertheless, the story's ending undermines and disrupts any convictions they may have to the contrary. It offers yet another reversal. The position the men occupy and what appears to be the sanctity of their patriarchal community remain vulnerable because the women wondered who would be Lena's next victim. With this ending, Hurston disrupts what we took to be the conventional throughout the story. While we definitely hear male egotism in the men's porch chat, we also witness a different matrix of female representation, one in which we see women as free agents as well. Lena is no mere vixen. She, like Isis and Janie, is "free of mind." Hurston may define the black woman as "de mule uh de world" in *Their Eyes,* but in "Spunk" Lena exercises as much agency as Spunk. Those attending Spunk's wake find that Lena "had filled the room with magnolia blossoms that gave off a heavy sweet odor" (32). She is not browbeaten like Janie, who is dominated by Joe Starks. Lena, unlike Spunk, is guilty of infidelity. She wants Spunk as much as he wants her, apparently at any cost, even the death of her husband. That Lena behaves like a black widow spider that will find yet another prey is suggested both by her active role in Joe's ultimate demise and by the "heavy sweet odor" in place to attract her next victim.

With her treatment and characterization of Sykes Jones in "Sweat,"[13] Hurston takes a more adamant position and makes a stronger statement against narcissistic male behavior, which is not exonerated by the patriarchal community, "the village men on Joe Clarke's porch" (76), who serve as narrators and moderators. Sykes's greatest desire is to replace Delia Jones, his wife of 15 years, with Bertha, a fatter, younger, and (to him) more attractive woman. Like Joe Kanty, Delia's weakness is her acquiescing personality; she, too, is described as habitually meek, having sagging, "thin, stooped shoulders" (74). Sykes physically and psychologically abuses her. He tells her that she is "one aggravatin' nigger woman" whom he now hates because, for him, she is no longer fat enough; certainly, she is not as fat as Bertha. He spends his time verbally abusing her and taunting her by exploiting and belittling her fear of snakes. Moreover, Sykes strongly objects to Delia's occupation as a laundress for whites. Although he finds it demeaning, she reminds him that they live in a home purchased with money she earned from this profession. She proudly tells him, "Mah tub of suds is filled yo' belly with vittles more times than yo' hands filled it. My sweat is done paid for this house and Ah reckon Ah kin keep on sweatin' in it" (75).

To execute his plans to oust and destroy Delia, Sykes brings home a six-foot diamond-back rattlesnake, which he keeps in a box placed in her daily path and eventually puts in the dirty clothes hamper. Delia discovers the snake while preparing for the next day's washing, but she escapes Sykes's sinister intention by running into the darkness of the night. When he returns to check on the outcome of his scheme, Sykes becomes the victim of his own nefarious plan. He is attacked by the snake while outside, Delia, lying in her flower garden, watches the rising sun and listens to his mournful cries for help, never going to his rescue. So she, like Lena, "kills" her lover.

Like Spunk, Sykes is driven by narcissism. His inflated ego, magnified by his having been taught to drive by a white woman from the North as well as by the attention he gets from Bertha, is the direct source of the shame he feels because of Delia's occupation. Although he has willingly accepted the benefits it affords over the years, his manhood remains debased by it. Again, despite the privilege they enjoy as members of their small patriarchal community, the men seem bound by a sense of communal morality. While they admire Delia for her fortitude, the porch guardians look upon Sykes with disgust, concluding, "He ain't fit tuh carry guts tuh bear" (77). Although they were more accepting of Spunk's behavior and display of virility, the men consider Sykes overbearing. Concluding that he is "too biggety to live" (78), they talk about taking him to the swamp and whipping him.

The obvious difference between the men's appreciation of Spunk and their disdain for Sykes is the high esteem in which the village men hold Delia. She commands their respect through her devotion to her church (she is a member in good standing at the local A.M.E. church), unyielding pursuit of her occupation, which allows them to realize semblances of the American dream of owning their own home, and commitment to Sykes. The men condemn him for the physical abuse he has used to ravage this once-beautiful woman. They explain, "[Sykes] done beat huh 'nough tuh kill three women, let 'lone change they looks" (77). Again, as in "Spunk," the men readily conclude that despite their practiced and accepted code of virility, they are still bound by the moral parameters of their community, irrespective of the obvious privileges they enjoy.

Only when Sykes brings the snake into her private Garden of Eden does Delia's love turn to hate. She tells him, "Ah hates you tuhde same degree dat Ah useter love yuh. Ah done took an' took 'til mah belly is full up tuhmah neck" (81). Joe Clarke's statement seems to justify Sykes's death and Delia's refusal to come to his rescue. He says, "Tain't no law on earth dat kin make a man be decent if it ain't in 'im" (77). Indeed, Sykes's death clearly signifies the triumph of good over evil, as well as the restoration of the village. Delia, a symbol of goodness, love, and faith, experiences rebirth and renewal as she emerges from her flower bed, listening but unmoved by Sykes's inevitable and violent demise.

In contrast to "Spunk" and "Sweat," Hurston's "The Gilded Six Bits" clearly explores and celebrates, through Missie May and Joe, a relationship in which neither misogyny nor narcissism occupies a meaningful place.[14] Reciprocity abounds in their life of domestic tranquillity. Missie lords over their simple but sunshine-filled home, which she keeps clean and beautiful. "Everything clean from the front gate to the privy house. . . . Fresh newspaper cut in fancy edge on the kitchen shelves" (86). She venerates what is clearly her "commercial" space. She tells Joe, "Ah'm a real wife, not no dress and breath. Ah might not look lak one, but if you burn me, you won't git a thing but wife ashes" (88). Joe, who works at the local fertilizer plant, respects this position and shows his appreciation and commitment by bringing home his weekly earnings. However, that their marriage is more than a business venture is signified by the chocolate kisses and pockets full of love tokens she discovers, along with the currency, during their playful bantering. Their friendly combat illustrates the equitable roles they share as well as celebrates their love.

This seemingly unblemished relation is almost bankrupt, however, when Joe returns home early from work to find Missie May in their bedroom in a compromising situation with Slemmons, a northern entrepreneur who has opened his own ice-cream parlor in their small community. Missie May is attracted to Slemmons's sartorial splendor, to his urban sophistication, and specifically to the golden piece, a ten-dollar coin he wears for a tie pin. Despite the corruption of the sanctity of their humble home and bedroom, however, semblances of their ideal life and home reappear months later, after Missie May gives birth to a son that resembles his father, Joe.

In her best-known short stories, then, Hurston focuses on domestic relationships, but as Lillie P. Howard notes, "instead of portraying marriage [excessively] romantically, . . . Hurston presents it frankly, replete with infidelity, jealousy, violence, and hatred."[15] The position of Hurston's narrators is clearly one in which marriage is perceived and presented as inevitably short-lived if respect, trust, and understanding are absent. Although Missie May brings infidelity into the domestic space she shares with Joe, it is important to note that Joe loves her and is willing to try to understand her behavior. It is indeed significant that he does not abandon his wife or home. To some degree, he is not unlike Joe in "Spunk," who tries to restore his marriage to Lena despite her public behavior with Spunk. However, unlike Lena, Missie May remains at home, committed to her husband.

Joe responds with a more passively aggressive behavior. Although he appears to accept Missie May's explanation that her motives were altruistic, he denotes, by leaving under their pillow the coins he took from Slemmons during their brief struggle, how ephemeral materiality can be: the coins are gilded! The silent implications of his behavior are even more shattering, given Missie May's perception and definition of her role as housewife as a "business." The possibility that Joe redefined their home as a different kind of marketplace momentarily fragments Missie May: "He had come home to buy from her as if she were any woman in the long house. Fifty cents for her love. As if to say that he could pay as well as Slemmons" (96). Their problems are resolved when trust can once again reenter their relationship. In fact, any interim lost profits are not only restored but also increased with the expansion of their family. Clearly, Missie May misidentifies her horizon in reaching for a valueless prize. Consequently, she almost loses her position and the center of her own self-created and redefined world in the process.

Hurston's most lucid pronouncement on domestic relationships is clearly found in *Their Eyes Were Watching God*. Appropriately, "Hurricane,"[16] the short story excerpted from this award-winning novel, focuses on the recommitment Janie and Tea Cake make to each other during the height of a storm that results in his death. Janie marries Tea Cake after the death of her second husband, Jody Starks, her bee-man with whom she eloped to fulfill her adolescent fantasies of sex, love, and marriage after escaping potential bondage by her landholding first husband, Logan Killicks. Both Logan and Jody (whose "I god" outbursts signify his empowered position and communal stature of privilege as mayor) seem determined to lord over Janie, relegating her to the mule status her grandmother warned about.

Although Jody succeeds in robbing Janie of her voice and involving her in a loveless marriage of 20 years, Vergible Woods, known as "Tea Cake," though younger and penniless, comes into Janie's life and helps her restore her voice and fulfill her cherished dream. They travel to the Everglades, where she works with him on the muck, a long distance from the privileged throne and lifestyle Starks provided. She does not have to speak through Tea Cake, as she was expected to do through Jody Starks's "big voice." In fact, as far as Tea Cake is concerned, Janie has "de keys to de kingdom" (165).

Proprietorship becomes an issue for Janie and Tea Cake, but it is clear that Janie has not become merely another man's property. At different junctures in their relationship each seeks (re)confirmation from the other. When jealousy drives Janie to suspect Tea Cake of having an affair with Nunkie, another field worker, she confronts him, fights him, and then makes love to him. The gratification she achieves is equated to that of a victorious rooster that crows over its victim. She confirms that Tea Cake belongs to her and no one else. He verifies this when he tells her, "You'se something tuhmake uh man forgit tuhgit old and forgit tuhdie" (206). Similarly, jealousy leads Tea Cake to beat Janie. "Not because her behavior justified his jealousy, but it relieved that awful fear inside him. Being able to whip her reassured him in possession. No brutal beating at all. He just slapped her around a bit to show he was boss" (218). Tea Cake's action usurps not only the plans of possible suitors, such as Mrs. Turner's brother, but also wins him the respect of their community:

> Everybody talked about it the next day in the fields. It aroused a sort of envy in both men and women. The way he petted and pampered her as if those two or three face slaps had nearly killed her made the women see visions and the helpless way she hung on him made men dream dreams. (218)

Wendy J. McCredie correctly notes that "The first fight [in which Janie attacks Tea Cake] is for themselves, and the second for the outside world that only recognizes man's, Tea Cake's, authority to possess and protect woman."[17] In the confrontations in which domestic violence is accepted or normal, each party grants ownership rights to the other; bodies are not merely independently appropriated without consent.

Despite the compromise, however, one has to agree with Lloyd Brown that Janie's quest for the ideal involves "both a transcendental affirmation of her selfhood and an act of accepting conventional notions of womanhood."[18] Janie confirms as much when, in the midst of the storm, Tea Cake asks if she made the wrong decision by marrying him. She is almost philosophical in responding to him: "People don't die till dey time come nohow, don't keer where you at. *Ahem wid mah husband in uh storm, dat's all.* . . . We been tuhgether round two years. If you kin see de light at daybreak, you don't keer if you die at dusk" (235–36; emphasis added). After Tea Cake rescues Janie from a rabid dog (and is bitten during the process), Janie once again celebrates the special love they share rather than lamenting the sacrifices she has made in giving up the life of comfort she inherited from Jody. She tells him, "Once upon a time, Ah never 'spected nothin' Tea Cake but bein' dead from the standin' still and tryin' tuh laugh. But you come 'long and made somethin' outa me. So Ahem thankful fuh anything we come through together" (247). In the end, Janie is forced to kill Tea Cake to protect herself after he develops rabies. She is left with his living memory, as she finally successfully "pull[s] in her horizon like a great fish-net. Pulled it from around the waist of the world and draped it over her shoulder."[19] One has to agree with Molly Hite that Janie's "heterosexual idyll with Tea Cake is thus not the culmination of the plot, but a transformative moment that leads to the culmination."[20]

The resolution achieved by Janie and Tea Cake, as well as by Missie May and Joe, and the possibility of wholeness that now lies on their horizons is enhanced by the fertile agrarian soil of the southern folk community and life that surrounds them. It provides the diastolic and systolic beat and sounds, that is, the life-invigorating language of restoration that they know and speak. It is here, in this space, where Joe Clarke's porch is located, that language is shaped and that stories, "big lies," are told and roots are possible. Closure for Janie is not only her return to Eatonville but also the opportunity and her ability to tell her story, providing "de understandin' to go 'long wid it" (19).

The kind of resolution found in Janie's and Missie May's agrarian community and lives is not possible in the urban jungle, where a more naturalistic survival of the fittest rules. Hurston strongly suggests this in her treatment of heterosexual love in "Muttsy" and "Story in Harlem Slang," which are both set in the Jazz Age of New York's Harlem. Although Harlem is viewed as the promised land by black migrants who flock there, like Pinkie of "Muttsy"[21] and Jelly (Marvel) and Sweet Back of "Story in Harlem Slang,"[22] it remains no more than a habitat of sycophants and pimps, in which relationships can only be superficial.

Muttsy, Jelly, and Sweet Back are black males who hate to work. Whereas Muttsy becomes a professional gambler (despite his competence and reputation as a highly respected stevedore), zoot-suited Jelly and Sweet Back strut their stuff on Lenox Avenue, "sugar-curing the ladies' feelings," hunting for "dishes to dirty" (127–28). They willingly prey on women whom they expect to support them. Muttsy succeeds in winning Pinkie's love after he promises to give up his life of gambling. However, he reneges on his promise after their marriage and returns to his habit.

Jelly and Sweet Back's feigned friendship is as manufactured as their colorful suits. Their verbal duel and signifying game of the dozens are central to the turf battle their lifestyle mandates. This is evidenced when starvation drives them to hunt like foxes on the prowl:

> "Git out of my face, Jelly! Dat broad I seen you with wasn't no pe-ola. She was one of them coal-scuttle blondes with hair just as close to her head as ninety-nine is to a hundred. She look-ted like she had seventy-five pounds of clear bosom, guts in her feet, and she look-ted like six months in front and nine months behind. Buy you a whiskey still! Dat broad couldn't make the down payment on a pair of sox."

"Sweet Back, you fixing to talk out of place." Jelly stiffened.
"If you trying to jump salty, Jelly, that's your mammy." (130)

There can be only one conqueror. However, in the end both lose, as their intended victim readily identifies them and exposes them for what they are:

"Naw indeed!" the girl laughed harshly. "You skillets is trying to promote a meal on me. But it'll never happen, brother. You barking up the wrong tree. I wouldn't give you air if you was stopped up in a jug. I'm not putting out a thing. I'm just like the cemetery—I'm not putting out, I'm taking in! Dig?" (132–33)

Despite the misogyny and misanthropy encoded in the rich texture of Hurston's urban dialect, a sensitive and even sympathetic narrator explains at the end, "But Jelly's thoughts were far away. He was remembering those full, hot meals he had left back in Alabama to seek wealth and splendor . . . without working" (133). Provincial, superstitious, misogynist, and even segregated, the agrarian South remains whole and wholesome, an infinite space of possibilities, a fertile soil for navigating to and reaching one's horizon, where resolution, if not transcendence of variables that obstruct the path to more meaningful heterosexual relationships, is possible.

Notes

1. Hurston was not always honest about her age, offering several dates for the year of her birth. Although it is known that she was born on January 7, scholars generally list several dates, from 1891 through 1901. The year 1891 is used by her biographer Robert E. Hemenway; Henry Louis Gates Jr. and Anthony Appiah also use 1891 in their *Critical Perspective* volume on Hurston.

2. Alice Walker, "Looking for Zora," in *In Search of Our Mothers' Gardens: Womanist Prose* (San Diego: Harvest, 1983), 87, 86, 107.

3. For quite interesting views of Hurston and the writers of the Harlem Renaissance see Darwin T. Turner, *In a Minor Chord: Three Afro-American Writers and Their Search for Identity* (Carbondale: Southern Illinois Press, 1971), 89–120, and Arthur P. Davis, *From the Dark Tower: Afro-American Writers, 1900 to 1960* (Washington, D.C.: Howard University Press, 1974), 113–20. Langston Hughes's *The Big Sea* offers some personal remembrances as well.

4. The short-lived journal *Fire* was founded by Wallace Thurman. Hurston, along with Langston Hughes and Richard Bruce Nugent, was listed as associate editor.

5. Robert Bone, *Down Home* (New York: G. P. Putnam's Sons, 1975), 139–50, specifically 144.

6. *The Complete Stories,* comp. Henry Louis Gates Jr. (New York: HarperCollins, 1995), 1–16. All references are to this edition and will be incorporated into the text.

7. Ibid., 17–25. All references are to this edition and will be incorporated into the text.

8. A term first used by Alice Walker in "In Search of Our Mothers' Gardens" (1974), in *In Search of Our Mothers' Gardens*, xi–xii. *Womanist* is the opposite of *womanish;* it describes a

black feminist or feminist of color, "usually referring to outrageous, audacious, courageous or *willful* behavior"—qualities not typically attributed to women.

9. See " 'Intimate Things in Place': A Conversation with Toni Morrison," in *Chant of Saints,* ed. Michael S. Harper and Robert B. Stepto (Urbana: University of Illinois Press, 1979), 220–21.

10. Lloyd Brown, "Zora Neale Hurston and the Nature of Female Perception," *Obsidian* (Winter 1978): 39–45. Brown also notes that ironically this perspective leads not only to a "transcendental affirmation of selfhood" but, as in Janie's case, to "an act of accepting conventional notions of womanhood" (43).

11. Bone, *Down Home,* 145. There are serious problems with Bone's reading of this story as well. For example, he finds in Isis's fantasies, which he equates with Hurston's childhood fantasies, one of Hurston's "most potent fantasies . . . that of being white" (146).

12. *The Complete Stories,* comp. Gates Jr. , 26–32. All references are to this edition and will be incorporated into the text.

13. Ibid., 73–85. All references are to this edition and will be incorporated into the text.

14. Ibid., 86–98. All references are to this edition and will be incorporated into the text.

15. Lillie P. Howard, "Marriage: Zora Neale Hurston's System of Value," *CLA Journal* 21 (1977): 260.

16. *The Complete Stories,* comp. Gates Jr. , 149–61. All references are to this edition and will be incorporated into the text.

17. Wendy J. McCredie, "Authority and Authorization in *Their Eyes Were Watching God,*" *Black American Literature Forum* 16 (Spring 1982): 28.

18. Brown, "Zora Neale Hurston and the Nature of Female Perception," 43.

19. Zora Neale Hurston, *Their Eyes Were Watching God* (1937; rpt., Urbana: University of Illinois Press, 1978), 286.

20. Molly Hite, "Romance, Marginality, and Matrilineage: *The Color Purple* and *Their Eyes Were Watching God,*" in *Reading Black, Reading Feminist,* ed. Henry Louis Gates Jr. (New York: Meridian Books, 1990), 443.

21. *The Complete Stories,* ed. Henry Louis Gates Jr. and Seiglinde Lemke (New York: HarperCollins, 1995), 41–56. All references are to this edition and will be incorporated into the text.

22. *The Complete Stories,* comp. Gates Jr. , 127–33. All references are to this edition and will be incorporated into the text. This story was first entitled "Now You Cookin' with Gas." See *The Complete Stories,* 233–41. Its ending differs significantly from "Story in Harlem Slang." Though they remain pimps, the men are debased by the jobs available to them. Hurston includes a "Glossary of Harlem Slang" with both stories.

BIBLIOGRAPHY
◆

Writings by Zora Neale Hurston

BLAINE L. HALL

The following abbreviations are used to refer to the location of Hurston's manuscripts, if known.

CSJ   Fisk Charles S. Johnson Papers, Special Collections, Fisk University Library

FHSP   Florida Historical Society Papers, University of South Florida Library

HCU   Fla Hurston Collection, Rare Books and Manuscripts, University of Florida Library

HUAL   Alain Locke papers, Moorland-Spingarn Research Center, Howard University Library

JWJ   Yale James Weldon Johnson Memorial Collection, Collection of American Literature, Beinecke Rare Book and Manuscript Library, Yale University

LCAFS   Archive of Folk Songs, Library of Congress

BOOKS

Jonah's Gourd Vine. 1934. Reprint, with an introduction by Larry Neal, Philadelphia: J. B. Lippincott, 1971. Reprint, with a foreword by Rita Dove, New York: HarperCollins, 1990. Manuscript in Schomburg Collection, New York Public Library.

Mules and Men. Preface by Franz Boas. Philadelphia: J. B. Lippincott, 1935. Reprint, New York: Negro Universities Press, 1969. Reprint, with an introduction by Darwin Turner, New York: Harper and Row, 1970. Reprint, with a foreword by Arnold Rampersad, New York: HarperCollins, 1990.

Their Eyes Were Watching God. Philadelphia: J. B. Lippincott, 1937. Reprint, Greenwich, Conn.: Fawcett Publications, 1965. Reprint, New York: Negro Universities Press, 1969. Reprint, with a foreword by Sherley Anne Williams, Urbana: University of Illinois Press, 1978. Manuscript in JWJYale.

Tell My Horse: Voodoo and Life in Haiti and Jamaica. Philadelphia: J. B. Lippincott, 1938. Reprint, with a foreword by Ishmael Reed, New York: HarperCollins, 1990. Manuscript in JWJYale.

Moses, Man of the Mountain. Philadelphia: J. B. Lippincott, 1939. Reprint, Chatham, N.J.: Chatham Bookseller, 1974. Reprint, with a foreword by Deborah E. McDowell, New York: HarperCollins, 1991. Manuscript in JWJYale.

Dust Tracks on a Road. Philadelphia: J. B. Lippincott, 1942. Reprint, with an introduction by Darwin Turner, New York: Arno Press, 1969. Reprint, with an introduction by Larry Neal, New York: J. B. Lippincott, 1971. Reprint, with a foreword by Maya Angelou, New York: HarperCollins, 1991. Manuscript in JWJYale.

Seraph on the Suwanee: A Novel. New York: Charles Scribner's Sons, 1948. Reprint, Ann Arbor, Mich.: University Microfilms, 1971. Reprint, New York: AMS Press, 1974. Reprint, with a foreword by Hazel V. Carby, New York: HarperCollins, 1991. Manuscript in HCUFla.

I Love Myself When I Am Laughing . . . and Then Again When I Am Looking Mean and Impressive: A Zora Neale Hurston Reader. Edited by Alice Walker, with an introduction by Mary Helen Washington. Old Westbury, N.Y.: The Feminist Press, 1979.

The Sanctified Church. Edited and foreword by Toni Cade Bambara. Berkeley, Calif.: Turtle Island, 1981.

Spunk: The Selected Short Stories of Zora Neale Hurston. Edited and foreword by Bob Callahan. Berkeley, Calif.: Turtle Island, 1985.

The Complete Stories. Edited and foreword by Henry Louis Gates Jr. and Sieglinde Lemke; afterword by Henry Louis Gates Jr. New York: HarperCollins, 1995.

Zora Neale Hurston: Folklore, Memoirs, and Other Writings. Compiled by Cheryl A. Wall. New York: Library of America, 1995.

OTHER PUBLICATIONS

"John Redding Goes to Sea." *Stylus* 1 (May 1921): 11–22. Reprinted in *Opportunity* 4 (January 1926): 16–21. Reprinted in *The Complete Stories,* compiled by Henry Louis Gates Jr. and Sieglinde Lemke (New York: HarperCollins, 1995), 1–16.

"O Night." *Stylus* 1 (May 1921): 42.

"Poem." *Howard University Record* 16 (February 1922): 236.

"Drenched in Light." *Opportunity* 2 (December 1924): 371–74. Reprinted in *The Complete Stories,* compiled by Gates Jr. and Lemke, 17–25.

"Spunk." *Opportunity* 3 (June 1925): 171–73. Reprinted in *The New Negro,* edited by Alain Locke. New York: Albert and Charles Boni, 1925, 105–11. Reprinted in *Spunk: The Selected Short Stories of Zora Neale Hurston,* edited and foreword by Bob Callahan. Berkeley, Calif.: Turtle Island, 1985, 1–8. Reprinted in *The Complete Stories,* compiled by Gates Jr. and Lemke, 26–32.

"Magnolia Flower." *Spokesman* (July 1925): 26–29. Reprinted in *The Complete Stories,* compiled by Gates Jr. and Lemke, 33–40.

"The Hue and Cry about Howard University." *Messenger* 7 (September 1925): 315–19, 338.

"Muttsy." *Opportunity* 4 (August 1926): 246–50. Reprinted in *Spunk: The Selected Short Stories of Zora Neale Hurston,* edited and foreword by Callahan, 19–37. Reprinted in *The Complete Stories,* compiled by Gates Jr. and Lemke, 41–36.

" 'Possum or Pig." *Forum* 76 (September 1926): 465. Reprinted in *The Complete Stories,* compiled by Gates Jr. and Lemke, 57–58.

"The Eatonville Anthology." *Messenger* 8 (September–November 1926): 261–62, 297, 319, 332. Reprinted in *I Love Myself When I Am Laughing . . .,* edited by Walker, 177–88. Reprinted in *The Complete Stories,* compiled by Gates Jr. and Lemke, 59–72.

"Color Struck: A Play." *Fire!!* 1 (November 1926): 7–15.

"Sweat." *Fire!!* 1 (November 1926): 40–45. Reprinted in *I Love Myself When I Am Laughing . . .*, edited by Walker, 197–207. Reprinted in *The Complete Stories,* compiled by Gates Jr. and Lemke, 73–85.

"The First One: A Play." In *Ebony and Topaz.* Edited by Charles S. Johnson. New York: National Urban League, 1927, 53–57.

"Cudjo's Own Story of the Last African Slaver." *Journal of Negro History* 12 (October 1927): 648–63.

"Communication" [about the Fort Moosa settlement and Negro colony in Florida]. *Journal of Negro History* 12 (October 1927): 664–67.

"How It Feels to Be Colored Me." *World Tomorrow* 11 (May 1928): 215–16. Reprinted in *I Love Myself When I Am Laughing . . .*, edited by Walker, 152–55.

"Dance Songs and Tales from the Bahamas." *Journal of American Folklore* 43 (July–September 1930): 294–312.

"Hoodoo in America." *Journal of American Folklore* 44 (October–December 1931): 317–418.

"The Gilded Six-Bits." *Story* 3 (August 1933): 60–70. Reprinted in *I Love Myself When I Am Laughing . . .*, edited by Walker, , 208–18. Reprinted in *Spunk: The Selected Short Stories of Zora Neale Hurston,* edited and foreword by Callahan, 68–74. Reprinted in *Spunk: The Selected Short Stories of Zora Neale Hurston.* Edited and foreword by Bob Callahan (Berkeley: Turtle Island, 1985), 54–68. Reprinted in *The Complete Stories,* compiled by Gates Jr. and Lemke, 86–98.

"Characteristics of Negro Expression." In *Negro: An Anthology.* Edited by Nancy Cunard. London: Wishart, 1934, 39–46. Reprinted in *The Sanctified Church.* Edited and foreword by Toni Cade Bambara (Berkeley, Calif.: Turtle Island, 1981), 41–68.

"Conversions and Visions." In *Negro: An Anthology,* edited by Cunard, 47–49.

"Shouting." In *Negro: An Anthology,* edited by Cunard, 49–50.

"The Sermon." In *Negro: An Anthology,* edited by Cunard, 50–54.

"Mother Catharine." In *Negro: An Anthology,* edited by Cunard, 54–57. Reprinted in *The Sanctified Church,* edited and foreword by Bambara, 23–29. Reprinted in *The Complete Stories,* compiled by Gates Jr. and Lemke, 99–105.

"Uncle Monday." In *Negro: An Anthology,* edited by Cunard, 57–61. Reprinted in *The Sanctified Church,* edited and foreword by Bambara, 30–40. Reprinted in *The Complete Stories,* compiled by Gates Jr. and Lemke, 106–16.

"Spirituals and Neo-Spirituals." In *Negro: An Anthology,* edited by Cunard, 359–61.

"The Fire and the Cloud." *Challenge* 1 (September 1934): 10–14. Reprinted in *The Complete Stories,* compiled by Gates Jr. and Lemke, 117–21.

"Race Cannot Become Great until It Recognizes Its Talent." *Washington Tribune* (29 December 1934), n.p

"Full of Mud, Sweat and Blood" [review of *God Shakes Creation* by David M. Cohn]. *New York Herald Tribune Books* (3 November 1935): 8.

"Fannie Hurst." *Saturday Review* 9 (October 1937): 15–16.

"Star-Wrassling Sons-of-the-Universe" [review of *The Hurricane's Children* by Carl Carmer]. *New York Herald Tribune Books* (26 December 1937): 4.

"Rural Schools for Negroes" [review of *The Jeanes Teacher in the United States* by Lance G. E. Jones]. *New York Herald Tribune Books* (20 February 1938): 24.

"Stories of Conflict" [review of *Uncle Tom's Children* by Richard Wright]. *Saturday Review* (2 April 1938): 32.

"Now Take Noses." In *Cordially Yours.* Philadelphia: J. B. Lippincott, 1939, 25–27.

"Cock Robin, Beale Street." *Southern Literary Messenger* 3 (July 1941): 321–23. Reprinted in *The Complete Stories,* compiled by Gates Jr. and Lemke, 122–26.

"Story in Harlem Slang." *American Mercury* 55 (July 1942): 84–96. Reprinted in *Spunk: The Selected Short Stories of Zora Neale Hurston,* edited and foreword by Callahan, 82–96. Reprinted in *The Complete Stories,* compiled by Gates Jr. and Lemke, 127–38.

"Lawrence of the River." *Saturday Evening Post* (5 September 1942): 18, 55–57. Condensed in *Negro Digest* 1 (March 1943): 47–49.

"The 'Pet Negro' System." *American Mercury* 56 (May 1943): 593–600. Condensed in *Negro Digest* 1 (June 1943): 37–40. Reprinted in *I Love Myself When I Am Laughing . . .*, edited by Walker, 156–62.

"High John de Conquer." *American Mercury* 57 (October 1943): 450–58. Reprinted in *The Sanctified Church*, edited and foreword by Bambara, 69–78. Reprinted in *The Complete Stories*, ed. Gates Jr., and Lemke, 139–48.

"Negroes without Self-Pity." *American Mercury* 57 (November 1943): 601–3.

"The Last Slave Ship." *American Mercury* 58 (March 1944): 351–58. Condensed in *Negro Digest* 2 (May 1944): 11–16.

"My Most Humiliating Jim Crow Experience." *Negro Digest* 2 (June 1944): 25–26. Reprinted in *I Love Myself When I Am Laughing . . .*, edited by Walker, 163–64.

"Beware the Begging Joints." *American Mercury* 60 (March 1945): 288–94. Condensed in *Negro Digest* 3 (May 1945): 27–32.

"Crazy for This Democracy." *Negro Digest* 4 (December 1945): 45–48. Reprinted in *I Love Myself When I Am Laughing . . .*, edited by Walker, 165–68.

"Hurricane." Taken from *Their Eyes Were Watching God* (1937). Published in *Taken at the Flood: The Human Drama as Seen by Modern American Novelists*. Edited by Ann Watkins. Harper & Bros., 1946. Reprinted in *The Complete Stories*, edited by Gates Jr. and Lemke, 149–61.

"Bible, Played by Ear in Africa" [review of *How God Fix Jonah* by Lorenz Graham]. *New York Herald Tribune Weekly Book Review* (24 November 1946): 5.

"Jazz Regarded as Social Achievement" [review of *Shining Trumpets* by Rudi Blesh]. *New York Herald Tribune Weekly Book Review* (22 December 1946): 8.

"Thirty Days among Maroons" [review of *Journey to Accompong* by Katharine Dunham]. *New York Herald Tribune Weekly Book Review* (12 January, 1947): 8.

"The Transplanted Negro" [review of *Trinidad Village* by Melville Herskovits and Frances Herskovits]. *New York Herald Tribune Weekly Book Review* (9 March 1947): 20.

Caribbean Melodies for Chorus of Mixed Voices and Soloists. With accompaniment for piano and percussion instruments. Arranged by William Grant Still. Philadelphia: Oliver Ditson, 1947.

Review of *Voodoo in New Orleans* by Robert Tallant. *Journal of American Folklore* 60 (October–December 1947): 436–38.

"At the Sound of the Conch Shell" [review of *New Day* by Victor Stafford Reid]. *New York Herald Tribune Weekly Book Review* (20 March 1949): 4.

"Conscience of the Court." *Saturday Evening Post* (18 March 1950): 22–23, 112–22. Reprinted in *The Complete Stories*, compiled by Gates Jr. and Lemke, 162–77.

"What White Publishers Won't Print." *Negro Digest* 8 (April 1950): 85–89. Reprinted in *I Love Myself When I Am Laughing . . .*, edited by Walker, 169–73.

"I Saw Negro Votes Peddled." *American Legion Magazine* 49 (November 1950): 12–13, 54–57, 59–60. Condensed in *Negro Digest* 9 (September 1951): 77–85.

"Some Fabulous Caribbean Riches Revealed" [review of *The Pencil of God* by Pierre Marcelin and Philippe Thoby Marcelin]. *New York Herald Tribune Weekly Book Review* (4 February 1951): 5.

"Mourner's Bench, Communist Line: Why the Negro Won't Buy Communism." *American Legion Magazine* 50 (June 1951): 14–15, 55– 60.

"A Negro Voter Sizes Up Taft." *Saturday Evening Post* (8 December 1951): 29, 150.

"Victim of Fate." *Pittsburgh Courier* (11 October 1952).

"Zora's Revealing Story of Ruby's First Day in Court." *Pittsburgh Courier* (11 October 1952).

"Ruby Sane." *Pittsburgh Courier* (18 October 1952).

"Ruby McCollum Fights for Life." *Pittsburgh Courier* (22 November 1952).

"Bare Plot against Ruby." *Pittsburgh Courier* (29 November 1952).

"Trial Highlights." *Pittsburgh Courier* (29 November 1952).

"McCollum-Adams Trial Highlights." *Pittsburgh Courier* (27 December 1952).

"Ruby Bares Her Love." *Pittsburgh Courier* (3 January 1953).

"Doctor's Threats, Tussle over Gun Led to Slaying." *Pittsburgh Courier* (10 January 1953).

"Ruby's Troubles Mount." *Pittsburgh Courier* (17 January 1953).

"The Life Story of Mrs. Ruby J. McCollum." *Pittsburgh Courier* (28 February; 7, 14, 21, 28 March; 4, 11, 18, 25 April; 2 May 1953).

[The Trial of Ruby McCollum.] In William Bradford Huie, *Ruby McCollum: Woman in the Suwanee Jail*. New York: E. P. Dutton, 1956, 89–101.

"This Juvenile Delinquency." *Fort Pierce Chronicle* (12 December 1958).

"The Tripson Story." *Fort Pierce Chronicle* (6 February 1959).

"The Farm Laborer at Home." *Fort Pierce Chronicle* (27 February 1959).

"Hoodoo and Black Magic" [column]. *Fort Pierce Chronicle* (11 July 1958–7 August 1959).

"Cures and Beliefs." First printed in *The Sanctified Church*,. Edited and foreword by Bambara, 19–22.

"Father Abraham." First printed in *The Sanctified Church*, Edited and foreword by Bambara, 15–18.

"Negro Religious Customs: The Sanctified Church." First printed as "The Sanctified Church" in *The Sanctified Church*, edited and foreword by Bambara, 79–107. FHSP. Copy in LCAFS.

"Book of Harlem." First printed in *Spunk: The Selected Short Stories of Zora Neale Hurston*, edited and foreword by Callahan, 75–81. Reprinted in *The Complete Stories*, compiled by Gates Jr. and Lemke, 221–26. JWJYale.

"Isis." First printed in *Spunk: The Selected Short Stories of Zora Neale Hurston*, edited and foreword by Callahan,, 9–18.

"Black Death." Short story submitted to 1925 *Opportunity* contest. First printed in *The Complete Stories*, compiled by Gates Jr. and Lemke, 202–8. CSJFisk.

"The Bone of Contention." First printed in *The Complete Stories*, compiled by Gates Jr. and Lemke, 209–20. HUAL.

"Escape from Pharaoh." In *Moses: Man of the Mountain*. Reprinted in *The Complete Stories*, compiled by Gates Jr. and Lemke, 178–92.

"Harlem Slanguage." First printed in *The Complete Stories*, compiled by Gates Jr. and Lemke, 227–32.

"Now You Cookin' with Gas." In *The Complete Stories*, compiled by Gates Jr. and Lemke, 233–41.

"The Seventh Veil." In *The Complete Stories*, compiled by Gates Jr. and Lemke, 242–60. HCUFla.

"The Tablets of the Law." In *Moses: Man of the Mountain*. Reprinted in *The Complete Stories*, compiled by Gates Jr. and Lemke, 193–201.

"The Woman in Gaul." In *The Complete Stories*, compiled by Gates Jr. and Lemke, 261–83. HCUFla.

UNPUBLISHED MATERIALS

"Under the Bridge." 1925. Short story.

"The Ten Commandments of Charm." 1930. Essay.

" Spear." Play. To be produced in 1998. In possession of Wyatt Houston Day.

"Barracoon." 1931. Biography of Cudjo Lewis, 117 pp. HUAL.

"The Chick with One Hen." Character sketch, 2 pp. JWJYale.

"Eatonville When You Look at It." 2 pp. In "The Florida Negro."

"The Elusive Goal—Brotherhood of Mankind." Essay, 18 pp. HCUFla.

"The Emperor Effaces Himself." Character sketch, 7 pp. JWJYale.

"The Enemy." Personal experience, 10 pp. HCUFla.

The Fiery Chariot. Play in one act, 7 pp. HCUFla.

"The Florida Negro." Manuscript prepared by ZNH and others for the Florida Federal Writers' Project. 183 pp. FHSP.

"Folklore." 11 pp. In "The Florida Negro." Copy in LCAFS.

"Goldsborough." 1 p. In "The Florida Negro."

"Herod the Great." Biography, 269 pp. HCUFla.

"Joe Wiley of Magazine Point." Folklore, 5 pp. HUAL.

"Maitland." 2 pp. In "The Florida Negro."

"The Migrant Worker in Florida." Journalism, 7 pp. HCUFla.

"Mule Bone: A Comedy of Negro Life." 1930. Play in three acts written with LH. Mimeographed copy in HUAL. Act 3 was published in *Drama Critique* (Spring 1964): 103–7.

"Negro Folk Tales." Folklore, 2 pp. LCAFS.

"Negro Legends." Folklore, 7 pp. LCAFS.

"Negro Mythical Places." 3 pp. In "The Florida Negro." Copy in LCAFS.

"Negro Work Songs." Folklore, 5 pp. LCAFS.

"New Children's Games." 9 pp. In "The Florida Negro."

"Polk County: A Comedy of Negro Life on a Sawmill Camp, with Authentic Negro Music." 1944. Play in three acts written with Dorothy Waring. JWJYale.

"The South Was Had." Essay, 7 pp. HCUFla.

"Take for Instance." Spessard Holland. Essay, 11 pp. HCUFla.

"Turpentine." 3 pp. In "The Florida Negro."

"Uncle Monday." 2 pp. In "The Florida Negro."

"Unique Personal Experience." 11 pp. HCUFla.

"Which Way the NAACP." Essay, 14 pp. In possession of Marjorie Silver, Ft. Pierce, Fla.

Index

♦

The General Editor

♦

Dr. James Nagel, J. O. Eidson Distinguished Professor of American Literature at the University of Georgia, founded the scholarly journal *Studies in American Fiction* and edited it for 20 years. He is the general editor of the Critical Essays on American Literature series, published by G. K. Hall/ Macmillan, which now contains more than 130 volumes. He was one of the founders of the American Literature Association and serves as its executive coordinator. He is also a past president of the Ernest Hemingway Society. Among his 17 books are *Stephen Crane and Literary Impressionism; Critical Essays on "The Sun Also Rises"; Ernest Hemingway: The Writer in Context; Ernest Hemingway: The Oak Park Legacy;* and *Hemingway in Love and War,* which was selected by the *New York Times* as one of the outstanding books of 1989 and which has been made into a major motion picture. Nagel has published more than 50 articles in scholarly journals and has lectured on American literature in 15 countries. His current project is a book on the contemporary short-story cycle.

The Volume Editor

◆

Gloria Cronin is professor of English at Brigham Young University, where she teaches critical theory; postcolonial literature and theory; and African-American, Jewish-American, women's, and twentieth-century American literature. She is the author of numerous articles and chapters. Her book-length publications include *Saul Bellow: An Annotated Bibliography* (1987), *Sixty Other Jewish Fiction Writers: An Annotated Bibliography* (1991), and *Small Planets: Saul Bellow as a Short Fiction Writer* (forthcoming in 1999). Professor Cronin is editor of the *Saul Bellow Journal* and an executive board member of the American Literature Association, and she runs international Web sites for the Saul Bellow Society and the American Literature Association.

ISBN 0-7838-0021-5

90000

9 780783 800219